Archaeological Researches in Retrospect

EDITED BY

Gordon R. Willey

WINTHROP PUBLISHERS, INC.
CAMBRIDGE, MASSACHUSETTS

Library of Congress Cataloging in Publication Data

Willey, Gordon Randolph
Archaeological researches in retrospect.

Includes bibliographies.
1. Man, Prehistoric—Addresses, essays, lectures.
2. Indians—Antiquities—Addresses, essays, lectures.
3. Archaeology—Addresses, essays, lectures. I. Title.
GN739.W54 913'.031 73–20134
ISBN 0–87626–044–X
ISBN 0–87626–043–1 (pbk.)

17 Dunster Street, Cambridge, Massachusetts 02138

 Printed in the United States of America. 10 9 8 7 6 5 4 3 2 1.

Contents

Introduction, **Gordon R. Willey** / ix

The Southwestern United States

Early Development in Mogollon Research, **Paul S. Martin** / 3

Prehistoric Europe

Prehistoric Europe: The Economic Basis, **Grahame Clark** / 33

Northeastern Iraq

The Iraq Jarmo Project, **Robert J. Braidwood** / 61

Paleolithic Europe

The Abri Pataud Program of the French Upper Paleolithic in Retrospect, **Hallam L. Movius, Jr.** / 87

The Eastern United States

The Adena Culture, **William G. Haag** / 119

The Peruvian Coast

The Virú Valley Settlement Pattern Study, **Gordon R. Willey** / 149

California

Studying the Windmiller Culture, **Robert F. Heizer** / 179

Mesoamerica

Reflections on My Search for the Beginnings of Agriculture in Mexico, **Richard S. MacNeish** / 207

The Sudan

Meroe in the Sudan, **Peter L. Shinnie** / 237

Between the Indus and Euphrates

Excavations at Tepe Yahya, **C. C. Lamberg-Karlovsky** / 269

Glossary / 293

About the Contributors

Paul S. Martin

b. 1899, Chicago, Illinois. *Education:* University of Chicago: Undergraduate and Graduate work; Ph.D., Anthropology (1929). *Positions:* Curatorial, State Museum, Denver, Colorado, and Field Museum of Natural History, Chicago, Illinois. Currently, Chairman Emeritus, Department of Anthropology, Field Museum. *Special Interests:* Archaeology, Southwestern United States, particularly behavioral patterns in the archaeological record and their applicability to contemporary social problems. *Field Work:* Wisconsin, Illinois, Yucatan, Colorado, New Mexico, Arizona. *Publications:* include *Handbook of North American Archaeology* (1933); *Lowry Ruin in Southwestern Colorado* (1936); *The SU Excavations at a Mogollon Village, Western New Mexico* (1940); *Anasazi Painted Pottery* (with Elizabeth Willis, 1940); *Digging Into History* (1959); *Late Mogollon Communities* (with Rinaldo and Barter, 1957); *The Archaeology of Arizona* (with Fred Plog, 1973).

Grahame Clark

b. 1907, Shortlands, Kent, England. *Education:* Cambridge University: Undergraduate and Graduate work; Ph.D., Anthropology (Archaeology and Ethnology, 1933). *Positions:* Teaching, Department of Anthropology, Cambridge University. Currently, Disney Professor of Prehistoric Archaeology, Cambridge University. Master of Peterhouse. *Special Interests:* European prehistory, especially ecological studies of the Mesolithic cultures of Northern Europe. *Field Work:* Cambridgeshire, Star Carr, Greece, Scandinavia. *Publications:* include: *The Mesolithic Age in Britain* (1933); *The Mesolithic Settlement of Northern Europe* (1936); *Prehistoric England* (1940); *Prehistoric Europe: the economic basis* (1952, 1965); *Excavations at Star Carr* (1954); *Archaeology and Society* (3rd. ed., 1957); *World Prehistory* (1961); *World Prehistory: A New Outline* (1969); *Aspects of Prehistory* (1970); *Star Carr: A Case Study in Bioarchaeology* (1972).

Robert J. Braidwood

b. 1907, Detroit, Michigan. *Education:* University of Michigan: Undergraduate and Graduate work. (Architecture and Anthropology); University of Chicago: Ph.D., Oriental Languages and Literatures and Anthropology (1942). *Positions:* Faculty appointments in Anthropology and Oriental Institute, University of Chicago since 1941. Oriental Institute field staff since 1933. Currently, Oriental Institute

Professor of Old World Prehistory and Professor, Department of Anthropology, University of Chicago. *Special Interests:* Middle Eastern archaeology, origins of agriculture. *Field Work:* Iraq, Syria, Iran, Turkey, Illinois, New Mexico. *Publications:* include *Archaeologists and What They Do* (1960); *Prehistoric Investigations in Iraqi Kurdistan* (with Bruce Howe, 1960); *Courses Toward Urban Life: Archeological Consideration of Some Cultural Alternatives* (with Gordon R. Willey, 1962).

Hallam L. Movius, Jr. *b.* 1907, Newton, Massachusetts. *Education:* Harvard University: A.B. (1930); M.A. (1932); Ph.D., Anthropology (1937). *Positions:* Research and Faculty appointments, Peabody Museum and Department of Anthropology, Harvard University since 1936. Currently, Professor of Anthropology, Harvard. *Special Interests:* Old World Paleolithic archaeology, with investigations in Ireland, Southeastern Asia and Europe. *Field Work:* Czechoslovakia, Central Europe, Palestine, Ireland, Burma and Java, Eastern France, Western Europe, field director, Abri Pataud Project (1958–71). *Publications:* include numerous monographs, and *The Irish Stone Age, Its Chronology, Development and Relationships* (1942); *Early Man and Pleistocene Stratigraphy in Southern and Eastern Asia* (1944); *Stone Age Site in Tangier* (with B. Howe, 1947).

William G. Haag *b.* 1910, Henderson, Kentucky. *Education:* University of Kentucky: B.S. (1932); M.S. (1933); University of Michigan; Ph.D., Anthropology (1948). *Positions:* Curatorial and teaching, Department of Anthropology, University of Kentucky, 1937–49; Associate Professor of Anthropology, University of Mississippi, 1949–52. Currently, Alumni Professor of Anthropology, Louisiana State University, Baton Rouge; State Archaeologist of Louisiana. *Special Interests:* Archaeology, Southeastern United States, West Indian Archaeology, osteological analyses of Pre-Columbian dogs. *Field Work:* Tennessee, Alabama, Kentucky, Mississippi, Louisiana, Cape Hatteras, Carolina coast, Mexico, St. Lucia and Martinique, Nicaragua. *Publications:* include *The Fisher Site, Fayette County, Kentucky* (with W. S. Webb, 1947); *The Jaketown Site in West-Central Mississippi* (with J. A. Ford and P. Phillips, 1955); *The Archaic of the Lower Mississippi Valley* (1961).

Gordon R. Willey *b.* 1913, Chariton, Iowa. *Education:* University of Arizona: A.B. (1935); A.M. (1936); Columbia University: Ph.D., Anthropology (1942). *Positions:* Instructor in Anthropology, Columbia University, 1942–43; Anthropologist, Bureau of American Ethnology, Smithsonian Institution, 1943–50; Overseas fellow, Cambridge University, 1968–69. Currently, Bowditch Professor of Mexican and Central American Archaeology and Ethnology, Peabody Museum, and Department of Anthropology, Harvard since 1950. *Special*

Interests: Archaeology, Middle and South American, settlement patterns, urbanism. *Field Work:* Peru, Panama, British Honduras, Guatemala, Nicaragua. *Publications:* include *Excavations in the Chancay Valley, Peru* (1943); *Prehistoric Settlement Patterns in the Virú Valley, Peru* (1953); (ed.) *Prehistoric Settlement Patterns in the New World* (1956); *Method and Theory in American Archaeology* (with P. Phillips, 1958); (ed.) *An Introduction to American Archaeology* Vol. I., (1966), Vol. II. (1971).

Robert F. Heizer *b.* 1915, Denver, Colorado. *Education:* University of California, Berkeley: A.B. (1936); Ph.D., Anthropology (1941); University of Nevada: D. Sci. (hon.) (1965); *Positions:* Teaching, Department of Anthropology, University of California, Berkeley since 1946. Currently, Professor of Anthropology and Coordinator, Archaeological Research Facility, University of California, Berkeley. *Special Interests:* Archaeology of Western North American and Mesoamerica, ethnography of North America, natural science applications to archaeology. *Publications:* include *A Guide to Archaeological Field Methods* (rev. ed., 1967); *The Archaeologist at Work* (1959); *Prehistoric Rock Art of Nevada and Eastern California* (with M. A. Baumhoff, 1962); *An Introduction to Prehistoric Archaeology* (with F. Hole, rev. ed., 1973); *Almost Ancestors* (with T. Kroeber, 1968); *The Other Californians* (with A. Almquist, 1971).

Richard S. MacNeish *b.* 1918, New York City. *Education:* University of Chicago: Graduate and Undergraduate work; Ph.D., Anthropology (1949). *Positions:* Senior Archaeologist, National Museum of Canada, 1949–62; Head, Department of Archaeology, University of Calgary, 1964–68; Director, R. S. Peabody Foundation for Archaeology, Andover, Massachusetts, since 1968. *Special Interests:* Archaeology, of Eastern United States; Plains; Canadian Northwest and Arctic; Mesoamerica and Peru; origins of agriculture; rise of civilization. *Field Work:* Eastern North America, Arctic, Mesoamerica, Peru, Southwest, Great Plains; Northwest Boreal Forest. *Publications:* include *The Prehistory of the Tehuacan Valley* series (1966–1974).

Peter L. Shinnie *b.* 1915, London. *Education:* Oxford University: Undergraduate work in Oriental Languages (Ancient Egyptian and Coptic), M.A. (1941). *Positions:* Commissioner of Archaeology, Sudan Government, 1947–55; Director of Antiquities, Uganda, 1957; Professor and Head of Department of Archaeology, University of Khartoum, 1966–70; Professor and Head of Department of Archaeology, University of Calgary since 1970. *Special Interests:* Archaeology, the Sudan, especially Meroitic and Medieval Nubian cultures, beginnings of agriculture and early cultures of West Africa. *Field*

Work: The Sudan. *Publications:* include *Meroe: The Civilization of the Sudan* (1967); *African Iron Age* (1971).

C. C. Lamberg-Karlovsky

b. 1937, Prague, Czechoslovakia. *Education:* Dartmouth College: Undergraduate work. University of Pennsylvania and Yale: Graduate work, Ph.D., Anthropology. University of Pennsylvania: Anthropology (1965). *Positions:* Teaching, Department of Anthropology at Harvard since 1965. Currently, Professor of Anthropology, Harvard. *Special Interests:* Archaeology, Middle East.

Introduction

Archaeologists know that there is, indeed, in the historian, Lynn White's words, "a changing past." While the measurements of a pyramid are immutable and the contents of a tomb remain the same, our perspective on these data and the interpretations that we derive from them are constantly being seen anew from the never-static present. The truism that the past is always seen through the eyes of the present, led me to think that it might be interesting, especially in view of the fact that archaeology is now going through a phase of critical self-examination, to ask a number of archaeologists to reflect on some of their past researches and to set down their thoughts from the vantage point of the immediate present. Each such personal view, in its microcosm, may contribute toward an understanding of transformations within the discipline as a whole.

In following up this idea I then invited nine archaeological colleagues (with myself being the tenth member of the group) each to prepare an article which would be a retrospective appraisal of a research project which they had undertaken in the past. Such an undertaking could be a specific dig, a series of related digs, a regional study, or a work of synthesis—but, in every case, it would involve researches in which the particular archaeologist had played a major role. I further asked that each article be addressed to certain questions. What were the original motivations of the research or the problems? What strategies were employed in the investigations? How were the results perceived at the time? And, finally, I asked each author for a critique that would consider such things as how the research plan looks to him now and how, with the advantages of hindsight, and in view of the changes that have come about in archaeology since the original research, he might do things differently.

To promote as free-flowing a retrospection as possible, and to make for interesting as well as instructive reading, I suggested that the style of the articles be informal or semi-formal, with the apparatus of scholarship, including footnotes and heavy referencing, kept to a minimum. I defined the audience for the articles as mainly an undergraduate college one; students with a beginning interest in archaeology. At the same time, I made clear that I did not want a simple "popular" essay, but rather a statement that could be read also by fellow professionals for substantive archaeological information, historical perspective, or both.

The assignment, which seemed straightforward enough at the time I made it, was only deceptively easy. Perhaps I could have made it easier if I had been more detailed and specific, more confining in my original instructions. I am glad, in retrospect, that I was not.

I suppose that one universal characteristic of archaeologists is their extreme individualism. I could have tried the patience of my collaborators by asking for editorial revisions, by attempting to standardize their retrospections. But to do so would have been to choke off spontaneity, or to force "spontaneity"—a contradiction of terms. As the reader will see, some of the contributors have written in an almost "free-associational" manner while others have been considerably more restrained. Some of the articles are quite openly self-critical and revisionistic; others are much less so. All of them, however, overtly or covertly reveal changes in the attitude of archaeologists toward their data, even where the perspective of retrospection goes back only a few years.

All of these papers were prepared either in late 1972 or early 1973, and they were written, insofar as I am aware, without any consultations among the several contributors. I even prepared my own article before I read any of the others. This volume contains, therefore, highly individualistic, indeed idiosyncratic, retrospective views of research archaeology dating back over the past ten to forty years.

In selecting the contributors for a retrospective book, a primary criterion is necessarily age. So, nearly all of the archaeologists I chose are senior scholars. They range from their early seventies to their middle fifties, and all have long professional experience in the field of archaeology. I made one exception, however, for it struck me that it might be interesting to have one junior member in the group, someone who is now currently engaged in his first major research. Retrospection is not altogether a prerogative of the old, and I like the idea of having a "prospective" statement in this setting of retrospective ones. My instructions to this author were somewhat different from those given to the rest of us, and I will explain them farther along. In making my selections I paid some attention to geographical and chronological coverage. With only ten papers this coverage could not be very thorough, but I have managed a division between Old and New World areas and a time and culture type range that goes from the Paleolithic to the threshold of early civilizations and beyond. While individual background and training is, of course, of utmost importance in how an archaeologist views his data, I must confess that I made no conscious effort to be selective in this regard when I sent out my invitations. Now, in looking over the list, it appears that there are eight Americans, all of them American-trained in university anthropological departments where archaeologists are, perforce, subjected to a certain amount of social anthropology and ethnology. This includes two people who have pursued Old World Middle Eastern archaeology, a field in which fine arts and linguistic backgrounds are more common than those of general anthropology. The two English archaeologists are both British-trained—one at Cambridge, in a general anthropological department, the other at Oxford in Oriental Languages. In broader intellectual context, I would say that all ten of us are essentially historically-oriented; however, we have all been sensitive to other emphases in archaeology which have become increasingly important over the last quarter-century, and most of us exemplify, in our work, the transition that has been taking place in archaeology from its more limited descriptive-distributional-chronological goals to those concerns with function and process that have come to be referred to as the "new archaeology."

For the archaeologically uninitiated, or the beginning student, this "new archaeology" may be defined by the following attitudes. The emphasis is on the elucidation of cultural process. This is to be done in a general framework of cultural evolutionary theory and, more specifically, in accordance with systems theory. There is also a strong ecological bias and a deductive, or "hypothesis testing," approach to the data of prehistory. The "new archaeology" also makes heavy use of the findings of the physical and natural sciences; it uses statistical procedures. None of the papers in this volume is fully within the scope of the "new archaeology" as so defined. This, of course, is not surprising, since most of the research described was carried out before 1960. In varying degrees, however, all of the papers either foreshadow certain "new archaeological" features or otherwise incorporate them.

The articles in this book are ordered chronologically, based on the ages of the archaeologists or on the dates of their researches. This arrangement has some historical interest, although the academically distinct research traditions represented in the book tend to blur an historical perspective. In writing this introduction, though, I have compromised with the book's arrangement by taking up and briefly discussing the papers under a series of problem themes.

One such theme is that of basic cultural definitions. The two otherwise quite different papers of Movius and Haag seem to me to take such definitions as their basic concern. To Movius, in his work at the Abri Pataud in southwestern France, this concern has focused on lithic typology. In reading the Movius paper one has the sense of an archaeologist attempting to break out of the confines and constraints of a firm and limiting scholastic tradition. Prior to the beginnings of Movius' investigations, French Paleolithic archaeology was characterized by the "type fossil" artifact concepts of the French Paleolithic archaeologists, Breuil and Peyrony, and even before them of de Mortillet. This formal, almost "stylistic," way of type definitions set the boundaries for such controversies as the Perigordian-Aurignacian debate which Movius describes. Movius felt that such a typology was inadequate, and he constructed one through a detailed attribute analysis of the individual implements. By studying the statistical clusterings of the attributes, with their norms and ranges, he hoped to arrive at the "constructional idea" of the toolmakers in the belief that such recurrent groupings of the data would reflect, in his words, "social alignments." In retrospect, Movius sees his typological procedures as the fundamental long-term contribution of Abri Pataud excavations. Movius carried out his Abri Pataud studies in the 1950's and 1960's, after extensive Paleolithic experience in the Old World, including field work in southeast Asia and Ireland. His typological approach was revolutionary in this Old World context. While a similar approach was advocated in New World pottery studies by the American archaeologist, A. C. Spaulding, as early as 1953, such classificatory procedures have not yet been put into practice on the scale that Movius is attempting in France. To date, his work has been reported only in a preliminary way, but, as he indicates, the final monographs by him and his associates are now ready for the press. In further reflecting on the Abri Pataud work, Movius stresses its environmental reconstructive aspects, made possible by the concerted efforts of archaeologists and natural scientists. In looking back, he admits that detailed provenience data on cultural debris from various cave floor levels would have been of value in aiding cultural interpretations. This data had not been processed at Abri Pataud because of its time-consuming expense. He notes the spall-reconstruction of flint artifacts by the French archaeologist, Pincevent, and the microscopic studies of wear on flint tools of the Russian archaeologist, Semenov, as research advances that he would incorporate in future Paleolithic work. One also comes away from the Movius article with the feeling that Movius wants to wring more "social" interpretation from his Paleolithic data than he has been able to do; his traditional archaeological caution holds him back. It is, of course, a dilemma which he shares with most of us.

A quite different recounting of archaeological cultural definitions is Haag's story of the pursuit of the Adena culture in the Ohio Valley and, particularly, in Kentucky. The background to the Adena study was in the romantic "Mound-Builder" tradition which first took form in the early nineteenth century. While at the end of this century reputable scientific opinion no longer held "Mound-Builder" or "mysterious lost race" theories of the origins of the Ohio Valley mounds, there still had been little attempt to sort out regional or chronological distinctions among the mounds and their contents. Research along these lines advanced but slowly in the early twentieth century. W. C. Mills, an Ohio archaeologist, was perhaps the first to conceive of distinct cultures in the area, of which the Adena was one. A serious difficulty was the apparent inability of the investigators to do anything about archaeological chronology. Haag's involvement in Adena research began in the early 1930's, and during this decade and into the 1940's, he served as an assistant to Major W. S. Webb, a physicist turned archaeologist, who was making great contributions to archaeology in Kentucky, Tennessee, and the Southeast. Haag's statement is informal and modest in tone—overly modest, in fact, for he had a key role in the development of our knowledge of Adena, as well as other southeastern United States archaeological cultures. In looking back, he sees the archaeology of that area in the 1930's and 1940's as being little more than trait listing; however, he admits that the archaeologists who were then of the younger generation made significant contributions in chronological organization of the area through stratigraphy and seriation and in the development of a systematic pottery typology. Ecology, settlement patterns, attempted social reconstructions—all of which would be a part of any 1970's attack on the Adena culture—were barely touched upon thirty years before.

The articles of Peter L. Shinnie, C. C. Lamberg-Karlovsky, Robert J. Braidwood, and Richard S. MacNeish have as their common denominator the study of site chronology and culture development. Shinnie's excavations at Meroe, in the Sudan, extended over five seasons and have only just been concluded. Meroe had been excavated by the archaeologist, Garstand, many years before, and Reisner, the great Egyptologist, had also obtained tomb collections and data there. The site is a key one for the central Nile and for the understanding of relationships to sub-Saharan Africa. Shinnie was primarily interested in sequence and stratigraphy in the residential part of the ancient city, where no work of this kind had been done before. In reading Shinnie's paper one has the feeling that there is a very strong Egyptian archaeological tradition, a "mind-set" which has long been focused on tomb contents, temples, palaces, and hieroglyphic inscriptions and that this had had pervasive influence on everything—from field digging techniques to overall problem conceptions. Shinnie's residential refuse tests appear to break with this tradition, at least to a degree. In retrospect, he calls for more residential settlement data than he obtained, for more data on ecology and past environment, and for attention to outlying or regional settlement patterns beyond the confines of the city proper.

Lamberg-Karlovsky's original research design for Iran was the investigation of connections between Mesopotamia and the Indus Valley—an essentially historical problem placed in the conceptual framework of Mesopotamia as the "nuclear center" of civilizational development for the entire Middle East-Indus area. Tepe Yahya, heretofore unknown, was the largest site or "tell" in its region. Lamberg-Karlovsky's large-scale, deep-digging operation at the site was pointed toward stratigraphic sequence and substantial architectural or building-level recovery. About midway through his third season there (in a program which began in 1967 and is still continuing) he began to find things which transformed his ideas about the rise of Middle Eastern civilization. Instead of seeing early civilization as something that sprang from a single Mesopotamian cell, he began to visualize it as a process which has as its precondition a number of cells, regions, or nucleus sites, interacting and interchanging among themselves, through trade and other mechanisms, so that his original research motivations began to shift away from chronology, *per se,* to themes of process. The investigation at Tepe Yahya, which so far has seen only preliminary publication, is still continuing. Lamberg-Karlovsky discusses the intended course of his Tepe Yahya work for future seasons. Among other things, he mentions a shift from the site proper to a regional settlement pattern study.

Lamberg-Karlovsky is the younger generation archaeologist to whom I referred a few pages back. As mentioned, my instructions to him were different from those given to the other authors. In lieu of a retrospective statement, I asked him for a "prospective" one in which, looking ahead twenty years hence, he attempts to evaluate his work at Tepe Yahya as it may then be seen by the coming generation of archaeologists. What might he have done that was not done? What will be sought by the "up-and-coming" archaeologists of the future? I will not anticipate here his interesting speculations.

While both Braidwood and MacNeish are concerned with chronology and culture development in the broad sense, their researches were aimed at a more specific problem within this range—that of agricultural origins. Prior to his work at Jarmo, Braidwood had had

Near Eastern archaeological experience with Oriental Institute teams and had been a student of the late Egyptologist, Henri Frankfort. But he also had anthropological training. He began the Jarmo excavations in Iraq in the late 1940's, and continued them into the 1950's. The outlines of his results are now well-known to his archaeological colleagues through a series of preliminary papers, although the final monographs on Jarmo are still to appear. The Jarmo region was picked with a definite strategy in mind. Braidwood reasoned that the alluvial flats of the Tigris-Euphrates system were not the likely place for agricultural beginnings but, rather, for agricultural expansion under irrigation at a somewhat later period in human technological and social development. Instead, it was his hypothesis that the "hilly flank" country bordering the great river plains would be the more likely place of first crop domestication. Braidwood's work was revolutionary in the context of a Mesopotamian archaeological tradition which, to that time, had been preoccupied largely with great monuments and textual materials. Among other things, Braidwood instigated an interdisciplinary approach to problems of plant and animal domestication, introducing specialists in botany, zoology, and other natural science fields into what had been the predominantly "humanistic" Middle Eastern archaeological setting. In looking back over the Jarmo work, with the perspective of the intervening years and in the light of his continuing researches on the same general problems in Iran, Braidwood is self-critical about a number of things, including his excavation and recovery techniques. He makes some pertinent observations on the old Jarmo-Jericho dispute which flared so brightly in the 1950's, and he reflects on the accidents of archaeological discovery which direct so much of our thinking. Probably more than any other archaeologist of his time, Braidwood has prepared the way for the advances and changes in archaeology that have come in the last decade. I think that this will be seen more clearly when some of the dust of battle between archaeological generations has settled.

MacNeish's search for Mesoamerican agricultural beginnings started in the late 1940's in Tamaulipas, Mexico. Although he does not allude to it in his article, MacNeish's original reasons for going to Tamaulipas were, I believe, to search out connections between Mesoamerican and Southeastern United States cultures. The dry cave discoveries of maize and other plants, in Preceramic contexts, were a bonus that turned him in this new direction—one that he has followed since with great success, especially in the Tehuacan Valley of southern Mexico. This Tehuacan research, which is the focus of his article, is now in process of publication. Meanwhile, MacNeish has moved on to Peru to continue the early agricultural search. MacNeish's self-criticism in his article is much concerned about the nature and organization of interdisciplinary research in archaeology, considering both its theoretical and practical aspects. He contrasts the way he organized such research in Tamaulipas with the improved procedures for Tehuacan, but he also indicates that he is still not satisfied. There is a very strong ecological dimension to MacNeish's work. He looks with great favor on what botanists, geologists, palynologists, and a host of others from the natural and physical sciences may contribute to archaeology. In contrast to this, there is a negativism about the potential contribution of social anthropology-ethnology to the problems of prehistoric cultural interpretation.

Grahame Clark and Robert F. Heizer have both been involved with Mesolithic, or "Mesolithic-type," cultures—Clark in northern Europe and Heizer with the Archaic cultures of California. As the relationships between peoples and their natural environments are easily observed on this level of cultural development, it perhaps follows naturally that both are very ecologically-oriented and, in their respective parts of the world, have been pioneers for this kind of archaeology. Clark, a student of Miles Burkitt, and influenced also by V. Gordon Childe, began Mesolithic archaeology as a research student at Cambridge, following along traditional typological investigations. He broadened these horizons considerably, however, in the early 1930's when he worked with the geologist, Godwin, on fenland pollen studies and archaeology in East Anglia. There had been an earlier tradition in environmental archaeology in Britain, of which Sir Cyril Fox was the principal exponent, but Clark, in his collaborations with Godwin, went well beyond this in the recreation of prehistoric environments and in the studies of the causative effects of environment upon culture. He drew the results of much of this together in his book *The Mesolithic Settlement of Northern Europe,* in 1936. In his present article he traces with great care, and with documentation, his intellectual development as an archaeologist. As he says, early on he conceived of archaeology on its three dimensions of "straight archaeology" (the space-time ordering of types or forms), ecology, and social context. His realization of the importance of the latter is attested to by his book, *Archaeology and Society,* which was published in 1939, just before World War II. After the war, Clark continued with research and teaching, especially in connection with the excavations at Star Carr. His *Prehistoric Europe,* the synthesis which forms the basis for his present retrospective essay, can be seen as a logical development of his distinguished career. As he says, his attitude in *Mesolithic Settlement* had been to view culture change as a straight reaction to natural environmental change; in *Prehistoric Europe* he sees the relationships between culture and environment as much more complex and involving reciprocal needs. At this point it is significant that he gives credit to social anthropological concepts, particularly those of the British social anthropologist, E. E. Evans-Pritchard. It is a characteristic in Clark's career that he has been constantly seeking that proper balance in archaeology between humans' reaction to their natural environmental setting and their adjustments to their social contexts.

The development of a systematic archaeology in California had lagged behind the growth of the discipline in the adjacent Southwest, or in Mesoamerica, and Heizer's career in California prehistory began at just about the time that the first efforts at establishing a regional chronology were made in the 1930's. Heizer did some field work then, and after the war returned to both field and laboratory research which eventuated in his major publication on the Windmiller culture in 1949. The Windmiller culture was the earliest discovered at that time in the northern interior valleys of California, marking the beginnings of the long California Archaic cultural tradition which was also known from the San Francisco Bay shell mounds where the archaeologists Uhle and Nelson had dug many years before. Kroeber, a well known anthropologist, had always maintained that the extraordinary conservatism of the prehistoric California Indians frustrated attempts at establishing archaeological sequences. This was true, to a degree, but Heizer's typological and stratigraphic analyses were able to overcome this limitation. Prior to the development of radiocarbon dating, Heizer collaborated with S. F. Cook in the study of chemical changes in bone composition in a search for a relative dating scale. He also turned to other physical and natural sciences, especially in analyses of food remains that were an attempt to give California prehistory an ecological dimension. In retrospect, he sees this early environmental archaeology of the 1940's as crude and simplistic; nevertheless it marked a beginning, as well as a new way of looking at the data. Similarly, his attention to obsidian, including a search for sources and a tentative plotting out of trade routes, foreshadows very recent work done along these lines in many places in the world. In concluding this retrospective paper Heizer emphasizes the importance of pushing toward new frontiers of investigation, even when the techniques for the solution of problems are not yet refined or immediately at hand. In this way the archaeologist sets up problems and is readied for new technical advances as these come along in other sciences.

The two papers by Paul Martin and myself share the theme of a search for archaeological-social organizational correlates, and, more specifically, for manifestations of these in prehistoric settlement patterns. Martin came into Southwestern United States archaeology in the late 1920's, just after Nelson, A. V. Kidder, the distinguished Southwestern archaeologist, and others had pioneered stratigraphic archaeology in that area. His earlier work in the Ackmen-Lowry region of Colorado was, by his own admission, vague in its sense of problem—or at least in stated problem—pottery stratigraphy and chronology was the main goal. Even at that time, though, Martin was concerned with what could be called the functional aspects of his data so that by the end of the 1930's he was hinting at relationships between architectural forms and prehistoric social units. He mentions, in the present paper, Robert Redfield's social anthropological scorn for archaeology as a kind of "trade school" activity, and, undoubtedly, this University of Chicago professor's teachings had served as something of a goad to Martin to look for the non-material aspects of culture behind the potsherds and the kiva walls. Although Martin says that he tended to scorn social theorizings and speculations in his archaeology after 1940, bowing to the dictum of the archaeological profession of that time to dig cleanly and think cautiously, this is not altogether convincing. While it is true that his avowed problems remained essentially historical—Mogollon origins, relationships, and chronology—the other kind of problem must have nagged him, for in 1950 he devoted a chapter in one of his site reports to the daring theme of prehistoric Mogollon social organization.

Martin's retrospective tone and attitude toward archaeology are highly optimistic. He believes firmly that there is much of the non-material past that can be resurrected from the material record. He speaks of his own conversion to a "processual" view of archaeology as dating from the mid-1960's, but some may feel he is overly modest in this regard. Certainly among the senior American archaeologists of today he is a principal forerunner of such a view. At the same time, Martin is open-minded about the courses which archaeologists may pursue toward processual goals, accepting even those of a more traditional "humanistic" sort. As he says, it will probably turn out that there are "many roads to the truth."

My own settlement and social organizational concerns were also set in a context of historically-directed, chronology-minded archaeology. When I turned to functional interpretation of the Virú Valley settlements in Peru, I operated almost entirely with a kind of settlement typology that was informed (and also undoubtedly misinformed) by general comparative analogy. I had little recourse to specific historical ethnology or to ecology. If I see others as being overly ecological, overly natural-science-minded, then in the Virú study I must accuse myself of having been obsessed with the social dimension of culture to the detriment of ecology. This balance should be righted for Virú, and perhaps it will be now by the work of others.

In summary, these retrospective papers delineate a series of transitions in the practice of archaeology over the past few decades. Not all of these transitions started from the same base line. Haag's investigations marked a passage from a somewhat antiquarian-oriented "Mound Builder" archaeology to a systematically defined grouping of prehistoric cultures. Movius initiated a more sensitive typology to replace a Paleolithic tool classification of a rigid "horizon-marking" kind. Shinnie helps widen the dimensions of a text-bound, monument-minded Egyptology to a more inclusive, "population-wide" archaeology. Lamberg-Karlovsky has begun to change the outlook of a diffusionist-oriented Middle Eastern culture history to a more sophisticated processually-concerned one. In the Middle East and in Mesoamerica, Braidwood and MacNeish, starting from conventional chronological and developmental points of view, went on to revolutionize archaeological thinking about such important happenings as the beginnings of plant and animal domestication. In Britain and northern Europe, Grahame Clark had the advantage of a well-grounded typological-chronological base, and he built on this both culture history and culture explanation through his examinations of the interplay of culture and natural environment. Heizer's Californian archaeological base was much less developed when he started, so that he had much of the typological and chronological groundwork to lay before he could go on to culture and environmental studies; however, his work of the 1940's made an important beginning in this direction. In the Southwestern United States and in Peru, Martin and I began to grope our way, through functional analyses of architectural and settlement forms, toward a better understanding of prehistoric cultures. Such are the highlights of the researches of ten archaeologists; their individual stories follow.

THE SOUTHWESTERN UNITED STATES

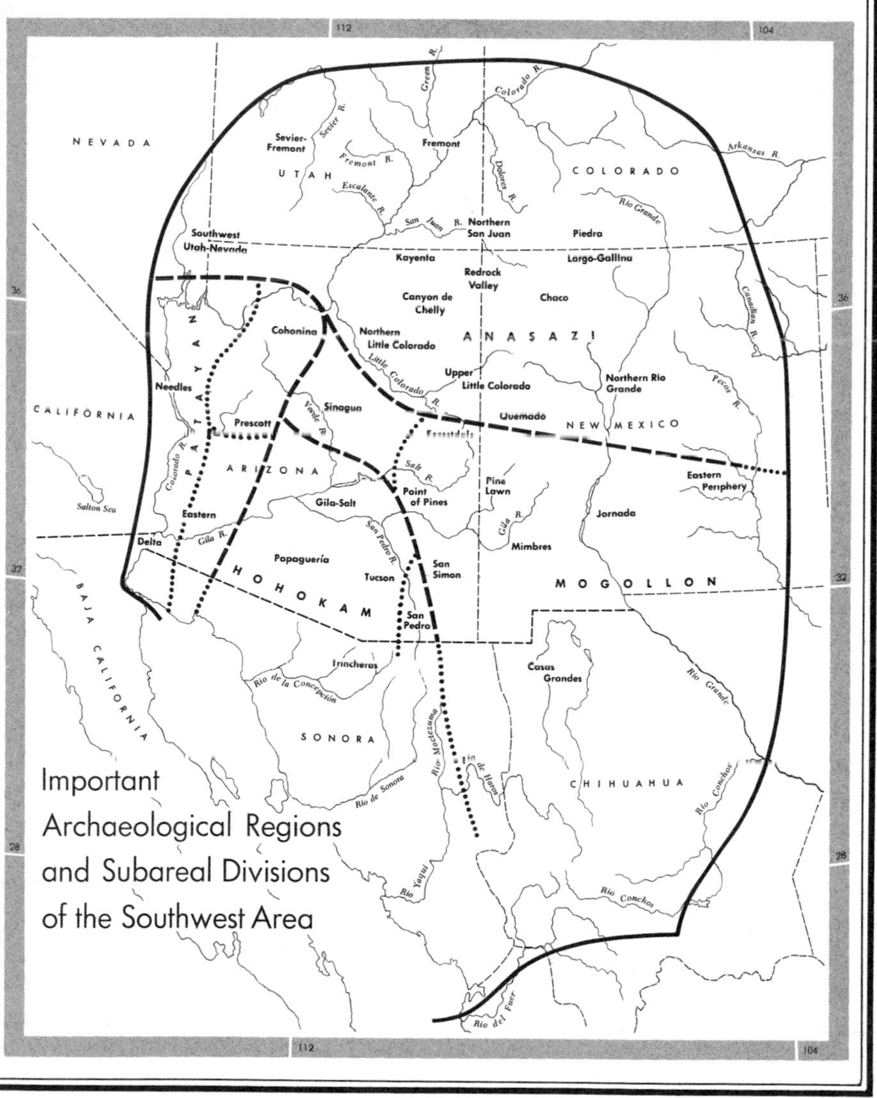

Important Archaeological Regions and Subareal Divisions of the Southwest Area

(preceding page)

Map of the southwestern archaeological area, illustrating major subareas and regions. Martin's early work was in the Ackmen-Lowry country of southwestern Colorado, which is in the general northern San Juan region. His later Mogollon investigations centered in the Pine Lawn region of western New Mexico. From Gordon R. Willey, *An Introduction to American Archaeology,* Vol. I (Englewood Cliffs, N.J.: Prentice-Hall, Inc., 1966), p. 180.

Early Development in Mogollon Research

PAUL S. MARTIN

Introduction

While still a graduate student I had the great opportunity of going to Yucatan as an archaeologist on the staff of Carnegie Institution of Washington. I was overwhelmed by the elegance of our quarters at Chichen-Itza and the very strict protocol: comfortable quarters for the bachelors with showers and flush toilets; tea at 4:00 p.m., in dress white coat, trousers, shirt and a necktie; dinner at 6:00 p.m. in the same full dress—no shedding of jackets in hot weather; the necessity to speak elegant Spanish, because we often had distinguished Latin-American guests; the after-dinner coffee on the *corredor;* the archaeologist Earl Morris at one end of the long table and Dr. Sylvanus G. Morley at the other end with about thirty archaeologists and other staff (nurse, secretaries, etc.) sandwiched in between; rising at 4:00 a.m. breakfast at 4:30; starting work at 5:00 a.m.—all of which was done to escape the tropical heat; linen table clothes and napkins with Maya glyphs embroidered on them; table silver with the name of the Institution engraved on it; Chinese houseboys to wait on the table and to clean our quarters. Such elegance took away my breath, but Morley believed in doing things in the grand style and I must say it was impressive.

The work that the expedition was concerned with consisted mainly of excavating and restoring ceremonial buildings. My own work was concerned with regrouping a mosaic of stone depicting warriors and eagles that had tumbled off the Temple of the Warriors, of which Morris was in charge and which was the big task of the moment. It was dull work and held none of the glamor I had expected. Later I was placed in charge of clearing a small temple called Temple of the Interior Atlanteans Figures. Still later I was placed in charge of excavating and completely restoring a small but gem-beautiful temple at old Chichen-Itza. Three doorways had once

Headpiece: Black-on-White pottery jar in the Mogollon-Anasazi tradition. (Courtesy, Field Museum of Natural History, Chicago.)

existed over which lintels of stone were imbedded and, on all three exposed surfaces, Maya hieroglyphs had been carved. Two were in good condition but the third was not at first found. Hence, the temple was called Temple of the Two Lintels and sometimes referred to as Paul Martin's Temple.

As noted earlier, our work stressed the restoration of ceremonial temples for tourist purposes; but at no time did we look for the remains of the Maya common man nor did we advance any hypotheses as to the beginnings or decline of this great city of the Itza family. It would be difficult to procure funds today for such colossal digging with nothing to show for it but beautiful temples, ball courts, and pyramids. I do not belittle the work as I enjoy looking still at restored temples. However, I would not be happy with work that produced such sterile results—even as far as history was concerned.

In the interim, I contracted malaria, worms, and amoebic dysentery. I was ill for a long time, getting down to ninety pounds. Finally, I was persuaded to give up my ambition to be a Mayologist and to return to the University of Chicago to finish up a dissertation on a non-Maya subject and to find another job.

I completed my residence requirements by taking a job as State Archaeologist of Colorado. By undertaking excavations for the State Historical Society, I was encouraged to believe that I could obtain a suitable dissertation later. In those days dissertations were concerned less with *problems* than with history. My doctoral dissertation was on the "Origin of the Kiva." I have not had the guts to look at it since because Dr. Bob Redfield scorned it and archaeology. In this he agreed with Chancellor Hutchins of the University of Chicago, who thought of archaeology as a "tool course" fit only for vocational schools. I think that with today's advances in theory, he would change his mind and admit that archaeology is a field of anthropology and hence a social science.

I reluctantly accepted my post as State Archaeologist since I liked Maya research and had enjoyed my four seasons at Chichen-Itza enormously. Soon, however, I received a most kind invitation from Dr. A. V. Kidder to attend a conference of southwestern archaeologists and ethnologists at Kidder's field station at Pecos, New Mexico.

My superiors at Denver thought I should attend the conference. Needless to say I would not have missed it for anything, as the conference marked the beginning of a series of annual meetings still called the "Pecos Conference." Further, it was the first time that all workers in the Southwest got together to thrash out their problems, to pool their knowledge, and to forge a synthesis of Southwestern culture-history—one that still serves well in many situations. It was an historic event—unique, informal, and greatly inspired and influenced by Kidder's guidance and leadership—qualities that were strong but not tyrannical. Kidder never insisted on his point of view although he freely gave of his profound experiences. Up to this time, the entire Southwest was thought by many to be an area dominated by one culture. There were a few, H. S. Gladwin, Director of the Gila Pueblo Research Laboratory especially, who dissented, but at the time of this first conference, he lacked convincing data to demonstrate his arguments.

As noted above, the archaeologists present at this conference forged a synthesis that came to be called the "Pecos Classification" and that even today has much value and is freely used by many workers in the field for a quick and handy reference to a culture stage. It was discovered later on that this classification did not apply equally well to all parts of the Southwest; it was especially applicable for the northern part of the area—the homeland of the Anasazi of "Pueblo" culture. Its supreme value was that it brought order out of chaos and placed cultures relative to one another in a rough lineal framework. Later on after Dr. Douglas' tree-ring calendar was announced and accepted, dates were assigned to the various stages in the Pecos Classification.

To go back a bit, I would say that my being invited was pure luck as I was a greenhorn with only a little experience in the mounds of Illinois and the Mayan cities. Here I had a chance to meet all the eminent archaeologists and ethnologists of the time. I could mix freely and informally with them at meals and during our discussion times, as we lounged under the pinyon trees on the mesa and in our sleeping quarters. I was housed with A. L. Kroeber, T. T. Waterman, Joe Spinden, who had a leak in his air mattress and swore at it every night, Earl Morris and Karl Ruppert! Imagine my feelings of awe at being permitted to share bunk space with them. The excitement of those moments and of the conference are still as fresh in my mind now as they were in 1926.

Among other things, my superior in Denver, the President of the Historical Society, wanted me to seek advice on whether digging in southwestern Colorado was worthwhile! He also wanted to know whether there were sites that the Society (relatively poor) could afford to excavate. Little did I know then, as I did later after conducting several archaeological surveys, that there were literally hundreds of small sites, large ones and the now famous Hovenweep Group of tall-standing walls, towers both round and square. Fewkes, at

FIGURE 1
Excavation of a kiva. (Courtesy, Field Museum of Natural History, Chicago.)

the time Chief of the Bureau of American Ethnology, Smithsonian, had seen these sites about 1916 but few other archaeologists had.

After the conference ended I set out by bus and train to Durango, Colorado where I rented an old car in which to conduct my exploration. I drove first to Mesa Verde National Park. The road up to the park was a one-way trail and very slippery due to recent rains. I had never driven on mountain roads before and I was frightened beyond words!

A few days later, I descended McElmo Canyon to search for sites and a camping place. A trader, John Ismay, spent several days showing me around, but water for a camp was a difficult problem. I then moved up to Ackmen (now defunct) about thirty miles northwest of Cortez, Colorado to call on a local archaeologist, Courtney Dow, who had been pleading with the Historical Society to send a representative to his area to see "his" ruins, about 300 of which he had mapped.

The plan delighted me, an abandoned shack was available for camp headquarters, we could board at a local rancher's house and labor was plentiful, as it was a depressed period. The local farmers needed aid badly.

The biggest ruin in the area—Lowry Ruin—was too big for us to tackle with limited funds, but plans were made for the next spring to excavate several of the small sites that abounded.

During the next two seasons we excavated five villages of the unit type, twelve kivas and seven square houses. All kivas were connected by subterranean tunnels either with adjacent rooms or towers. One large pueblo of twenty-two rooms possessed two kivas built within the room block. This large pueblo was built on the edge of the canyon and had no towers. The function of the towers is not known, but since they did not appear to have any defensive purposes but were connected to kivas, one wonders if they served any ceremonial function.

The purposes of these digs were vague. Essentially, I was digging for specimens for the Museum, and because, aside from work by Prudden in the early 1900's, little research had been done on sites of this time period (about A.D. 1000). Mostly, we dug out of curiosity, for fun, for specimens, and to write the historical details for these sites and for this time period. Actually, we added a fair amount of information to the study of cultural process and the social grouping of the early history of the Anasazi.

It was the work of T. Mitchell Prudden in the early 1900's that suggested to me that the boundaries of architectural units might be used to indicate the boundaries of social groups. For decades, archaeologists had been eager to perceive what social groups were and what bearing these ancient groupings had in forming modern southwestern societies. The evidence, if converted into an ethnographic context, might be valuable in making cross-cultural comparisons. Prudden's work demonstrated that the pueblos of the northern San Juan watershed, where he carried on his researches, consisted of one general or standard structure—the unit type pueblo that probably housed one family unit, and larger pueblos which were made up of several such structures. Certainly our work demonstrated that a "unit type" consisted of a pueblo of about six to ten rooms with one kiva. Where more rooms were involved, more kivas and towers accompanied them. Further, the complete unit type was often surrounded by a low, compound wall that perhaps seemed to set off one clan or extended family structure from another.

After two years with the Colorado State Historical Society, I was offered a job with the Field Museum of Natural History as replacement for Duncan Strong, who was leaving to teach at the University of Nebraska. My title was Assistant Curator of North American Archaeology. After a year, I was able to persuade the Museum to let me return to the Southwest for the express purpose of excavating Lowry Ruin, named after a former homesteader.

Lowry Ruin and the Anasazi Culture

When I first saw the ruin, I thought it must be two or three stories high, but I was not aware that the site sat on a low natural mound. I also overestimated the number of rooms present by about 10 percent. But I was eager to dig a "big" ruin—a desire that later dissipated! Little did I realize that four years of digging would mean about three additional years of analyzing the data!

I assembled a crew, the most important member of which was Al Lancaster who later assisted Joe Brew at Awatovi, and who then went on to become famous for digging and restoration work for the National Park Service. Al had been assistant foreman during the two years we worked in unit-type pueblos and had demonstrated his alertness and ability to "see" things that I would have missed.

Soon after we started work at Lowry, we ran into trouble. A new homesteader, Jasper Foster, did not comprehend that his homesteading rights did not extend to either the ruins or to the mineral rights of the tract of land. His first expression of hostility was to split all our shovels one night, and to saw our pick handles into pieces. When I went over to his house to protest this vandalism I was run off with a shotgun. Foster's next act was to take pot shots at us as we dug, and each time we had to drop down into a room for protection. I obtained permission from the sheriff to carry a gun in the car. One day Foster ambushed me as my car meandered around the sage brush. He sprang from behind a bush and jumped upon the running board of the car, threatening me with a large piece of pipe. I slipped across the seat and out the other door, taking my gun with me. I was shaking too hard to have hit him, but Foster did not know that and stayed his distance.

I decided that somehow we must put an end to all this foolishness, so I went to Watson Smith, who had joined our team and Jess Nussbaum, who was superintendent of Mesa Verde National Park, for advice. Jess suggested calling in a Federal Marshal from Denver, which we did. The marshal impressed Foster and eventually we made a "settlement," which consisted of buying ten acres of Foster's homestead—although he had no legal right to sell to us; nor did we have the right to buy from him. Fortunately, this illegal arrangement brought an end to our quarrel—thanks to Watson Smith—and digging proceeded without any more trouble.

What were the original motivations of the research at Lowry Pueblo? To be honest, I fear some of them were the result of my callow youth: the desire to make a name for myself by aping Kidder, by digging a big ruin and to run substantial stratigraphies to solve some of the ceramic problems of the area; to obtain a goodly amount of loot for the Museum, for I was, at the time, very museum-minded; and because it was a challenge for a novice to be in charge of ten workmen, to have a pueblo of about thirty rooms to excavate as well as a great kiva. There were few young men of my age (about thirty years) that were entrusted with a job of such magnitude. As time went on, I became aware of many other serious problems that needed answering. I suppose basically the biggest problem I wanted to solve was that of the culture-history or time-space systematics. This was the sort of problem that most of my elders and contemporaries were engaged in and since I was just fresh from the enormous influences of the Pecos Conferences of 1926-1930 this was not surprising. We were all eager to help fill in the time gaps in the Pecos system and to see if the postulated historical sequences of that system were reasonable and whether the facts accorded with the theoretical outline of the Pecos Classification. The idea of sampling or of testing hypotheses never occurred to us—if indeed any one of us knew of these matters. Other motivations will be mentioned in the section on results.

The two principal strategies involved were: 1. to gather all possible data; and 2. to dig the entire pueblo—rooms, kivas, and the great kiva.

Upon the advice of Dr. Kidder and Dr. Nussbaum we decided to dig two long trenches, starting them some 200 feet from the mound and running them diagonally in order to intercept the southwest and northeast corners of the main building. Later, several trenches were driven through the main refuse dump located on the southwest corner of the pueblo. In the two major trenches, we found that the undisturbed surfaces ascended about fifteen to seventeen feet. Although the mound stood thirty feet above the plains, only thirteen feet of it was debris. In other words, before the pueblo was erected, the knoll on which it stood was about seventeen feet high. In the long exploration trenches we found four pit houses, which we did not dig, several kivas, and under some of the rooms we found some remains of earlier walls and structures.

Since we wanted room-refuse taken away as far as possible from the main structure, we went to Rico, a nearby mining town and purchased a mine dump car and several hundred feet of rails. All dirt in the rooms was removed by shovel from levels and thrown up on top of the mound. Since this excavation took place long before the days of bulldozers and back hoes, we used a team and Fresno scraper for moving the refuse as it was thrown up on the mound. The team and scraper, with drivers, went round and round, picking up the

FIGURE 2
Excavation of a pueblo room. (Courtesy, Field Museum of Natural History, Chicago.)

loose dirt and dumping it down a wooden chute below which the empty mine-dump car stood awaiting a load. A gentle push started the car rolling down the slope. At the bottom of the gradient stood a buffer which tripped the dumping mechanism and allowed the dirt to fall through the trestle. It was an easy, quick, effective way of removing the room-fill. Later, when we worked the rooms at the north end of the pueblo, we used wheelbarrows because we forgot to leave enough base or surface to allow a team of horses to ambulate without falling into deep rooms.

Excavations in all areas were carried on in such a way that the horizontal and vertical placement of every artifact was known. A map of each room was made that indicated placement and size of doorways, beam sockets, beams, vents, and fire pits. Each room was photographed from a tower. Thus, a total of thirty rooms some two stories high, eight kivas, bins, and a great kiva were excavated. Kiva "A" was superimposed over a much earlier one—"B." From the abutments and bonding sequences a building sequence was established which had five stages. It was fairly apparent that the pueblo growth was due to an increase in number and size of families. The evidence at the time of excavation seemed to indicate that the site was abandoned from time to time. I rather doubt this now, although sections may have been abandoned. Apparently, the population was never very large since parts of the town were obsolete and unused. My guess in 1936 was that at the maximum, it consisted of only fifty or sixty people.

One aspect of our excavation at Lowry Pueblo that was a real contribution to the engineering knowledge of the people was a thorough and intensive study of all masonry. In this project, I was guided by Laurence Roys who had made a similar study of the engineering knowledge of the Maya. Since that study of masonry, the search for abutments and bonding is being revised today. I am proud that I had a part in this initial study. Roys divided the masonry at Lowry Pueblo into Chaco-like and non-Chaco-like.

Because of the presence of the Great Kiva, Chaco-like masonry and some Chaco-like pottery, I had speculated that a colony of people from Chaco Canyon had emigrated to the area and established what we now call Lowry Pueblo. Today, I seriously doubt this hypothesis and am of the opinion that what I called "Chacoan" was merely a widespread fashion of the time although the impetus might have originated in Chaco Canyon, for it was a formidable aggregation of people, numbering perhaps 10,000 to 50,000 individuals. Aztec Pueblo is also supposed to be "Chacoan" in part, but here again I think the Chaco style of masonry and pottery was a widespread style of the time. This does not mean that Chaco people were wandering here and there and establishing colonies. Just as Black-on-White pottery was common all over the Anasazi area, albeit with distinctive but related designs, so was the "Chaco" style widespread without any implication of movement of people. Another example is the spread of the Chavin cult art style in a comparatively short time over an area encompassing much of modern Peru and extending as far north as Ecuador and as far south as Bolivia. Certain ceramic design elements and stylistic traits associated with Chavin seem to have spread far beyond the actual core of the cult. Just how the enormous spread took place is unknown, but it probably was not due to conquest.

We obtained relatively few tree-ring dates from the ruin because pinyon and cedar were the woods commonly used for roof construction. The few dates that we did obtain fix the position of the building as being between A.D. 1086 to 1106; but my feelings are that the pueblo was probably in existence between A.D. 950 to 1200.

Some thousands of sherds were collected stratigraphically from which I was able to suggest the rise and fall in popularity of particular types. A type called Mancos Black-on-White appeared at Lowry during the decline of Lino Black-on-Gray pottery. This is the ware that appears to have Chacoan decorative motifs. McElmo Black-on-White preceded the Mesa Verde pottery.

Reflections on Lowry Ruin Processes

The more we worked, the more explicit some of our problems became. One of them was that the work would contribute towards the discovery of some of the forces which caused the gradual rise of the Pueblo Indians from a lower to a higher cultural state. Today we would call this cultural dynamics. We were interested in gathering facts in order to derive historical conclusions. Today this would be more or less frowned on. The mere gathering of facts leads one into a morass unless one has a problem or hypothesis. Certainly the facts we gathered in the 1930's did not lead to the solution of any problem that would satisfy a contemporary anthropologist. True, we did contribute to the history of the area and this was worthwhile, but we could have made a greater contribution to anthropology and the solution of contemporary environmental and societal problems if we had used the scientific method. We should all use our resources and wits in discovering the laws that govern contemporary society so that we can legislate more wisely. Archaeology covers thousands of years of human behavior and the laws that we formulate can be tested over and over so that our relief programs, for example, will not be a mish-mash of sentiment and experiments. Archaeologists will have to use their imaginations and conceive of hypotheses that we can deal with and that can contribute to human welfare and happiness.

In short, I would sum up the results of our excavation at Lowry Ruin as being historically sound and representative of the 1930's, but lacking in conceiving of archaeology as anthropology and therefore as a social science. This is a comment that has the merit of hindsight. Many of the ideas expressed above are recent, and perhaps not more than twenty years old, hence I cannot be blamed for not having had foresight. My remarks stem from a revaluation of the report on Lowry Ruin and are therefore retrospective.

The Mogollon Region

After having investigated the Anasazi in Colorado for twelve seasons and having excavated a range of sites, from the earliest known site to the latest (from circa A.D. 600–700 to A.D. 1200), I felt the need to change areas and to move on to new challenges and different problems. In 1939, John Rinaldo, my colleague, and I moved everything to an area near Reserve, New Mexico. I had been hoping to find an "unexplored" area and Emil W. Haury and Ted Sayles, at that time archaeologists at the Gila Pueblo recommended the northern part of the Mogollon area in New Mexico—a culture area which up to that time had barely been touched. Haury had excavated two sites (Mogollon 1:15 and the Harris Village); the Cosgroves, the Swarts Ruin; Wes Bradfield, Cameron Village; Paul Nesbitt, the

Mattocks Ruin; and J. W. Fewkes, Hough and Kidder had all done work in the area. With the exception of Hough, Haury, and Nesbitt (at Starkweather Ruin), all the researches had been carried on in the southern or Mimbres portion of the Mogollon region. No work since Haury's had been done north of Glenwood, New Mexico. Hence, here was a virgin tract that contained many early Mogollon ruins as I knew from the large surveys of Gila Pueblo by Dr. Haury.

Further, although I blush to admit it, I was tired of the sage brush environment of Colorado and wanted to be in a pine forest—certainly the height of nonsense when one is supposed to be a scientist!

The Mogollon culture had been recently delineated as a separate branch by Haury, and his taxonomy and his theories were being combatted. Hence I was eager to help substantiate his ideas, if possible. Also, little was known about the antecedents of the culture that Haury had unearthed.

To seek for the earliest aspects of the Mogollon culture was another reason for our choosing Pine Lawn Valley, near Reserve, New Mexico.

The site that Haury and Sayles suggested we first look at was located three miles west of "the Saw Mill." We had a difficult time finding the site because the saw mill that Haury and Sayles referred to had been moved! When we finally located the ruin we were delighted with it because it was strewn with small bits of plain ware sherds (afterwards called *Alma Plain* and *Alma Rough*), was located on a low ridge, and appeared to include fifteen to thirty pit-house depressions, one of which was much larger than the others. We called the site the SU site, the brandmark of the old Stevenson-Underwood ranch.

The local Forest Ranger helped us select a most attractive site for our field station—a site just across the road from the Pine Lawn Tourist Camp where we could obtain water, milk, and food. It was an ideal arrangement that worked admirably for fifteen years. Joe Weckler, my assistant, and I, purchased lumber from the nearby saw mill and in three weeks' time built a most comfortable cabin of five rooms, with fireplace, root cellar for photography, and several other smaller buildings. We purchased a 500 gallon tank for water storage and perched it on a hill so that we could have running water in the kitchen and at the showers. The water for the tank had to be hauled from the nearby store and was discharged into the storage tank by gravity.

In examining the first report on this area I note that in my introduction I mention some of the reasons for moving: that archaeologists were then becoming aware that the entire Southwest was not just one culture—the Anasazi, with "aberrations" or "special developments" elsewhere; that Abajo Red-Orange pottery was related to Mogollon Red-on-Brown pottery; that I wanted to broaden my knowledge of the Southwest by expanding my "frontiers." In my second report, I asserted that although we had dug eight houses (out of a possible twenty-six), we needed more data before we could make valid generalizations about a new culture. We also announced a new slant on our research: namely, we hoped to gather information that would help shed light on how SU Indians lived, how they grouped themselves socially and how they solved their economic and food problems, why they lived in a town and whether they had developed religious concepts.

In the synthesis of the second report, I defined the Mogollon culture, set forth a set of dates with phase names; compared the traits of the Mogollon, Basketmaker and Hohokam; pointed out that a certain amount of psychological inertia had to be overcome when a new idea is advanced and that I was one of those that did not easily accept new ideas.

I characterized the Mogollon culture as an undeveloped, unsophisticated, unalloyed, unvarnished, homespun kind of culture with no striking or dramatic features. The general pattern was unadorned and lowly and based on almost minimal requirements. It was homogeneous and non-expansive in that it probably sought no, or few contacts with other cultures. I conjectured that the people were mild, timid, and retiring. The traits that appeared in their region (houses, agriculture and pottery), were not reworked and were not stamped with strong Mogollon character or woven into the Mogollon pattern. I felt that the Mogollones never became accustomed to agriculture or with house-building but continued to love and use their old household "gods"—stone artifacts inherited from their Cochise ancestry. When Anasazi influences later drifted into their areas, the resistance of the Mogollon was so mild that the Anasazi culture became the dominant one. This was my evaluation of the Mogollon in 1943.

In general I would still agree with this evaluation, although I might state the ideas more simply. Certainly much of the Mogollon culture remained apparently static and styles of stone tools remained pretty much unchanged for centuries.

In the third and final report on the SU site, I summed up the results of this remarkable site. We excavated all the pit houses we could find—twenty-six, in all—and this gave us a certain confidence in house-types and settlement pattern. The houses were semi-subterranean (pit houses), more or less roundish, with short or long tunnel entrances mostly facing east; ranged in diameters from about 4.0 meters to 7.0 meters and in depth, all were about 1.0 meter. The largest one measured 10.0 meters in diameter and about 75 centimeters in depth. The interior equipment was different from all other pit houses in addition to being larger. Next to the wall and spaced equi-distant were five log-shaped grooves. In these, one could discern impressions of bark. The function of these grooves is unknown. Its size and log grooves, plus a firepit that was lacking in some of the other houses, caused me to wonder if this was a ceremonial room. If not, it must have housed an extended family and that arrangement differed from all other SU houses.

The settlement pattern was more or less determined by the long, narrow ridge on which the village was located. Most of the houses clustered about the central area of the ridge with the kiva or ceremonial room at one end of the village and the other, smaller houses scattered about in an irregular fashion with no discernible regularity.

The dates on the site ranged from about A.D. 380 to 500, and the phase was called *Pine Lawn.*

We had a few answers to the questions stated earlier. Chances are that one nuclear family lived in each house. The ground plan does not suggest any special social groupings or breakdown into clans. But, it is possible that the village was composed of one or more extended families; or the arrangement may have been similar to the camps of hunting and gathering bands—that is, several patriarchal families related through the father line and living together in a village. We know that they grew corn, beans, squash; collected and ate wild plant food, and hunted deer, bison, antelope, fox, Jack Rabbit, turkeys and birds.

We conjecture that they had developed religious ideas because of the presence of a large ceremonial pit house and because several of the burials were provided with mortuary offerings (pottery and shell bracelets).

We don't know why they lived in villages, but since it seems that most human beings like propinquity or living in groups, this may have been a reason for villages. Protection from enemies and the sharing of food may have been other reasons.

Here again, I would criticize our work for not having specific hypotheses to guide it. As it was, we were merely collecting data for historical purposes—a good enough reason, but not sufficient in terms of contemporary philosophy. Fortunately, we did record our data in fairly full detail so that they can be used now for testing hypotheses.

After spending three seasons on the SU site, we chose sites that appeared to be later in time, in order to provide historical data for a sequence extending from about the time of Christ to A.D. 1200. At our next site (dated A.D. 750–800), we excavated thirteen pit houses that we classified as belonging to the San Franciso phase. In this report there is a section entitled "Problems." In it I state that our objectives were to fill in a 400 year gap in the local sequence of the Pine Lawn Valley; again, time-space systematics. Some of the questions I asked seem somewhat unimportant today. These are as follows: 1. Were there transitional types of house structures between Pine Lawn and Three Circle phases? 2. Was there evidence of abrupt change in milling tools and methods, or was the change a gradual one? 3. Could we find evidence of an increased use of agriculture? 4. Was there any evidence that smudged pottery came in about A.D. 850 or prior to that? 5. Did Alma Rough disappear when textured wares came into fashion? 6. Did the Chiricahua people linger on in the valley from about 1500 B.C. right up to the beginning of the Pine Lawn phase (A.D. 1)?

We did not find answers to all of these somewhat inconsequential questions, but we came up with some hypotheses, a few of which I shall cite.

1. Pit house shapes changed from round to rectangular about A.D. 800.
2. Some houses were provided with fewer floor pits but were provided with wall niches instead.
3. House size decreased from an average of 6.2 meters in Pine Lawn phase to 5.3 meters in Three Circle phase. This might have meant a change from extended family residence to nuclear family residence pattern.
4. But most important, we found kiva features in some houses—deflectors, ventilators, fireplaces and sipapu. Were these true kivas?

In the meantime, we had become aware by means of surveys that in addition to the many pit house villages in the area, there were also many surface villages with masonry walls—that is, pueblos. Often associated with some of these were large and small rectangular kivas. Some of these pueblos were merely four to six rooms; others thirty to forty rooms. But the most startling fact about these villages was that the pottery was different from that found in and about pit house villages. In the latter, the painted pottery consisted of Mogollon Red-on-Brown, Three Circle Red-on-White, Mimbres Black-on-White, and textured wares. These are standard pottery type names in Southwestern archaeology and each has a particular role in defining prehistoric cultures by period and area. But on the pueblo sites—that is, sites with surface rooms and walls of stone masonry—we note that although some of the ancient Mogollon textured wares lingered, there appeared Black-on-White wares the origin of some of which was definitely Anasazi and from the Gallup-Chaco areas in New Mexico; the other (Reserve and Tularosa Black-on-Whites) were also northern in origin—possibly from Klagetoh or the Puerco River Valley.

The earlier of these pueblos were erected with crude masonry walls composed of small, unshaped boulders set at random, laid in copious amounts of mud mortar, but the painted pottery was made up of the older Mogollon textured types and a sprinkling of Lino Gray and Wingate Black-on-Red, and Reserve Black-on-White. Along with these occurred Red Mesa, Kiatuthlanna and Mimbres Bold Face and White Mound Black-on-White types. This would place the beginnings of the Reserve phase at about A.D. 800. Thus, the first buddings off of northern peoples and the need of northern Anasazi people to spread to new, less-crowded territory took place probably as early as A.D. 800 or 900 or even earlier.

Thus it would seem that a momentous event took place—an alien people with a "different" way of life moved into the Mogollon territory. Although this is not direct evidence of such a migration, it comes close to it.

From our present perspective the migration seems to have been as follows: the Anasazi people, who inhabited the Zuni-Klagetoh, Manuelito-Gallup-Chaco areas of the Little Colorado River Basin of western New Mexico and eastern Arizona were apparently increasing in numbers. As their numbers increased, they began spreading or "budding off" and moving into new territories—especially north and south. "Budding off" means that a newly married couple, who live in an already crowded region, would naturally want their own farm. To obtain land already not claimed, they would move into a different territory—in this case the choice Mogollon area. This area was well-watered, attractive, and thinly populated. This, perhaps, is a possible explanation of the Anasazi expansions into the Mogollon heartland. Whatever the explanation, we find incontrovertible evidence that the Anasazi, or their relatives moved southwards. Some of the evidence has been alluded to but let me briefly sum it up. We find many Mogollon traits displaced—pit houses, some tools, some pottery types and some pottery shapes. Added to the Mogollon inventory and displacing some ideas are the following: surface pueblos with masonry walls and contiguous rooms, arranged in a cellular fashion; Black-on-White pottery of a novel style; rectangular Great Kivas with masonry walls, a firepit, "foot drums," a broad ramp entrance opening to the east, and

benches; small rectangular kivas constructed within the block of living rooms, so that the kiva was more or less surrounded by family dwellings. Each small kiva was provided with a ventilator, fire screen or deflector, firepit and sometimes a bench or an "altar"—that is, a deep recess constructed over the ventilator tunnel. In several such kivas, we found painted stone ceremonial objects—an effigy of a bear, a round sun-disc; tubular tobacco pipes of enormous size. All of these were painted in colored stripes—black, yellow, red, and green.

As time went on, the pueblos became larger (Higgins Flat Pueblo, about eleven rooms; Apache Creek Pueblo, about thirty-six rooms; and Valley View Pueblo, about twenty-five to thirty-five rooms; Hooper Ranch, about fifty rooms; and Table Rock Pueblo, forty rooms).

Along with the surface rooms and small kivas built within the house block, we also found that subterranean structures survived. We called them "pithouse kivas," although we do not know what their function was. They were about 6.0 meters square, the floors of which were about 1.5 meters below the surface. These were provided with a fire pit, a ventilator, mealing bins or flour receptacles and milling stones. Many were found at Apache Creek and some of them are similar to the subterranean structures found in the Kayenta area and reported by Lindsey.

Before I proceed with our further work in the Mogollon area I should like to pause briefly here and make an observation about my work—an observation made by my friend Jeff Reid.

In Retrospect

From 1930 to about 1939, my reports often ended with a section labelled "Conjectures" or "Synthesis." In these sections I summed up our results but also added sections that might be dubbed imaginative, fanciful, or visionary. In these latter sections, I can detect interests, or ideas in embryo that I later developed and some of which I still hold. But from about 1940 throughout all the reports on the SU site, I tended to shrink from expressing any radical ideas. The three reports on that early Mogollon Village— the SU site—are generally merely straightforward, factual reports with few conjectures, speculations, or surmises. (It is true that the second report on the Mogollon work does contain a section in which I attempt to characterize the character of the Mogollon culture; but it is a somewhat feeble, unaccented attempt lacking the boldness of my previous essays.)

I am perplexed about why I slackened and permitted my views

to take on a pseudo-objectivity, to become sterile and unoriginal. I am not at all sure that I understand this lapse. As I think about it now I can only make three guesses. One reason is that my previous reports had drawn a considerable amount of criticism and ridicule. I was told that my reports lacked objectivity; and to be "scientific" and unbiased, one should present only facts and not make any "interpretations." I had thought that by presenting all the cold data as carefully as possible and by then separating my "conjectures" very carefully from the actual details, I was not overstepping the bounds of propriety. Anyone could then take our "facts" and make his own interpretations. But, perhaps, I had unwittingly violated some unwritten code. The second reason may have been that I entertained mixed feelings about the Mogollon culture. For example, we did not yet know enough about this newly established taxonomic unit and hence could not afford to speculate about it, and, that since the Mogollon culture was not universally accepted, I should stick to the facts. Certainly, compared to the older and better established Anasazi culture, we knew considerably less about the Mogollones. Lastly, I felt my reports were out of line with others. Actually, I do not know the reason for permitting my imagination to run out.

At any rate, by the time I published a kind of synopsis of the sites of the Reserve phase, I was in full chase again after the spoor of the Mogollon life ways.

In 1950 my colleague and I published a report that included a chapter entitled "Conjectures concerning the social organization of the Mogollon Indians." It was the ultimate in this kind of essay. It was an attempt to probe deeper into the culture by making a series of inferences concerning the social organization of an extinct society. We assessed the value of every bit of detail that we had excavated in seven years. I was eager to perceive trends in culture growth by interpreting the raw data at hand. We did this by tracing the trends in architecture from about A.D. 300 to A.D. 1100, in the frequency of metates per house through time, the number of artifacts in houses through time. From these data we postulated a change from bilateral descent in the hunting-gathering stage that dated from about 1500 B.C. to A.D. 500 to the rise of matrilocal extended families that continued to evolve up to and beyond A.D. 1000. I shall not attempt to present our arguments but would merely like to point out that this attempt was regarded as a series of postulates, and an attempt to achieve a greater understanding of and time depth for the social organization of the Mogollones. I felt that this trial had merit over a mere description of bare material remains. I also had the impression that such an attempt to reconstruct the total culture could best be done by means of a study of pan—Southwestern culture patterns. In the light of my most recent change—a change from a philosophy that invoked only culture history, to one that calls for a study of why and how culture changes, I consider this chapter on the social organization of the Mogollon Indians as dramatic, prophetic, and a milestone in Southwestern archaeology. I think it was the first attempt in recent times to reconstruct prehistoric social organization in the Southwest and to make archaeology a social science with relevance for contemporary problems. But even this novel attempt was too much for some archaeologists. I remember being invited to present a guest seminar at a large university. After my presentation of our data and postulates, the instructor said: "Interesting. But don't you think it is too soon to make such conjectures?" This seemed like such rampant conservatism that it caused me to become dissatisfied with traditionalism and to be fearful of becoming fossilized.

Meantime, I longed to find perishable materials—the kind of objects one might find in a dry cave. Our surveys had turned up a rock shelter called Tularosa Cave, high upon a hill-side. The opening was minimal—just large enough for a man on his belly to crawl into. On the surface were a few bits of encouraging evidence—ash deposits, a few sandals, and bits and pieces of string, sherds, and reeds. We also knew that Hough, of the United States National Museum, had sampled this cave and had been fortunate to find perishable objects of wood, skin, fiber and plant material. Up to this time (1950) we had confined our digging operations to open sites, in which were preserved only tools of stone and bone, pottery and house forms. We hoped for and needed two requisites to round out our image of the prehistoric Mogollon culture. One was a stratigraphic sequence in order to test out typological sequences that we had developed from excavating scattered open sites. The other was a representative collection of perishable Mogollon materials in order to show us the other side of the coin. Up to this time, we had only seen the non-perishable objects of the culture, but we needed to know more. We needed to know, for example, what kinds of foods they ate; what sorts of clothing they wore; what objects they fashioned from wood, fibers and plant materials; and what their weapons were. In short, did the Mogollones make and use objects other than stone, bone and fired clay?

Tularosa Cave

In the Tularosa Cave we found what we were looking for, and in abundance. The specimens came out in the tens of thousands, and we had to wire Chicago for extra catalogers. The Cosgroves had dug several dry caves in the area, but the rich yield of Tularosa Cave far eclipsed any other in the Mogollon area.

I would like to present briefly the history of the cave deposits and the mechanics and almost insuperable difficulties of digging the bone-dry shelter.

Apparently, the cave had been occupied from time to time, but its size—about 9.0 meters long by about 5.0 meters wide, precluded large groups of people. The bulk of the fill was ashey, the particles of which were so small and dry that it behaved like talcum powder. If one walked or crawled from front to rear, an impenetrable cloud of powder arose and it required about forty minutes for the pulverized, ashey particles to settle. Imagine the difficulties in working under these conditions! But, actually, it was a blessing because such desiccation meant almost perfect preservation of all perishable objects.

As I noted earlier, the cave was choked with ashey fill and debris from floor to ceiling—a depth of about 3.0 meters. Since no electricity was available and since we could not afford a portable generator, we used very large re-chargeable flashlights for illumination and special respirator masks and goggles. The masks were provided with filters that were changed several times daily. As a result of our precautions, no one suffered any ill effects from the dust. We excavated by means of natural levels—a method that possessed both advantages and drawbacks. On the whole it worked well. The cultural sub-divisions were made on the basis of statistical tabulations of pottery types which changed proportionally and markedly from level to level. The lowest levels of the cave (the bottom four to six levels) contained no pottery whatsoever. Such levels were classified as Pre-Pottery and were dated by Carbon 14 measurements as being about 350 B.C. ±200 years. The Pre-Pottery materials were sub-divided by Carbon 14 dates and by levels. Some Pre-Pottery levels from other caves in the area dated back to about 800 B.C. ±200 years (O'Block Cave).

Up to this time and even now the earliest pottery-producing site had been dated at about A.D. 400-500. On the basis of radiocarbon dates from dry caves, the earliest brown-ware pottery may be dated as early as 500 B.C. to 150 B.C. This does not mean that the earliest Mogollon pit houses yielding only plain brown pottery are necessarily as old as 500 B.C. But it does indicate that plain brown pottery was present in the Pine Lawn area as early as 150 B.C. or even 500 B.C.

What was so remarkable about the artifacts that were obtained from Tularosa and other caves?

Our typological sequences were demonstrated to be correct and valid. This is especially true for the ceramic and lithic sequences—the only two that had been established in open sites. The dates for ceramics and lithics—dates established by many radiocarbon measurements from the various cave levels—have served as chronological anchor points for the entire Pine Lawn sequence and by extrapolation for other points in the Mogollon area.

But the richness of the other artifacts needs only to be mentioned to whet the reader's appetite. Here are a few of the significant finds: hundreds of tools of stone and bone—manos, metates, projectile points, drills, shell bracelets, dice, animal effigies; thousands of pieces of cordage made from vegetable fibers and human and animal hair; knots in the cordages of every type known today, including "granny" knots. Of special interest were thirteen large snares found in the lowest levels and provided with figure-of-eight or slippery hitch knots, probably used for snaring deer or antelope; sandals of textiles, leather, fibers; cloth of fibers and cotton; atlatls, bow and arrows, digging sticks, tablitas, reed cigarettes in which tobacco was smoked, a medicine man's charm bag of muskrat skin, baskets, wooden utensils, burden straps, cradles, matting, two desiccated bodies, and over 30,000 corn cobs(!), some of which date from the earliest levels. From this vast number of corn cobs, it is hoped that botanists can derive useful information about the early ancestors of maize.

We discovered that the Mogollon Indians possessed ceremonial equipment; that they treated the dead with tenderness and possible affection; thay they believed in life after death (mortuary offerings); that they were not essentially neat or tidy; that psychomatic medical practices were in vogue; and that they played games.

From the data at the cave, I suggested that up to about A.D. 1 there was a relatively uniform food gathering culture that existed throughout the Great Basin; that the Southwestern cultures, hence, were largely derived from the earlier and widespread hunting and gathering economy, and that there were periods of stability and instability. The latter was especially reflected in the period of about A.D. 500–700 at which time all of the material culture seemed to have reflected change, because after that time there were additions, subtractions and regrouping of traits. This was especially true in that during this period there was a larger yield of wild plants and a reduction in the remains of cultivated plants (corn, beans, squash).

TABLE 1
Culture Chronology Chart for the Southwest, with principal subarea columns.

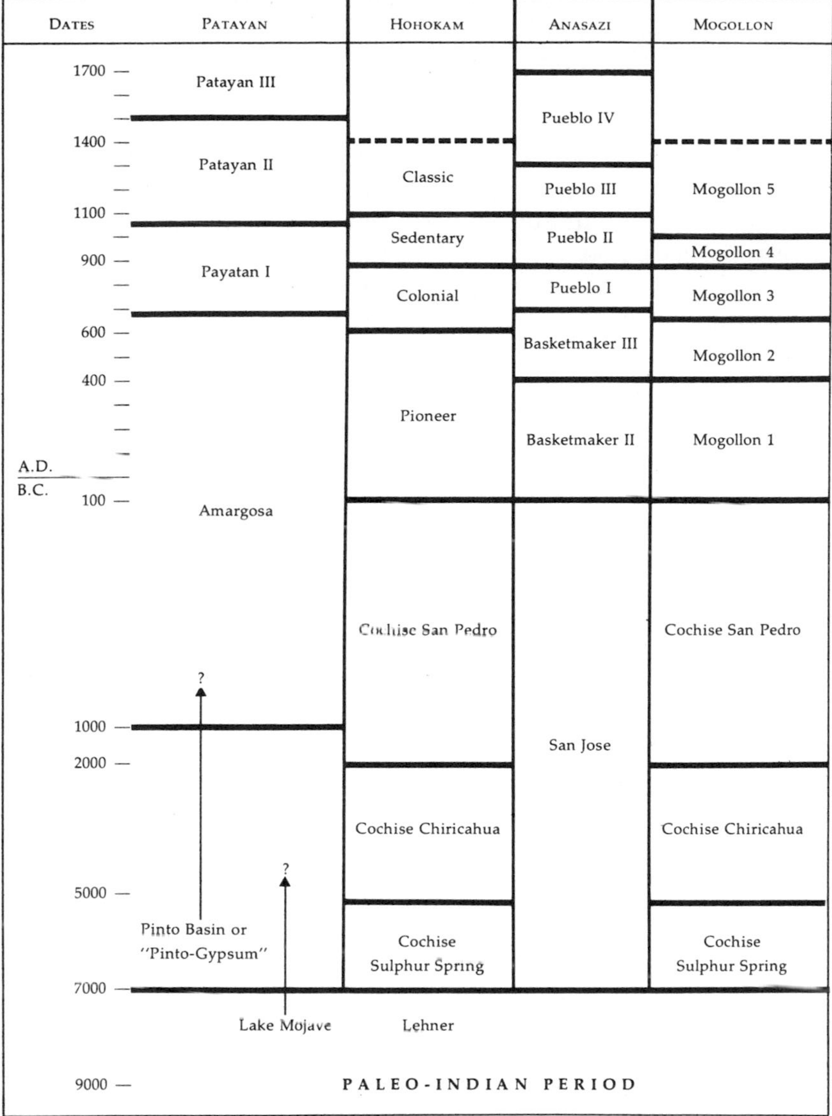

From Gordon R. Willey, *An Introduction to American Archaeology*, Vol. 1. (Englewood Cliffs, N.J.: Prentice-Hall, Inc., 1966), p. 188.

In other words, there was a significant modification of the subsistence patterns—that is, reduction in the use of cultivated plants to an increase in the consumption of wild foods and plants. In short, there was a regression towards an earlier form of subsistence—a return to a hunting and gathering existence. Why this happened is a mystery. We can find no evidence of change in the rainfall pattern. But it does show how easily the Mogollones adapted to stress. This adaptation brought about other changes, for we found that at this period (A.D. 500–700), there were other shifts, substitutions, and borrowings from without. Shortly after this "depression," we find Anasazi houses, pottery, and types of tools penetrating the Mogollon heartland. There are cultural dynamics in this situation that are not understood or explained. This is certainly a problem for future archaeologists to pursue. The solution may well have a bearing on our own cultural problems. Certainly, we merely exposed the existence of the issue but in no way have explained it.

I would like to detour here for a moment to present my latest views about the variety in Southwestern cultures.

Summary of the Southwestern cultures

A few pages back I suggested that the various cultures of the Southwest—Mogollon, Hohokam, Anasazi, Patayan, etc. (See also Table 1.)—were all derived from a much earlier and widespread way of life—a hunting and gathering means of subsistence. This is sometimes called the Desert culture that extended from Canada to Mexico (and into Mexico) in the Great Basin that lies between the Sierra and Rocky Mountain chains. But, if all the Southwestern sub-cultures arose from this Desert culture base why is it that they can be differentiated and why do they appear to be so different from each other?

An expert can readily distinguish between the material facets of these sub-cultures. But, actually, there is a parallelism or likeness between them all. For the most part, the "differences" between the different pottery types, houses and tools of the sub-cultures probably reflect the existence of functionally different ecological niches. Such differences as we note refer to varieties in the form of cultural activities and artifacts but do not necessarily indicate differences in the ways cultural activities are or were linked to local ecological communities. For example, if two cultural systems base their subsistence on hunting and gathering, and if one group inhabits a jungle and the other a desert environment, one would expect the procurement of food and activities concerned with the processing of foods to be carried out in special and different ways. Their daily activities would have special adaptive forms and styles that would be related to the gross differences in the environments and the foods being exploited. Since both cultural systems are classed as hunting and gathering societies, they in reality and in actuality occupy similar ecological niches in their different environments. Thus, form and style of houses, and the variety in the various aspects of the material culture would be functional. Hence, the stress we have placed on the taxonomic variations has been over-emphasized to the point that we fail to see that functionally the differences are not so distinctive. We have blurred the similarities in favor of specific details.

Show Low

In 1956, having explored or dug sites in all time ranges, we decided to move westward into Arizona, near Show Low. This region, too, was virtually unexplored.

The bedrock in this area is lava and is very hard to drill. It took a month to deepen the town well to 380 feet. After that we felt more relaxed and my colleague John Rinaldo began making an archaeological survey of the nearby area. To our great surprise we found that this whole region was also Mogollon. The earliest houses were pit houses containing the typical plain brown and plain red ware. Preceding the pit houses, we found evidence of the Desert culture (hunting and gathering) lasting up to about 1200–1500 B.C. Whether there was a hiatus of many centuries before the Mogollon people moved in is not known. We dug early pit houses that were dated by Carbon 14 to about A.D. 850–950. The Anasazi painted pottery that occurred in these houses suggests that these dates are close to the correct range.

Dr. William Longacre joined the staff next year and spent the following four years conducting a survey of the immediate area—St. Johns, Springerville, Snowflake, McNary, Pinetop and Show Low. We excavated a series of the sites he located, ranging in time from A.D. 800 thru 1350. Our operations had expanded to include pollen analysis and computer statistical tests on the pottery from Carter Ranch Site by the archaeologists Freeman and Brown. A nearby dry lake was cored and the data permitted Dr. Richard H. Hevly to suggest inferences about the climate and changes therein for a period running from late Pleistocene to Recent or for about 6,000 to 10,000 years. It was apparent from the various studies that Anasazi traits had penetrated the area as early as A.D. 850 and continued to increase up to the time of abandonment or about A.D. 1450. The archaeologists, Cooley and Hevly, had worked out the geology and depositional environment of Laguna Salada—a nearby ephemeral lake—and Longacre, another archaeologist, had contributed an essay on the sociological implications of the ceramic analysis and a synthesis of Upper Little Colorado prehistory including an estimate of the population trends. These reports were all significant because they included new types of studies and analyses never before linked to an archaeological report.

But about 1964–1965, Longacre had decided that he was finished with traditional archaeology, which emphasized only cultural history. He further decided that if I wanted him to continue to work for and with me that I had to forsake my old ways and adopt a contemporary view of archaeology. He was very patient with me and bore my hostility and outrage with great calm. Although I was indignant at this student who was flouting all my long-held beliefs and traditions, I was secretly very relieved to leave a fossilized philosophy. For some time I had been growing weary of culture history, of writing reports that lacked purpose, of carrying on a scholarly job that was completely cut off from social science and from relevance to contemporary problems. I felt that if I would not make contributions to the study of human behavior and discover the laws that governed human actions, I might as well capitulate and hand over to a younger, more innovative generation. Hence, I was happy to accept the precepts of Binford, Longacre, Hill, Fritz, and other younger men. I have detailed this change from traditionalism to a newer philosophy elsewhere and will not devote further space to this "revolution." But since then, I have taken more satisfaction in my research and feel that with my colleagues I have made some worthwhile contributions.

As a result of this transformation, our next site—Broken K Pueblo—was excavated in 1963 by James N. Hill according to the newer principles—random sampling, sociological implications, and restructuring of all of our ideas. Hill has amplified on all this in a publication issued by the University of Arizona in 1970.

In 1965, as a result of a suggestion by the Director of the Field Museum, E. Leland Webber, I was able to propagate these ideas even further by applying for and receiving a grant from the Undergraduate Research Participation Program of the National Science Foundation.

Since then we have received eight more grants from this same program and as a result have turned out some eighty-eight students who have been permitted to choose independent research topics based on the scientific method. They have learned the enchantment of working on their own with guidance, when needed, from a young innovative staff of graduate students who were pursuing similar pathways. In the meantime, the staff has written some eighteen theses and dissertations. Thus, in the space of about ten years, we have been able to make contributions to the corpus of anthropological knowledge and have provided some eighty students with fresh ideas, independence and a chance to make substantive contributions of their own. The versatility and inventiveness of these undergraduates in creating imaginative, original hypotheses for testing and demonstrating has both astonished and pleased me. For a report to be published by Field Museum Press, I wrote a chapter on our philosophy of education at Vernon Field Station. In its conclusion I said "We try to present science as an open system, without 'true' or "right" answers. We encourage students to investigate problems, solutions to which will help make the complexities of the present as well as the prehistoric world—more understandable."

I think we are succeeding to some degree. We are becoming aware that the scientific method with its creation of an hypothesis, test implications and so on may not be the only approach to good archaeology. We have emphasized the processual view or the study of the reasons for changes in culture through time. But there is the humanistic approach; the focus of social organization as a method of getting at human interactions; and many other ways of getting at the explanation of human behavior which is one important aspect of the millenia of human history at our command. We do not feel we have *the* answer. My guess is that there are many roads to truth.

References

COSGROVE, H. S. AND C. B.

1932 The Swarts Ruin. Papers of the Peabody Museum of American Archaeology and Ethnology, Vol. 15, No. 1. Cambridge, Mass., Harvard.

HAURY, E. W.

1936a Some Southwestern Pottery Types. Medallion Papers 19

1936b The Mogollon Culture of Southwestern New Mexico. Medallion Papers 20.

HOUGH, WALTER

1903 Archaeological Field Work in Northeastern Arizona, Expedition of 1901, Museum—Gates Expedition. Report of the U.S. National Museum of 1901.

MARTIN, PAUL S.

1929 The 1928 Archaeological Expedition of the State Historical Society of Colorado. Colorado Magazine 6; 1: 1–35.

1936 Lowry Ruin in Southwestern Colorado. Anthropological Series, Field Museum of Natural History 23; 1.

1943 The SU Site. Excavations at a Mogollon Village, Western New Mexico: Second Season 1941. Anthropological Series, Field Museum of Natural History 32; 2.

MARTIN, PAUL S.; LLOYD, CARL AND SPOEHR, ALEXANDER

1938 Archaeological Work in the Ackmen-Lowry Area, Southwestern Colorado, 1937. Anthropological Series, Field Museum of Natural History 23; 2.

MARTIN, PAUL S.; LONGACRE, WILLIAM A. AND HILL, JAMES N.

1967 Chapters in the Prehistory of Eastern Arizona, III. Anthropology 57.

MARTIN, PAUL S. AND RINALDO, JOHN B.

1939 Modified Basket-Maker Sites, Ackmen-Lowry Area, Southwestern Colorado, 1938. Anthropological Series, Field Museum of Natural History 23; 3.

1940 The SU Site. Excavations at a Mogollon Village, Western New Mexico, 1939. Anthropological Series, Field Museum of Natural History 32; 1.

1947 The SU Site. Excavations at a Mogollon Village, Western New Mexico: Third Season 1946. Anthropological Series, Field Museum of Natural History 32; 3.

1950a Turkey Foot Ridge Site, A Mogollon Village, Pine Lawn Valley, Western New Mexico. Anthropology 38: 2.

1950b Sites of the Reserve Phase, Pine Lawn Valley, Western New Mexico. Anthropology 38: 3.

1960a Excavations in the Upper Little Colorado Drainage, Eastern Arizona. Anthropology 51: 1.

1960b able Rock Pueblo, Arizona. Anthropology 51: 2.

MARTIN, PAUL S.; RINALDO, JOHN B. AND ANTEVS, ERNST

1949 Cochise and Mogollon Sites, Pine Lawn Valley, Western New Mexico. Anthropology 38: 1.

MARTIN, PAUL S.; RINALDO, JOHN B. AND BARTER, ELOISE R.

1957 Late Mogollon Communities: Four Sites of the Tularosa Phase, Western New Mexico. Anthropology 49: 1.

MARTIN, PAUL S.; RINALDO, JOHN B. AND BLUHM, ELAINE A.

1954 Caves of the Reserve Area. Anthropology 42.

MARTIN, PAUL S.; RINALDO, JOHN B.; BLUHM, ELAINE A. AND CUTLER, HUGH C.

1956 Higgins Flat Pueblo, Western New Mexico. Anthropology 45.

Martin, Paul S.; Rinaldo, John B.; Bluhm, Elaine A.; Cutler, Hugh C. and Grange, Roger, jr.
1952 Mogollon Cultural Continuity and Change: The Stratigraphic Analysis of Tularosa and Cordova Caves. Anthropology 40.

Martin, Paul S.; Rinaldo, John B. and Longacre, William A.
1961 Mineral Creek Site and Hooper Ranch Pueblo, Eastern Arizona. Anthropology 52.

Martin, Paul S.; Rinaldo, John B.; Longacre, William A.; Cronin, Constance; Freeman, Leslie G., jr. and Schoenwetter, James
1962 Chapters in the Prehistory of Eastern Arizona, I. Anthropology 53.

Martin, Paul S.; Rinaldo, John B.; Longacre, William A.; Freeman, Leslie G., jr.; Brown, James A.; Hevly, Richard H. and Cooley, M. E.
1964 Chapters in the Prehistory of Eastern Arizona, II. Anthropology 55.

PREHISTORIC EUROPE

(preceding page)

Map of the main vegetational zones of Europe. From Grahame Clark, *Prehistoric Europe: the economic basis* (London: Methuen & Co., Ltd., 1952), p. 10.

Prehistoric Europe: The Economic Basis

GRAHAME CLARK

Introduction

In a field as inherently difficult as Prehistoric archaeology, in which we seek to recover the history of preliterate societies, a terrain with few signposts and almost limitless horizons, it is important at all times to know precisely where we stand and how we have come to be where we are. The history of research is a history of false trails as well as breakthroughs into new territory and it is important for the individual explorer not only to chart his own course but to be aware of the explorations of others. Only in this way is it possible to draw the maximum profit from the experiences, adverse or favorable, of the totality of competing, but also in a larger sense cooperating, individuals working in any particular field of archaeology. And it need hardly be added that experiences in one field may often be found to apply with varying degrees of qualification to cognate or even quite remote fields of archaeology. There is room, therefore, for a more technical kind of historical dialogue in the field of archaeological research than is commonly found in the literature. The history of archaeology in relation to other fields of inquiry and to the general movement of ideas need not be and indeed rarely is written by scholars dedicated to fundamental research in any particular branch. As the subject grows in maturity, on the other hand, a new need has become apparent, the need for a more technical assessment of the process of research in particular fields. Such treatment of particular aspects of archaeology, if successfully accomplished, ought to make us more effective because more consciously orientated towards purposeful goals.

The authors best qualified for the historical appraisal of particular fields are probably those who have held to a particular line and have made their position clear in a series of publications over a

Headpiece: Swedish Bronze Age rock engravings of fishermen. From Grahame Clarke, *Prehistoric Europe: the economic basis* (London: Methuen & Co., Ltd., 1952), p. 86.

period sufficiently long to have witnessed basic changes in the course of archaeology. In my particular case I have been asked to explain why and how I came to write *Prehistoric Europe: the economic basis* and how the approach and concept embodied in it have contributed to and been modified by the onward progress of research. The first part of this assignment is the easier and the one the author is best qualified to discuss, and for that reason the one to which my attention will be directed.

A book is often said to be the child of its author. In reality the relationship is much closer. A parent contributes genes to his offspring, but the outcome is the product of a genetic mixture of overwhelming complexity extending backwards to countless generations. An author, on the other hand, at least has the illusion of being more in control of his product. Yet the words he inscribes on blank pages, though they are his and his alone, embody thoughts which, whatever the individual twist, derive to a greater extent than he can probably bring himself to admit from his social environment and his own historical context in the evolution of that environment. The fact remains that an author is an individual and a book the expression of an individual's point of view at a particular juncture of time under specific circumstances. It would be as false to pretend to a god-like independence of milieu as it would be to suggest that books emerge apart from their authors in response to influences or movements in the realm of ideas. A factual account of how I came to write my book is bound nevertheless to be autobiographical or a piece of pretentious humbug. Since authors stand in as much need of self-deception as the next man—and probably a good deal more so—it is well to recognize the dangers of reminiscence. The only objective manner of avoiding or at least of reducing the benefit of hindsight is to quote from books and articles written by myself and published at successive dates before 1952. By the same token, changes in my own way of looking at things at least can be documented from publications published since or in press.

The careers of most academics necessarily begin with a period of more or less intense specialization. The ever-increasing degree of specialization and the growing volume of publication necessitates choosing a restricted topic if worthwhile results are to be achieved within a prescribed period. In winning their doctorates, candidates are found to cut deep grooves as they penetrate the outer layers of academically approved doctrine and seek to explore some aspect of inner reality. The danger is that having succeeded, they fail to extract themselves from the grooves of their own creation. One reason for this is that they are too often unconscious of being walled in.

Mesolithic Research in the East Anglican Fens

Before describing how I personally succeeded in discarding my Ph.D. shield, perhaps a word should be said about how I came to acquire it. The subject of my initial research—Mesolithic Britain—was suggested by my teacher Miles Burkitt in the Department of Archaeology and Anthropology at Cambridge. In those days at Cambridge, Miles was required to cover the whole field of prehistory up to the time when metallurgy was established. In attempting this he was made keenly aware of the fault or gap between the Old Stone Age (Paleolithic) and the New (Neolithic), something thrown into strong relief by the different training and objectives of those primarily engaged in one or the other. Because he had to teach both he was all the keener to try to restore or discover the continuity of prehistory. To this end he undertook surveys of the data recovered since the beginning of the century on the European continent, which appeared to be of intermediate age and to date from the earlier part of Post-glacial times. One reason why he put me on to the task of investigating the evidence for a Mesolithic phase in Britain was that the most common clues would lie in the most durable residue, namely flint industries. As an undergraduate I had already been a passionate connoisseur for more than a decade, a result, perhaps, of having attended boarding schools from the age of seven, each of them situated on chalk downs (Sussex and Wiltshire), which were rich in flint industries.

My first task was a typological one. I had to comb through collections of flints, mostly collected by amateurs from the surface, to seek for parallels with Mesolithic material from Continental Europe. Other than this collection of Mesolithic material there were a small number of lithic assemblages obtained in the course of limited and not very sophisticated excavations and a few stray finds of antler and bone artifacts. It was on the slender basis of mere typological analogy, lacking stratigraphical or any other kind of dating that I presented the case for a Mesolithic phase of settlement in Britain (1933) and in particular for the presence in eastern England of flint industries and barbed antler and bone points resembling those excavated in Denmark and known as "Maglemosian." The comparative abundance of the material presented gave some ground for confidence but I was only too keenly aware of the need for an adequate chronological frame of reference.

The introduction of the technique of pollen analysis to Britain by Dr. and Mrs. Harry Godwin was to provide the best means for testing my hypothesis. By one of those contingencies which so often affect the course of research, a barbed point of "Maglemosian" type was dredged from the bed of the North Sea between the Leman and Ower Banks by the trawler *Colinda* in September 1931. This discovery was just in time to be included in an appendix to my first book and, what is more important, occurred precisely at the moment when the Godwins were ready to apply their new technique. The new find, although differing in detail from those already known from Holderness, Yorkshire, and from the Thames Valley, strongly reinforced the notion that the Maglemosian culture extended across the North Sea at a time when the southern part of the sea was a vast freshwater fen. In their classic paper of 1933 (Godwin 1933:36-48), the Godwins were able to show that the North Sea specimen and that from Skipsea, Holderness, belonged to an early and late phase of the Boreal period, respectively; that is, that they were chronologically comparable with Maglemosian finds in Denmark. The analyses also gave some insight into the type of forest vegetation prevailing during the period when Britain formed an integral part of the North European Plain.

Godwin and I—he was already an established lecturer in the Department of Botany and I was still a research student in Archaeology and Anthropology—first came into contact through a common interest in the Fenland. This was the nearest point to Cambridge where a well-developed sequence of Post-glacial deposits of a kind likely to produce archaeological specimens in deposits containing identifiable pollen was known to exist. Cyril Fox (1923) had shown nearly ten years previously how Neolithic, and to a lesser extent Bronze Age finds, thickly clustered on the sandy Breckland, extended into the peat zone of the southeast Fenland. There seemed every hope that the area round Shippea Hill would provide opportunities for locating archaeological material from these periods in deposits capable of investigation by pollen analysis. Even more to the point, so far as I was concerned the Breckland contained in the Wangford-Lakenheath dune area a classic site for Mesolithic flints. There was a prospect that traces of this phase of settlement might also be located in the Fen sequence. A good deal was known about the Post-glacial stratigraphy of the Fenland thanks to the opportunities provided by the extensive cuts needed to maintain effective drainage. Skertchley's geological memoir showed that in the southeastern part of the basin including the Shippea Hill area, two major peat layers were commonly separated by a thick deposit of clay. The problem was how to establish the context of successive phases of human settlement to this well-defined stratigraphy. Since settlement in the Fenland has always been closely linked to waterways, an obvious lead was to follow the extinct course of the Little Ouse, which traversed the Shippea Hill Fens in the form of a low silt bank or "rodden." The decisive clue came with the discovery of a mixed assemblage of flints on the surface of sand ridges on either side of the former channel of the Little Ouse on Plantation and Peacock's Farms, Shippea Hill. The first find was made in 1931. The Fenland Research Committee was formed in 1932 under the Chairmanship of the distinguished paleo-botanist Sir Albert Seward, who then held the Chair of Botany at Cambridge, to insure that all the available skills of Quaternary Research were brought to bear on exploiting the potentials of the region (Phillips 1951: 158-273). Working as a team, Godwin and I succeeded before the end of 1934 in defining the ecological contexts of three phases of settlement—Late Mesolithic, Early Neolithic and Early Bronze Age—in the Shippea Hill Fens, by locating the peripheral scatter of waste from each phase of settlement, the first two at successive levels in the Lower Peat, the third in base of the Upper Peat and by seeing how these fitted into the sequence of vegetational history defined by pollen analysis (Clark 1935: 284-319). We had also by this time tied in an Early Mesolithic flint assemblage at Broxbourne in the Lea Valley between Cambridge and London. By the time this work had to come to an end in 1940 the sequence had been carried down to the Roman occupation of the Fenland. Although much of the basic work in the field and the laboratory fell to Godwin and myself,we received much help from working as members of a group. Much of the benefit accrued from the informal gatherings held each term to discuss research prior to publication and to enlist specialist aid in analyzing finds. Experience of this teamwork in Quaternary Research was an enduring influence.

Although drawn to Quaternary Research initially as a means of dating and validating traces of Mesolithic settlement, involvement soon made me aware of the importance of the environment in its own right as something to which man had necessarily to adapt. This made me impatient to see what had been achieved in the study of Mesolithic settlement in the countries which pioneered pollen analysis. In 1933 and 1934 opportunities were taken to visit excavations and museums in Denmark, Germany and Sweden. On my return I wrote a new book to show what had been achieved in these countries by viewing the archaeological data in its appropriate environmental setting (Clark 1936, 1969). The book's publication showed a fuller appreciation of the need to take account of the widest range of material equipment and in particular of objects made from antler, bone, bark, wood and other organic substances. Even more importantly, it revealed a real if still unsophisticated appreciation of the significance of physical environment: the change from Paleolithic to Mesolithic, for example, was viewed as in essence the outcome of adaptation to the new Post-glacial forested landscape. There was even a glimmer of an appreciation, evidenced, for example, by the fauna lists in Appendix One, that the people who practiced industrial traditions in the context of Post-glacial environment actually lived by exploiting its resources.

Archaeology and Society

Before this book appeared another decisive influence already had been at work and had made it possible to step out into a more spacious field. In 1935 I had been appointed to a lectureship at Cambridge. Experience of teaching soon awakened me to an awareness that archaeology was in effect a process of deploying techniques to increase knowledge of social life, something which in the ecstasy of classifying microliths in the cloistered world of a research student I had tended to overlook. The shock of having to teach novices after a spell of individual research, is the greatest help in dispelling thesis neurosis. At such a juncture the effects of earlier training tend to assert themselves. Following the English tradition which still prevails in essentials, I specialized during my last year at school primarily on one subject, in my case history, and it was as a historian that I spent my first two years at Cambridge, since archaeology and anthropology in those days only rated half a course. It is so general in the United States for Prehistoric archaeology to be taught in the context of anthropology, that it may be worth emphasizing that Cambridge is one of the very few centers in Europe where this happens. I owe much to my training in history, which has always made me more interested in prehistory than merely in Prehistoric archaeology, and but count myself doubly fortunate to have been brought up during the second half of my undergraduate training spent in the Department of Archaeology and Anthropology, on Radcliffe-Brown and Malinowski—and in due course on Evans-Pritchard and Thomson—as well as on Breuil and Childe. With such a training it was impossible to be content for long with ordering vestiges of material culture. When my time came to teach I was concerned to emphasize that archaeological fossils are social fossils and that what prehistorians were concerned with was in the final resort the process of social evolution. That is why I called the book I wrote for students at this time *Archaeology and Society* (1939), a book by the way, which after a third of a century remains obstinately alive. It seems hard to recall that the opening sentences of this book

"Archaeology is often defined as the study of antiquities. A better definition would be that it is the study of how men lived in the past..." should once have had an almost prophetic ring. What is certain is that Chapter Six headed "Interpretation" contained in embryo the ideas developed in later writings down even to the diagrammatic model which in elaborated form illustrated and in a sense symbolized the theoretical position taken up in my Reckitt Lecture for 1953 (Clark 1953: 215-238).

Prehistoric Europe: the economic basis

If it had not been for the outbreak of war in the very year that *Archaeology and Society* appeared, *Prehistoric Europe: the economic basis* would probably have been written ten years earlier. Thus, when invited to contribute a book on *Prehistoric England* (1940) for a popular series—a task discharged while awaiting national service in 1940—I found myself organizing the chapters not chronologically but functionally. Chapter by chapter the evidence was reviewed for the food quest, dwellings, handicrafts, mining and trade, communications, hill-forts (defense), burial and sacred sites. The basic ideas and an accumulation of notes were there. In the years of tedium and frustration that followed they no doubt simmered, but they could not be nourished by reading or research. An indication that this was so is given by the publication, while on war service, of the first two of a series of preparatory papers, one on bees (Clark 1942), the other on water (Clark 1944). In the first of these I made it plain that I intended to change the course of archaeological research by concentrating on social activities rather than upon objects. In the opening paragraph of the paper on bees I wrote:

> As purveyors of honey and wax, substances rated high by early man, bees would seem to deserve more attention from archaeologists than they have in fact received. In this respect they serve to point a moral. The tendency has all too frequently been to concentrate on those aspects of ancient cultures which lend themselves most easily to classification, to the neglect of those which promise the closest insight into the working of the societies under review, thus inverting the true outlook of the archaeologist and turning him away from the activities of human beings to a world of abstractions. The thesis we would like to urge is that the prime concern of archaeology is the study of how men lived in society, of how within the social framework they have striven to satisfy and multiply their wants. From such a standpoint the means adopted to gratify the taste for sweet things, a taste shared by man and beast and physiological in its basis, merits

at least as much attention as current fashions in safety-pins and other topics beloved of "museologists." (Clark 1942: 215).

I ended the paper by expressing the essence of an ecological viewpoint, linking honey with land-utilization and beeswax with bronze-casting. I noted how "through the activities of bees, the pastoral background of Bronze Age Europe helped materially to fashion the most characteristic products of the period. Which tell us more, the bees or the bronzes? A question-begging question. In the study of any society, past or present, no aspect can safely be omitted, for all are interdependent.

The article on "Water in Antiquity" (Clark 1944) started off by recalling the basic importance of food and water "and the all-pervading influence upon outlook and social structure exercised by the methods adopted to insure (their) adequate supply." I acknowledged my debt to Social Anthropology implicitly by including myself among "those who approach prehistory from a functionalist point of view" and explicitly by making footnote reference to books by Audrey Richards on diet and work in primitive society. On the other hand, the general organization of this article running through from the Old Stone Age to the modern hydro-electric era showed plainly enough a concern with history. Yet the essence of this paper is again ecological: the sources, methods of lifting and modes of utilization of water are considered as developing through time, but in step with basic subsistence and settlement patterns and subject to the natural possibilities of regions.

The fact that in these papers and those which followed immediately after the war I was consciously urging the need to break away from object-fetishism, does not mean that I was turning away from archaeological material. Quite the contrary, my idea was to use this as a means of documenting social life. In interpreting objects I sought to use every archaeological means, including the associations and contexts of data and iconography, but equally historical sources whether from classical or medieval antiquity or even from recent times. Again I did not hesitate to draw upon the extraordinary wealth of information assembled by ethnologists. In using this last source I was always aware of the need for sophistication. The principles I followed were described in an article written shortly after the war though it was not published until 1951 (Clark 1951). I began by emphasizing the falsity inherent in any attempt to apply the concept of unilinear evolution to human affairs. Cross-cultural comparison might indeed be suggestive: it could hardly in the nature of the case be definitive. More cogent results were likely when the comparisons were made within the same environment and when there was clear evidence of historical continuity between them. When seeking to interpret data about past behavior and in particular about the way in which natural resources were utilized it was helpful to know how people occupying the same territory managed to provide for themselves before the rise of modern economies.

On resuming active scholarship after the war I lost no time in investigating the basic means of subsistence of prehistoric Europeans. The resulting papers fell into two groups: those concerned with hunting and catching activities and specifically with the exploitation of seals (Clark 1946) and whales (Clark 1947a) and with fowling (Clark 1948a) and fishing (Clark 1948b) and those connected with forest clearance (Clark 1945 a & b, 1947b), farming and stock-raising (Clark 1947c). Since the seal-hunting paper was the first of a series it may be taken as a type. Its purpose was made crystal-clear in the opening paragraph:

> The research, on which the present paper is based, is part of a program to further knowledge of prehistoric times by the study of social activities. Seal-hunting is here considered, not because it gave rise to objects which need classifying and dating, but simply because it was an activity of vital interest to certain coast-dwelling communities in northwestern Europe during the Stone Age. (Clark 1946: 12)

I then proceeded to indicate the basic sources of my study. Since I went on to define my problem as "basically biological" it is not surprising that I gave first place to zoology—to the identification of the seals from archaeological contexts and not least to the life habits of the various species which alone enables us "to visualize the opportunities open to the old hunters." Secondly, one depended on the findings of Quaternary Research both for dating stray finds and above all for information about contemporary coastlines. Thirdly, I drew upon ethnographic data bearing on the methods used to catch seals before the introduction of firearms: in this connection I make only circumspect use of data from Eskimo territory, relying much more heavily on information about the way in which seals were hunted and exploited in northern Europe itself during historical times as recorded by historians and modern ethnographers. Finally, as was invariably and necessarily the case, I relied upon the archaeological data itself, the cultural and chronological contexts of seal bones and of the equipment used to catch them, information tabulated in a schedule and incorporated in a series of maps.

In discussing whales, fowls and fish, respectively, as factors in the subsistence and technology of the prehistoric inhabitants of Europe, I relied on the same kind of criteria as I had done in the case of seals and went out of my way to emphasize the degree of continuity in exploiting these particular resources. A point that may bear emphasis in connection with these papers on catching activities is that by stressing activities I was incidentally able to throw light on the way particular categories of artifact were used. The connection between form and function was frequently confirmed. For example, the formal distinction between stout harpoon heads with prominent barbs and some arrangement at the base for securing to a line emphasized the association with seal bones and isolated skeletons and the more slender finely barbed spearheads with tangs adopted for hafting to a wooden shaft emphasized the frequent association with remains of pike. Again, the association of stag antler mattock heads with the skeletons of stranded whales argued that one use of these artifacts was to detach blubber or meat from the carcass. Even more interesting, the sizes and shapes of fish-hooks could sometimes be linked with the classes of fish for which they were designed. The other, and by far the most significant consideration, is the stress laid on the behavior and seasonality of the types of animal concerned, matters on which early man must have been well-informed as the price of survival and which provide us with a powerful key to the understanding of his way of life.

In considering the subsistence of people who practiced mixed farming, much of the emphasis lay in vegetation and in particular on the way early man cleared the land, grew his crops and provided improved grazing for his livestock. In measuring the progress and nature of land clearance by far the most informative technique was that of pollen analysis. To appreciate the problem I was faced with, it is necessary to recall the orthodox position set out by Cyril Fox and which received general assent in British archaelogical circles. In his work on *The Archaeology of the Cambridge Region* (1923), Fox observed that the earlier antiquities of the settled period were mainly concentrated on areas with light soils, mainly gravels, sands and chalk, which he termed a primary area of settlement. It was only later during the Roman period, but not seriously until Saxon times, that the heavier clay lands, commonly termed the secondary area of settlement, began to be taken up on any scale. In due course Fox generalized this observation and applied it to Britain as a whole (Fox 1932). The correlation was valid enough. Unfortunately, Fox went a step further and supposed that the primary zone was occupied first because it was free of forest or at least only lightly covered, whereas the secondary area was avoided by prehistoric man because it was forested. This supposition carried conviction because common observation showed that the present day woodlands were frequently (but of course by no means invariably) situated on clay lands whereas heaths and the chalk downland were commonly (though again by no means invariably) free of forest. From this it became common practice to "restore" forests to distribution maps on the basis of geology and, conversely, to depict lighter formations as though these were free of forest. Thus, by a circular argument, when distributions of artifacts dating from the Neolithic to the Pre-Roman Iron Age were plotted they were almost invariably found to occur in "open" country. The doctrine that forests were inimical to primitive farmers, one that could hardly have been entertained for a moment by anyone aware of the most elementary accounts of horticulturalists in the heavily forested areas of Africa, southeast Asia or South America, was also dominant on the European mainland during the early decades of the twentieth century. R. Gradmann and his followers, observing that traces of the earliest farmers were found on the loess and other formations presently supporting a mixed association of shrubs, grasses and bushes, supposed that farming spread on formations that carried relicts of a *Steppenheide* vegetation (Gradmann 1906).

In order to understand the conditions under which farming economy was pioneered in temperate Europe it was necessary to understand what ecological conditions really were like during Neolithic times. There was one simple way to test the assumptions of Fox and the hypothesis of Gradmann and that was to discover by means of pollen analysis what kind of vegetation was in fact growing on the loess, light soils and calcareous formations at the time they were settled by Neolithic man. The result of systematic work carried out over a broad area of temperate Europe including Britain has been to show that at the peak of Post-glacial temperature when farming began in this part of the world the landscape was in fact dominated by forest which spread far and wide broken only by mountains, marshes, lakes, rivers and their flood plains and the sea coasts. Loess, chalk and breckland heath were alike forested. In so far as they are open today this is because they were among the first to be farmed. The first task of the Stone Age farmers was precisely to clear the forest, a long process in which several phases can be detected (Iversen 1941). In the same manner it was necessary for me to clear away misconceptions which stood in the way of understanding. So far from the forest being a barrier to farming, the earliest regime in temperate Europe was based on felling and burning, the regime of *brandwirtschaft;* and it was only when pressure of population caused the system to break down that permanent clearance and the creation of fixed fields and meadows began. It was into this picture that the cultivation of cereals and the maintenance of livestock (Clark 1947c), the twin pillars of mixed farming, had to fit.

The years 1945-48 which saw the publication of the papers on different aspects of subsistence were crowded ones. The war-time interruption had made men of my generation anxious to push ahead with their own work, but organized teaching had to be resumed and given an impetus and in my own case there was need to give a renewed impulse to *The Proceedings of the Prehistoric Society* which somehow had been brought limping through the war. Over and above this were the excavations which I regarded as part of my duty to carry on during the long vacation as a means of training students but which also could be used to demonstrate in practical terms the priorities in research that stemmed directly from the notions set out in my writings. It was no accident that the summers of 1949, 1950 and 1951, the years I was writing *Prehistoric Europe* saw me at work in a waterlogged hole in the peat at Star Carr in East Yorkshire (Clark 1954, 1971). The same preoccupation that drove me to mine and quarry the literature and museum collections for information about how men exploited natural resources to maintain social life made me anxious to obtain the same kind of information for myself by means of excavation. Again, there was a certain justice in choosing a Mesolithic site for my demonstration. During my time as a research student twenty years previously I had been confined to the typological study of the most durable lithic residues and was helped out only by a few stray finds of antler and bone work. While teaching I had emphasized the need to remedy this situation by paying close attention to the conditions which determined the survival of a broader range of data and spelled out the potentialities in temperate Europe of sites where water-logging had inhibited or at least slowed down the process of bacteriological decay. It remained an objective to find such a site and when John Moore first showed me Star Carr in 1948 I realized that here was the chance I had been seeking. By systematically uncovering this site by the former Lake Pickering, one had the opportunity to recover at least some of the organisms on which Mesolithic man subsisted and at the same time of securing a far wider range of the equipment by which he adapted to and utilized the resources of his environment. The idea that most artifacts at least on Stone Age sites relate to the manipulation of environment is enough to indicate that research on a site like Star Carr needed to be carried out within the framework of interdisciplinary research. This was fortunately available. The work of the Fenland Research Committee was, as we have seen, essentially complete by 1940 and when Quaternary Research was revived at Cambridge after the war its horizons were altogether wider. The sub-Department of Quaternary Research was instituted at Cambridge in 1948. In 1949 and again in 1950 and 1951 members of its staff were on the site at Star Carr and in due course contributed significantly to the final publication.

When I came to write the preface to *Prehistoric Europe* I made it clear that I hoped to bring "into focus two distinct lines of vision, those of the natural scientist and of the historian." I was concerned to show not only how men sustained life but how over a period extending from the Late-glacial period to the foundation of cities in different parts of the Continent this life underwent progressive change. In defining the sources available for realizing this aim I distinguished the following main categories in my Introduction:

1. *Archaeological*
   - (a) Material equipment for which I emphasized the need to compensate for under-representation of the organic component and the importance of studying materials and techniques of production as well as finished forms.
   - (b) Representations in the form of rock-art, models, engravings on metalwork or graffiti on pottery.
2. *Ethnographic and Ethnohistorical*
   - (a) Direct observation or records by trained ethnologists of the practices and equipment of indigenous peasant communities more especially in Scandinavia, the Alpine region and central and eastern Europe.
   - (b) Uncritical but still useful records by early writers, ranging from Strabo and Tacitus to King Alfred's edition of the history of Orosius or Olaus Magnus' *History of the Northern Peoples* published in the middle of the 16th century.
3. *Biological*
   - (a) Biological data on archaeological sites mainly in the form of food-refuse.
   - (b) Changes in vegetation revealed by pollen analysis and reflecting changes in land utilization.

The first chapter entitled "Ecological Zones and Economic Stages" began by defining economy as "an adjustment to specific physical and biological conditions of certain needs, capacities, aspirations and values." This definition marked a considerable shift from the position taken up in *The Mesolithic Settlement of Northern Europe* in which changes in the cultural sphere were treated without comment as if they were straightforward adaptations to environmental change.

Instead the relations between culture and the different aspects of the environment were now regarded as reciprocal. A direct appeal was made to the equilibrium model worked out by Evans-Pritchard in relation to the Nuer of the Sudan, the implication being that the status quo at any particular time or place could be expressed only in terms of interaction between cultural equipment and the main components of the natural ecosystem. But such a model was seen to be valid only for a very brief time. It was useful as a tool for investigating the workings of a functioning system and helped to explain why archaeological assemblages might retain their integrity long enough to form recognizable archaeological stages. To account for change, on the other hand, it was necessary to envisage forces that made for temporary disequilibrium. As soon as a long period of time was considered—and my book avowedly concerned itself with a period extending from the Late-glacial to the foundation of cities—stress had to be laid on the dynamic character of the adjustment between culture, habitat and biome. Changes in total ecosystems comprising human cultures in the context of their particular habitats and biomes, might be expected to proceed from any one of several directions. The equilibrium could be affected and even upset by changes in the environment, by what might be termed economic dynamism caused, for instance, by taking up all the available land, or by the effect of some labor-saving innovation, or again by the effect of contact between distinct cultures. Nevertheless, it was maintained that the climatic and vegetational zones in which Europe could be divided imposed certain limits to economic exploitation at any particular stage of technology. These zones, which shifted notably from the Late-glacial to the Post-glacial were defined as from north to south Circumpolar (fjäll-tundra and coniferous forest), Temperate and Mediterranean. Peasant societies based on mixed farming were seen as expanding to the northern frontiers of the Temperate zone and towns as emerging first in the Mediterranean zone, only developing as permanent institutions much later in the Temperate and Circumpolar zones.

The bulk of the book was given over to reviewing the evidence bearing on different aspects of economic life arranged in broadly chronological order in each chapter. The most complete treatment was accorded to the food quest, two chapters being devoted to catching activities (inland; coastal) and two to farming (clearance and cultivation; crops and livestock). Next followed, in logical order, shelter (houses and settlements); technology comprising the apparatus used to manipulate the environment (one chapter on artifacts of stone, bronze and iron; the other on other crafts, mainly those concerning working organic materials); and lastly, two chapters on distribution (trade; travel and transports). In presenting this material, particular care was taken to provide detailed documentation in the form of references to the extensive literature and a large number of illustrations.

This was necessary if the book were to succeed in its prime purpose, which was quite simply to convince professional archaeologists that their subject held more interesting possibilities than categorizing data in terms of cultural definition and periodization.

Retrospect

I responded eagerly to the pronouncement in 1935 of a revered senior, A. M. Tallgren, who stated "Forms and types, that is products, have been regarded as more real and alive than the society which created them and whose needs determined these manifestations of life." (Tallgren 1937: 155)

From that time I began to accumulate notes bearing on the social function of archaeological data. As I've already mentioned, an invitation to write *Prehistoric England* for a popular series in 1939 gave me my first opportunity to try out a functional approach and the material for papers written while on war service (Clark 1940) were drawn from notes accumulated during the immediate pre-war period. *Prehistoric Europe* was written with a considerable head of steam. How far it contributed to breaking the professional routine of the previous three generations it is not for me to say. Probably it would be best to regard the book as itself part of a reaction to what I have elsewhere termed "Museological archaeology." This reaction, so eloquently called for by Tallgren, was already beginning and was bound to come first in a territory like Europe in which the main spatial and temporal sorting of the primary data had already been accomplished.

The best form of attack depends very much on the intellectual and social context of the field of operations. My book was written in an English academic context. This is an unpromising field for dialectic. On the other hand, it does respond to facts, provided these are adequately validated. Translation of the book into eastern as well as western European languages shows that it must have met a need which was already being widely felt. Essentially the book represented a marshalling of facts which, in their totality, made it evident how much information could be gleaned about economic life even from material recovered with other ends in view, and specifically economic archaeology. By helping to channel the objectives of archaeological research also it has influenced, though to a lesser degree than one had hoped, the choice of sites for investigation and the methods used. The excavations at Star Carr which were not completed soon enough for more than a passing reference, are a case in point. Another is the continued investment of research time on the peat deposits of the Somerset Levels of southwest England, an investment which has already yielded important dividends in advancing knowledge about the existence and construction of prehistoric causeways (Godwin 1960) and the practice of Neolithic archery (Clark 1963) and which promises even more valuable insights into the settlement and exploitation of the area by Neolithic and Bronze Age peoples. The systematic quest for sites offering the highest organic content is a logical and necessary counterpart of the kind of archaeology I was intent to foster. So long as archaeologists are absorbed in the preliminary task of establishing areas and distributions as they have to be in the initial stages of exploration in any area, there is a positive advantage in maintaining the ongoing ritual and getting on with the task of collecting stereotyped samples of a limited range of artifacts which because of their high survival value can be relied upon to recur. Once archaeology is regarded as a means of discovering how people lived, on the other hand, there was a powerful incentive to maximize the range of information by choosing the right kind of site and employing consistent and adequate sampling techniques. The choice of waterlogged sites in the temperate zone is only one example of what I mean by choosing the right kind of site. Even more important is the need to concentrate on settlements and either excavate these completely or sample them in such a way as to make it possible to infer within a reasonable error of probability the scale and plan of structures. Again, in so far as economic archaeology is concerned with the way in which communities exploited natural resources, it follows that it ought to be pursued in the context of Quaternary Research. The Somerset tracks, for instance, only make sense in the context of ecological circumstances. They can only be recovered by means of pollen analysis and similar techniques, just as frequently they can only be dated by this method or directly by radiocarbon analysis.

The most trenchant criticism I received when the book first appeared came from Gordon Childe: "Yes, Grahame, but what have you done about Society?" Childe was a good Marxist. He may well have had in mind a crucial passage from *Das Kapital* which presumably underlies the immense investment in Institutes of the History of Material Culture put forth by the Soviet Union and its satellites:

> Relics of bygone instruments of labor possess the same importance for the investigation of extinct economic forms of society as do fossil

> bones for the determination of extinct species of animals. It is not the articles made, but how they are made, and by what instruments, that enables us to distinguish different economic epochs. Instruments of labor not only supply a standard of the degree of development to which human labor has attained, but they are also indicators of the social conditions under which that labor is carried on. (Marx: 172)

A more wide-ranging criticism must be that the book was by its very nature too generalized, too divorced from actuality. Thus, in emphasizing the importance of studying archaeological and accompanying biological data in its ecological context, discussion was in practice limited to differences obtaining in the territories of four major macro-zones. Again, by abstracting the archaeological data from its social matrix and treating it as though it were the product merely of a generalized historical process, the social dimension of culture, the fact that archaeological, like anthropological data, in general, relates to specific communities was lost sight of. To conflate both the criticisms my treatment of the data inhibited consideration of it in terms of systems. With the benefit of hindsight it is easy to see this. Only two things need be said. These criticisms did not impair the immediate aim of the book, which was to make a very elementary, but in the context of the time, a very necessary point—namely, that even the data incidentally collected in the course of stratigraphic and culture-defining archaeology was capable of throwing light on the history of prehistoric economy. And, conversely, it implied that, if archaeologists were only to concentrate their attention on seeking answers to the right questions, there was every prospect of being able to throw far more light on the processes by which the prehistoric inhabitants of Europe exploited its resources in maintaining and improving their living standards. In other words, taking one elementary step did not preclude but made it easier to take further ones. In fact, certain further steps have been and are currently being taken, in some instances, even by the present author.

Star Carr

One way of making this last point is to compare the initial publication of the excavations at Star Carr (Clark 1954) with the treatment accorded after the lapse of nearly twenty years (Clark 1972). My prime objectives in excavating at Star Carr were to recover:

(a) an artifact assemblage of Early Mesolithic character combining equipment made from organic materials—antler, bone and hopefully wood

—as well as from flint and stone, under conditions allowing dating in relation to phases in the history of Post-glacial vegetation in Britain;

(b) food-refuse, notably in respect of discarded meat bones, which might throw light on subsistence economy;

(c) information about the scale of social unit involved and if possible about the type of structures in which people lived.

The site on the northern edge of the lake which during Late-glacial and Early Post-glacial times filled the Vale of Pickering was chosen after prolonged search because it seemed to fulfill the main condition of success, namely an archaeological level in water-logged deposits. The success with which the first objective was realized can be seen from Table I (Clark 1954), which brings out very clearly the way in which the excavation of this single site enlarged our knowledge of Pre-Boreal and Boreal settlement in England. Not least of the finds was the quantity of waste resulting from the manufacture of artifacts of antler on the site. A disappointment was the rarity of wooden objects, which might conceivably have been mitigated if we had thought of using water jets as an excavating tool. A substantial body of food-refuse was obtained, principally animal bones, but including traces of edible plant foods, which may or may not have been gathered for food. The area of the site, indicated by plotting flints and noting the extent of a rough timber platform (only the lakeside half of which survived) made it plain that not more than a micro-band of three or four nuclear families can have occupied it at any one time. No information about actual shelters was obtained, except the negative one that we found no traces of vertical or oblique stakes in the underlying platform, which was composed entirely of birchwood, weighted with stones and wads of clay.

The main purpose of the publication was to make details of the find available with a minimum of delay to interested scholars. For this reason it carried many illustrations and was basically descriptive. An important feature of the book, as of the research on which it was based, was that it was interdisciplinary and included chapters on stratigraphy and vegetational history, and on the animal remains, as well as on the archaeology of the site. The presence in the field team of one or more qualified paleobotanists insured that the stratigraphy was correctly established and samples taken from the positions best calculated to insure that the occupation was fitted in correctly. This was invaluable not merely from a chronological but also from an ecological point of view: it allowed us to visualize fairly accurately the conditions under which the people responsible for the Star Carr assemblage were living while they occupied the site.

Again, the identification of fruit and seeds gave us some idea of the plant food available at the time. The animal material was important because it marked an intermediate link in the food chain: on the one hand it gave us an idea of the kind of animals that fed on the vegetation revealed by pollen analysis and macroscopic identification—it was interesting to note for example the relatively high proportion of elk and aurochs and the low proportion of swine at a time preceding the formation of oak-mixed and older forests. On the other hand, it gave a direct insight into the range of animals exploited by the occupants of the sites as well as into their relative importance in the food quest. Yet very little was made of this in the original publication. As zoologists, Fraser and King were asked specifically whether they could pronounce on seasonality and whether they were able to show that the site was occupied during the winter and abandoned during the summer months. Important information was passed by, such as why this was the case, how it fitted in with the archaeological finds, where the hunters were during the rest of the year and in effect what the totality of information from animal bones and artifacts was able to tell us about the economic system. A certain amount of attention was paid to working out the calorific output of the animal material actually recovered from the site and this was shown to be enough, with certain corrections, to maintain a group of four nuclear families for over six years. This finding agreed well with the observed concentration of artifacts and the fact that stratigraphical evidence on the lakeward side was enough to indicate visits over a period of time. What was missing from the original publication on Star Carr agreed very well with what was lacking in *Prehistoric Europe*: in neither case was consideration paid to social groups in the round.

In the case of Star Carr an invitation to contribute to the McCaleb series of Modules in Anthropology (Clark 1972) gave me the opportunity to rethink the results free from the burden of presenting an adequate record of the primary data. In particular I had the chance to view what we had found in terms of the seasonal utilization of territory. In connection with his work on Paleolithic settlement at Epirus in northwest Greece, Eric Higgs had drawn special attention in association with C. Vita-Finzi to what he termed the catchment area of sites (Vita-Finzi and E. S. Higgs 1970) that is, the area within an hour or two's walk of the actual home base which was fixed at a particular spot. Calculations made in relation to the north side of the former Lake Pickering showed that the carrying capacity of the low ground at the time of the year when red deer were present there would have been sufficient to maintain a group adequately so long as it did not exceed a microband of three or possibly four nuclear families. A closer look at the red deer remains, which accounted for around two-thirds of the meat supply of the Star Carr encampment, brought out the important fact that those represented in the kill were predominantly adult stags. This fact went well with the circumstance attested by archaeology that a major industrial activity at the site was cutting strips from stag antler and fabricating these into barbed points for use as spearheads. This interpretation also agreed very well with the observation that during the winter when the herds come down to shelter on the lower ground adult red deer stags tended to occupy separate yards distinct from the hinds and young. Since at this time of the year most of the hinds were carrying young it was obviously consistent with good husbandry to concentrate on adult stags in winter, the time of the year incidentally when their antlers provided a valuable source of raw material. Where were the deer—and presumably their human predators—during the summer months? Or to put it the other way round, how far did the annual territory, that is, the territory exploited during the course of the year by the microband that wintered at Star Carr and doubtless other sites on the north shore of Lake Pickering, extend? To judge from available studies of red deer, notably those by Fraser Darling (1969) for Scotland and by Ingebrigsten (1924) for southwest Norway, the stags would have rejoined the herds and the animals would have moved up on to the lower slopes of the hills and progressively onto higher ground as vegetation ripened only to come down again at the approach of snow.

As is normally the case, once one has the key to the system—or better to begin with—once one has even formed a hypothesis to account for a limited range of facts—the chance comes to test it on its own terms. If in a territory of some marked surface relief, as we find in Yorkshire, we suppose that herds and their predators were exploiting high ground, does archaeology support this? In the case of Yorkshire the answer is surely, "Yes." On the very crests of the North Yorkshire moors or of the Pennines, lithic industries of Mesolithic aspect had long been known in localities which by common consent were too exposed to have been occupied by man during the winter months. Such industries were indeed among the first of their kind to be known in England. Because they differed in certain formal respects from those on lower ground they were generally attributed to distinct cultures: thus we had Tardenoisian industries on the high Pennines and Maglemosian ones on the low ground of East Yorkshire to go no further afield. Viewed bioarchaeologically (or by the archaeology of how individual communities in fact lived in their environments), it begins to look as if at least some of the Pennine industries relate to the summer hunting grounds of people who camped on lower ground during the winter. The microlithic and scraper component of the "broad-blade" group of Pennine industries could be lost in the lithic assemblage at Star Carr and such differences as we can see can be explained in ecological/seasonal terms. For instance, the absence of axes and adzes from the high Pennine sites above the tree-line is hardly surprising; nor is the much lower proportion of flint burins, which at Star Carr were linked with intense activity in working stag antler by the groove and splinter technique, since during the summer, antlers were still in the process of growth. One of the morals of the rethink of Star Carr is the need to correct generalized concepts like "culture" (e.g., Early Maglemosian) and environmental zones (e.g., Birch-pine forest) by getting down to basic bioarchaeology—the study of how communities lived—by exploiting the resources of specific territories. In the case of people who depended on animals that shifted their territories seasonally this implied moves of the home-base and its attendant resource territory over a more extensive annual territory.

A model of this kind explains something, but it is nevertheless inadequate for the basic reason that human societies, even at a comparatively elementary technical level, differ profoundly from the animal aggregations which serve them as prey. The predator in chief moves in an extra dimension, the dimension of social territory. Aggregations of mammals achieve human status to the extent that their behavior conforms to or reacts against social patterns, that is, patterns transmitted and added to by virtue of belonging to historically constituted societies. The integrity and cohesion of these societies both determines and is reinforced by a certain patterning of behavior in the same way that individuals signal their identity by conforming to (or of course dissenting from) social norms. Since human societies occupy and defend territory it is useful to speak of social territory as a third and peculiarly human level in the territorial hierarchy. At an economic level, one may define social territory as the territory drawn upon for resources by any community by virtue of belonging to larger social groupings. If in *Prehistoric Europe* I ignored these groupings, which define themselves in the archaeological record in a variety of ways but notably by virtue of sharing idiosyncratic features of style which suffice to reinforce a sense of social identity, I did so intentionally. My aim in writing the book was quite simply to wake archaeologists from a situation in which, to repeat Tallgren's words, "forms and types...[were] regarded as more real and alive than the society which created them." If it helped in any way to promote economic prehistory or bioarchaeology it did what I set out to do. Now a generation later one can afford to admit: yes, communities had to exist by utilizing natural resources and by deploying the appropriate techniques and artifacts, *but* they did so as communities, that is, as human, culturally defined, historically-based communities. From this it follows that form and style analysis, so long as it is pursued with the object of defining social territories and, as societies advanced in complexity, of defining classes, and not as an end in itself, retains a highly significant place in scientific archaeology.

It is possible and, as I tried to point out in *Prehistoric Europe: the economic basis,* highly desirable when one encounters artifacts to ask the question that a paleontologist asks of a fossil, "What was this *for*?" meaning something more than that this artifact or this fossil helps me to systematize or order my data as archaeologist or as paleontologist. An archaeologist, like a paleontologist, values the objects he handles, not only as a means of controlling his material, but as a means of gaining an insight into the lives of the organisms to which they relate—how they were structured, how they ate, what territories they occupied, how they adapted to environment and how they moved about it. But people are more complex beings than fossil mammals and archaeology is that much more difficult. It is concerned with a new dimension, a new territory. When we speak of use we must in the case of artifacts think not merely of material use, but of social, symbolic use. The fact that the vast majority of the finest artifacts were never intended to be used at a banal, material level does not mean that their makers were wasting their time or merely shaping prize museum specimens. These things had their uses but they were social uses. By isolating the socio-cultural from the economic factor I did what I intended to do, but in doing so did violence to the total reality. For instance, I devoted a chapter to what, drawing on the vocabulary of our own quite different type of society I termed "trade," without so much as recognizing that redistribution is not only a basic characteristic and mark of human society, but that patterns of redistribution satisfied social as well as merely economic purposes. I first woke up to the meaning of the patterns of redistribution to which archaeologists have been paying increasing attention as a result of spending a term in the Department of Anthropology at Otago working in a country with a strong ethnohistorical tradition. The paper I wrote on the so-called stone axe "trade" (Clark 1965) is one sign of awakening. At the present moment, half-way through my book on *The Older Age Settlement in Scandinavia,* I am beginning to appreciate more fully what Childe meant in 1952, when he commented, "Yes, Grahame, but what have you done about Society?"

References

Clark, Grahame

1933 The Mesolithic Age in Britain. Cambridge, Cambridge University Press.

1935 Report on Recent Excavations at Peacock's Farm, Shippea Hill, Cambridgeshire. Antiquaries Journal 15: 284–319.

1936, 1969 The Mesolithic Settlement of Northern Europe. Cambridge, Cambridge University Press. New York, Greenwood Press.

1939, 1947 Archaeology and Society. London, Methuen. 1960, 1965 New York, Barnes and Noble.

1940 Prehistoric England. London, Batsford.

1942 Bees in Antiquity. Antiquity 16: 208–215.

1944 Water in Antiquity. Antiquity 18: 1–5.

1945a Farmers and Forests in Neolithic Europe. Antiquity 19: 57–71.

1945b Man and Nature in Prehistory, with special reference to Neolithic Settlement in Northern Europe. University of London Institute of Archaeology, Occasional Paper 6: 20–28.

1946 Seal-hunting in the Stone Age of North-Western Europe, a study in Economic Prehistory. Proceedings of the Prehistoric Society 12: 12–48.

1947a Whales as an Economic Factor in Prehistoric Europe. Antiquity 21: 84–104.

1947b Forest Clearance and Prehistoric Farming. The Economic History Review 17: 45–51.

1947c Sheep and Swine in the Husbandry of Prehistoric Europe. Antiquity 21: 122–136.

1948a Fowling in Prehistoric Europe. Antiquity 22: 116–130.

1948b The development of Fishing in Prehistoric Europe. Antiquaries Journal 28: 45–85.

1951 Folk Culture and the Study of European Prehistory. *In* Aspects of Archaeology in Britain and Beyond. Essays presented to O. G. S. Crawford, W. F. Grimes, ed. London, Edwards.

1952, 1965 Prehistoric Europe: the economic basis. London, Methuen. 1966, Stanford, Stanford University Press.

1953 The Economic Approach to Prehistory. Proceedings of the British Academy 39: 215–238.

1954, 1971 Excavations at Star Carr, an Early Mesolithic Site at Seamer, near Scarborough, Yorkshire (with chapters by D. Walker, and H. Godwin and F. C. Fraser and J. E. King.) Cambridge, Cambridge University Press.

1963 Neolithic Bones from Somerset, England and the Prehistory of Archery in north-west Europe. Proceedings of the Prehistoric Society 29: 50 ff.

1965 Traffic in Stone Axe and Adze Blades. The Economic History Review 18: 1–28.

1972 Star-Carr: A Case Study in Bioarchaeology. Reading, Mass., Addison-Wesley Modular Publications: McCaleb Module 10.

COLES, J. M.; HIBBERT, F. A. AND CLEMENTS, C. F.

1970 Prehistoric Roads and Tracks in Somerset, England: 2. Neolithic. Proceedings of the Prehistoric Society 36: 125 ff.

FOX, CYRIL

1923, 1948 Archaeology of the Cambridge Region. Cambridge, Cambridge University Press, Maps I, II.

1932 The Personality of Britain. Cardiff.

FRASER, DARLING

1969 A Herd of Red Deer. Oxford, Oxford University Press.

GODWIN, H.

1933 British Maglemose Harpoon Sites. Antiquity 7: 36–48.

1960 Prehistoric Wooden Trackways of the Somerset Levels: their construction, age and relation to climatic cleavage. Proceedings of the Prehistoric Society 26: 1 ff.

GRADMANN, R.

1906 Beziehung zwsichen Pflanzengeographie und Siedlungsgeschichte. Geogr. Z. 12: 305–325.

HIGGS, E. S.

1971 Further information concerning the environment of Palaeolithic man in Epirus. Proceedings of the Prehistoric Society 37: 367–380.

1972 Papers in Economic Prehistory. Cambridge, Cambridge University Press.
Note the fact that the British Academy should have chosen to adopt an investigation into the Early History of Agriculture as its first Major Research Project is an interesting portent.

INGEBRIGSTEN, O.

1924 Hjortens Utbredelse i Norge. Bergen.

IVERSEN, J.

1941 Land Occupation in Denmark's Stone Age. Danmarks Geologiske Undersøgelse. IIR, 66. Copenhagen.

MARX, KARL
Das Kapital. Everyman Edition, Vol. 1. New York, E. P. Dutton.

PHILLIPS, C. W.
1951 The Fenland Research Committee, Its Past Achievements and Future Prospects. *In* Aspects of Archaeology in Britain and Beyond. W. F. Grimes, ed. London, Edwards.

TALLGREN, A. M.
1937 The Method of Prehistoric Archaeology. Antiquity: 152–161. See page 155. This was translated from the original written in French and published in Eurasia Septentrionalis Antiqua X (1935).

VITA-FINZI AND HIGGS, E. S.
1970 Prehistoric Economy in the Mount Carmel Area of Palestine: Site Catchment Analysis. Proceedings of the Prehistoric Society 36: 1–37.

NORTHEASTERN IRAQ

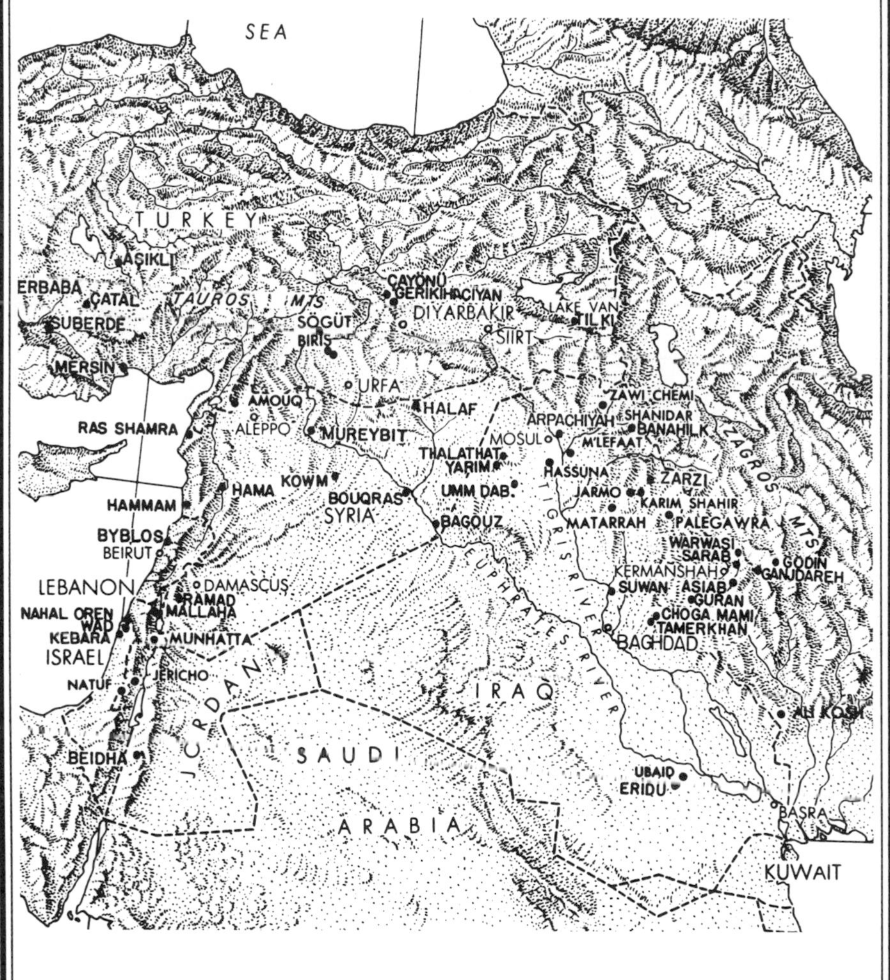

(preceding page)

Map of the locations of the better-known sites of the range from latest Paleolithic materials to those of the developed early-village communities in the nearer portion of southwestern Asia.

The Iraq Jarmo Project

ROBERT J. BRAIDWOOD

Jarmo is an early village site in the Chemchemal intermontane valley of the Iraqi Zagros range. It lies about 60 kilometers upslope and east of Kirkuk city in what is known traditionally as Kurdistan. The site is believed to yield the remains of a single but certainly developing cultural manifestation of the early-mid seventh millennium B.C. *(Libby). With its base camp at Jarmo, the Iraq Jarmo Project of the Oriental Institute, the University of Chicago examined not only Jarmo but several other late prehistoric sites, from the late 1940's to the mid-1950's.*

Avant Propos

A number of years ago, at an American Anthropological Association meeting in Chicago, the anthropologist, Margaret Mead, made an eloquent (but I suspect quasi-serious) plea that all ethnologists should preface their monographs with an abstract provided by their psychoanalysts. At least one recent book suggests that archaeologists may now be setting a fashion for self-analysis. Excavators do, indeed, often develop love affairs with some particular site.

Any retrospective essay such as this should begin, therefore, with a brief *vita*. Born in Detroit in 1907 and a product of its public schools, my collegiate career began with three years of architecture at the University of Michigan and one of outside office practice. The combination of a very indifferent academic record and the beginning of the 1929 Depression propelled me into another area early in 1930. In the autumn of that year, I went with a Michigan field staff, as "artist and surveyor," to Seleucia on the Tigris, south of Baghdad. My first published paper was on Parthian jewelry! I studied happily at the University of Michigan under Arthur Boak in history and under Carl Guthe and Leslie White in anthropology; my M.A. thesis, under Boak was on the economic organization of

Editorial Note: the author's preferred spelling, "archeology" has been changed throughout his chapter to conform to the accepted spelling of the book.

Headpiece: sickle and grain symbol.

the Seleucid empire. After a summer digging with the Chicago crew in Fulton county, Illinois, in 1933, I went to Syria that autumn for the Oriental Institute and have been on its payroll ever since. I studied history at the Oriental Institute under A. T. Olmstead, my Ph.D. dissertation, done under Henri Frankfort, concerned the basal materials of the Amouq sites, and my degree was granted by the Department of Oriental Languages and Literatures, although a third of the program was administered by the Department of Anthropology. In 1941, I had a happy summer under Paul Martin at the SU site in New Mexico, but that was my last effective New World experience. Since World War Two, I have worked again in Iraq, subsequently in Iran and most recently in Turkey. I would most like to be known as a culture historian and I reject the idea that historians are not interested in process. It amuses me that the Academy of Arts and Sciences classifies me under "Social Relations" but the Philosophical Society under "Humanities." I expect I may have been one of the cases Robert McC. Adams had in mind of ". . . a few individuals who manage to keep an uneasy foot in each camp . . ." (Adams 1968: 1188).

Gordon Willey's invitation to be retrospective first prompted me to read over various writings of mine committed during the years immediately following World War Two. I have come away from this dubious exercise with two feelings: the first being one of embarrassment over foolish guesses and oversights; the second being one of wry whimsy in finding many of the things I wrote to be well within what I take to be the spirit of the "new archaeology."

Naturally, what I wrote was not properly phrased since the new archaeology's "new speak" had not yet been invented. Nevertheless, my wife and I were already beginning to use the word "ecology" with some sense of its meaning in 1950, (Braidwood and Braidwood 1950: 194). In 1953 (Braidwood and Braidwood: 278) we even advertised the intention of an essay at ecological and cultural reconstruction, but quickly realized we did not know enough about the subject to write it. In 1959 in answer to a letter to the editor of *Kush* by A. J. Arkell, advising that I be "content" simply to "collect facts" and "carefully digest the facts collected by others," I wrote I would "much rather take a flyer now and then, marking it plainly a highly personalized fabric of hunches, test it as best I may by field research and drop it like a hot penny if it goes wrong!" (Braidwood 1959: 237) If only I had been prescient enough to say *hypothesis*, I could still march with the saints, but at least I did say *test*!

Actually, I don't mind being an "old"—or maybe better, "anomalous"—archaeologist. In the part of the world where I work, Arkell's desire for a far broader spectrum of evidence (which I am

TABLE 1
Chronological and developmental chart of Middle Eastern-European culture growth from the Late Paleolithic to the threshold of urban civilization (about 11,000 to 3,000 B.C.), as visualized by Braidwood in 1967.

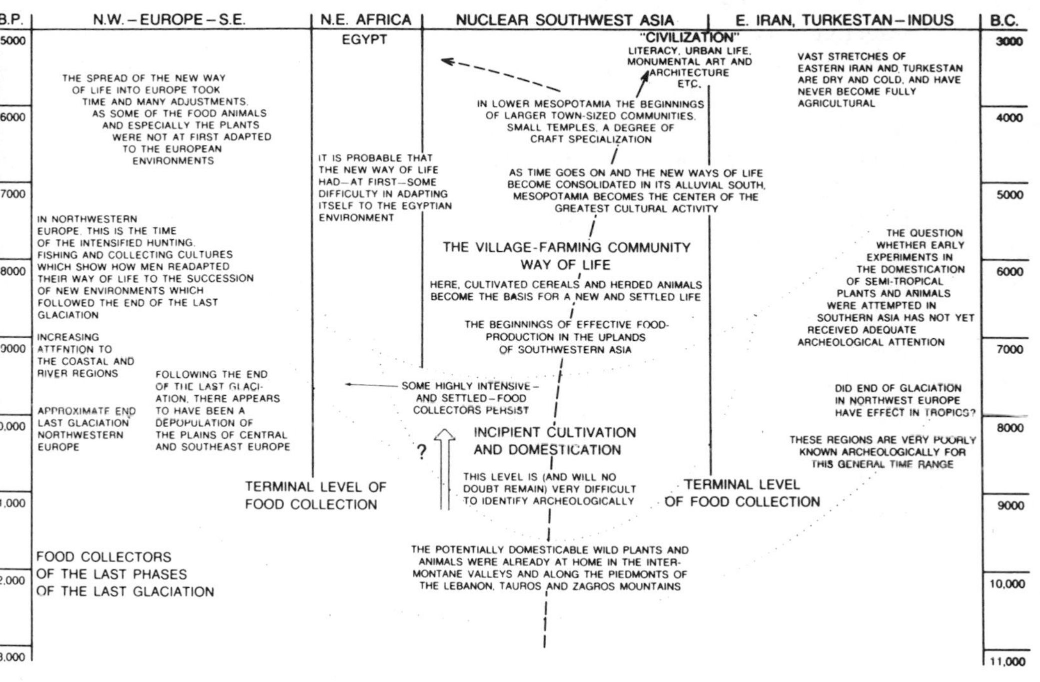

sure is what he really meant) plus certain political exigencies would seem to argue against any single set of formulae for archaeological research procedures. Some of the ideas involved here will be developed subsequently.

The Iraq Jarmo Project

It is doubtless best that I make clear at the beginning that the Oriental Institute's "Iraq Jarmo Project" concerned other sites than Jarmo alone. A preliminary account of our Iraqi field work, to the point of its interruption, was published in 1960 (Braidwood and Howe, *et al.*) and I myself, in 1972 (Braidwood: 310–20) did a brief review of all of the Prehistoric Project's field activities, as these relate (in my own judgment) to the general development of late prehistoric research in southwestern Asia. My primary concern here is with the Iraqi sites, but other site names will creep in. Our research goal in Iraq (as it has been subsequently in Iran and Turkey) was to gain an understanding of the beginnings and achievement of an effective food producing and village-farming way of life in southwestern Asia. The available evidence from Jarmo suggests a village of modest size which flourished for a relatively brief span of time after food-production had become relatively effective. Hence Jarmo itself is only part of the story of the Iraq Jarmo Project's field efforts, even if we did make our broadest exposures in Iraq at Jarmo.

The Iraq Jarmo Project was activated in 1947. Since at least 1944 (Braidwood, Tulane and Perkins 1944: 67), we had suspected a gap in the available later prehistoric sequences in southwestern Asia. Our 1947 proposal to the Iraqi Directorate General of Antiquities that we be allowed to work in the extreme northwestern corner of the country was declined on the ground that security was weak in that region. The Directorate suggested instead a Hassunan phase site, Matarrah, and the site of Jarmo, both in the Kirkuk region, where security was good. We perforce accepted their suggestion and requested excavation permits on both sites before we even left Chicago. With the exception of a site with Acheulean and pebble tools in the Barda Balka gravels, however, all the rest of the sites we subsequently examined in Iraq depended on our own survey activities.

That the excavation of Jarmo, the first instance of an early village site of its range of time to be examined in the trans-Euphrates region, came about as something of a fluke of the early post-war situation need not be a surprise. Such is one of the actualities of archaeological work in southwestern Asia. I often wonder how different our generalizations on the early village range in southwestern Asia might have been if it had been possible to begin in northwestern Iraq rather than at Jarmo.

Furthermore, as I suggested above, our excavations at Jarmo were interrupted before reaching even a reasonable level of completion. With the *coup d'état* which ended the monarchy in 1958 and subsequent unrest in the Iraqi Zagros, foreign archaeological activities in the Iraqi hill flanks were essentially terminated. In 1959, we shifted our activities to the Kermanshah Valley in Iran, although the Oriental Institute's budgetary label for the season still remained "the Iraq Jarmo Project"! During our three Iraqi field seasons, in 1948, 1950–51 and 1954–55, we were actually involved at Jarmo for a total of twelve months, of which perhaps a third involved only indoor processing during bad weather. We normally worked about thirty men.

I should recall at this point the genuine spirit of hospitality, active interest and helpfulness of the personnel of the Iraqi Directorate General of Antiquities. Much of our ability to carry through our field program effectively until the *coup d'état*, was due to their enthusiasm for our work. We were also blessed with a remarkably good sequence of staff members, both senior and junior. Neither can I overlook our remarkably fine Egyptian field superintendent, Abdullah Said Osman al-Sudani, or the half dozen highly-trained Shargati workmen recommended to us by the Directorate. Further, the local villagers were both friendly and intelligent and Abdullah and the Shargatis soon managed to make careful and trustworthy excavators of them. In retrospect, no expedition of which I have ever been part has been better served in the above senses.

An unhappy recollection, however, is the persistent concern we had over logistical matters. Until National Science Foundation aid became available in time for our final Iraqi season, a high proportion of our budgets was committed to staff travel and gear shipment. The only town of any size in the Chemchemal plain was too far from the sites; the two nearby villages were small and had no extra houses. Hence, we had to build our own expedition house. The weather was often tricky; our normally quite adequate do-it-yourself access road was sometimes mudded in or blocked by wadi floods for four to five days' time. With the expedition house handy to both Jarmo itself and a good well, we were happy even in isolation, but—with no assurance of a renewed budget at the end of the 1950–51 season—we had to demolish the house to recoup on its materials. This meant a tent camp in the spring of 1955. And above all, of course, the uncertaintyof long-range budgetary support (taken with the perpetual political uncertainties of that part of the world) tended to inhibit the making of long range operational plans on the sites. We doubtless should have been more trusting in this matter of planning but, as things turned out, it would not have done us much good.

The next really embarrassing aspect of the Iraq Jarmo Project's incompleteness is its lack of final publication. I am in the awkward position of being asked to be retrospective about a piece of field work which is not only incomplete in itself but of which a full description of the already excavated yield is not yet available. I would far rather be retrospective about the early Amouq materials. My wife and I completed our final obligations on them in 1960

(Braidwood and Braidwood). It seems to me now that we benefited from the enforced wartime pause in field activities (the Amouq field work itself ended in September, 1938) and that, as younger people with far less broad and fragmentary involvements, we were then able to accomplish most of the processing and descriptive writing on the Amouq materials by ourselves.

During the Iraq Jarmo Project years the situation increasingly changed. The broad interest the Iraqi sites themselves created, with their implications for the general problem of understanding the appearance of an effective food-producing way of life in southwestern Asia, tended to develop into a perhaps overly fashionable research focus. This very fortunately brought us funds (in the season by season sense), and senior research collaborators in the natural sciences and interested graduate students, but whatever success I seem to have had in orchestrating the activities of these senior and junior colleagues in the field does not seem to have carried over into holding all of them to the drudgery of producing finished final reports. With the graduate students, this has been particularly (and doubtless understandably) the case. We encouraged their use of portions of the Project's materials as the basis for theses and dissertations, with implications that their descriptive processing would become final reports and their conclusions would serve as their theses or dissertations proper. Too often, the descriptive processing sections have remained only rough drafts and, with their dissertations completed and degrees granted, the individuals have proceeded to develop their own careers elsewhere. I cannot really blame them—it was my mistake not to insist on a completed descriptive manuscript as well as a dissertation.

My Turkish colleague, Halet Çambel, criticizes the fact that our American pattern in archaeology tends to favor priorities on the career development of individuals rather than on long-range commitments to the completion of all responsibilities for a given site. There is certainly justice in her point of view, especially if seen from a milieu where, for example, the director of the Deutsches Archäologisches Institut's excavations at Warka, Iraq, observed quite seriously in the 1950's that his Institute anticipated completion of the site in about one hundred years. The French, as another example, industriously continue excavations begun at Ras Shamra, Syria, in the late 1920's and at Susa, Iran, begun in the late 1800's. It has been noted, however, that the milieu in which these foreign colleagues operate is one of persisting governmental support, which affords—among other things—a cadre of full-time career technicians, draftsmen and specialist processors and that the senior field staff also has little if any teaching or curatorial responsibilities at home.

I do not, however, mean to excuse myself from all culpability for the long delay of the final Iraq Jarmo Project reports. Most of the reports are already in the editor's hands and the end is in sight. I do think, however, that had we been able to persist in the Iraqi Zagros, much more would already be in print than our 1960 *Prehistoric Investigations*.

THE YIELD

Given the incompleteness of our final reporting, I might usefully summarize portions of our preliminary reports and also conclusions we have come to in further analyses of the materials. I shall let retrospection creep in as it may.

A brief general observation or two might come first, however. It would be very easy to make a long list of desiderata of evidence overlooked because specialized techniques of recovery had not yet been devised by the mid 1950's. For example, we did not use flotation to recover plant remains on any of our Iraqi sites. We did not take properly oriented baked oven floor samples for paleomagnetic analysis. We did not make a determined attempt to quantify the relative proportions of the remains of wild vs. domesticated plants or animals. We did not undertake intensive surface surveys of our sites before excavation. I, of course, wish now that we had. Were Sir Flinders Petrie, founder of modern archaeology in Egypt still alive, he would certainly also wish he had not given coffin wood and matting from his predynastic burials to his workmen for their tea fires! Who dreamed of radiocarbon age determination in the early 1900's?

A second general observation would be that only in the case of Bruce Howe's work at the small terminal Paleolithic cave site, Palegawra, were our exposures significantly proportionate to the overall site areas. Two points are in my mind here, for both of which I must assume that my readers have some comprehension of the nature of the multi-layered mud-wall and debris matrix of a typical southwest Asian mound. We take for granted that domestic structures (or structures with other purposes, *if* they indeed already existed!) were not arranged in regular geometric order and density within the confines of given prehistoric sites in southwestern Asia. Such is certainly the case if we extrapolate a village plan from such incomplete prehistoric exposures as we have or judge by reference to exposures made on sites of the literate ranges of time or—perhaps best of all—observe the simple present-day mud-walled peasant villages of the same general size and complexity in much of southwestern Asia. The orientation of the structures in an early village-farming community was undoubtedly not very regular, the spacing between structures was doubtless irregular and there were probably broad open areas scattered here and there within the original village plan. My first point, then, would be that *only* one or two modest sized exposures on a prehistoric village site may give a very unbalanced as well as incomplete notion of the original occupants' assemblage and activity localities and hence lead to skewed archaeological interpretations.

My second point of worry related to inadequate exposures is concerned with reckoning the relative times of occupation of structures (with their individual inventories of artifacts and hints of activities) of the same apparent "level" or "horizon" but appearing in different trenches on the same site. Sun-dried mud-brick or loaded-mud (touf) walls normally suggest short-lived structures. I have seen more than one still thriving village in southwestern Asia in which a quarter to a third or more of the village area had roofless mud-brick houses already slumping into abandoned ruins while the houses in the rest of the area hummed with life. A single 10.0 × 10.0 meter exposure (or even a pair of them) into such a site of seven thousand years ago would doubtless give an impression of a more tightly settled village plan and of a larger population than was actually the case. Relative elevations above sea level, however precisely taken, would be of no help; mounds are seldom horizontally stratified like cakes! Nor would any of the available age-determination procedures give the chronological precision we would need here. Given no later intrusions into it, a long and carefully studied profile in a connecting trench between the pair of 10.0 × 10.0 meter exposures would (to my mind) be our one possible salvation, but—ergo—this underlines my point of necessarily adequate exposures.

I am not satisfied that our work in Iraq provided us with really adequate exposures. Given the resources we had at the time in funds, trained staff and local workmen, and the careful pace at which prehistoric excavation must responsibly proceed, I would suppose we did as well as we could, but now wish we had exposed much more than we did.

From the point of view of problem orientation, our assumed baseline in the past was the terminal Paleolithic assemblage first described by Dorothy Garrod (1930: 8) from the Iraqi Zagros cave site of Zarzi. Zarzi lies about 35 kilometers north-northeast of Jarmo in the drainage of the Lesser Zab River. In Bruce Howe's spring survey of 1951, the talus yield of another small rock shelter, Palegawra ran heavily to Zarzi-like blade tools and microliths. Howe excavated a portion of Palegawra a month later and returned again for more digging in the spring of 1955. Palegawra opens to the southeast on a rocky spur extending into the Bazian plain in the Basira-Tauq Chai drainage. This intermontane plain lies upslope (east) of the Chemchemal plain and is separated from it by the Sagirma ridge, although the two plains have the same drainage. Thus, Palegawra is only about 26 kilometers east-northeast of Jarmo, but also only 26 kilometers south-southeast of Zarzi. The shelter has a maximum breadth of about 6.0 meters and extends about 5.0 meters into the rock; its maximum depth is slightly less than 2.0 meters of which there was some later disturbance in the uppermost 60 centimeters.

Howe's final descriptive report is essentially complete and a general description of the Palegawra occurrence appeared in our 1960 *Prehistoric Investigations*. In brief, the flint industry ran heavily to backed blades and microlithic bladelets; various end, round and other scrapers; simple, angle and polyhedral burins, and an assortment of microlithic geometric forms. Simple bone tools, beads and pendants of shell, bone, tooth and stone appeared, and there was a grooved rubbing stone, a polished celt, a quern fragment and a modest scatter of obsidian from well below the zone of upper disturbance. Reed and Turnbull's final report on the animal bones is complete and in 1967, Priscilla Turnbull (Turnbull: 4) published a note on the bones, accounting for the onager (*Equus hemionus*) as the most common hunted animal but indicating that wild sheep, wild goat and large red deer bones were numerous and that wild pig, wild cattle and gazelle were also present, along with some smaller mammals, land snails and crabs. We recovered little trace of vegetable foods but charcoal samples of oak, tamarisk, poplar and a conifer (*Juniperus*) were identified. Three radiocarbon determinations from Palegawra run gratifyingly in proper stratigraphic order (13,060 ± 110, 13,480 ± 75 and 14,210 ± 80 years B.P.).

It is unfortunate that the material from the Palegawra zone immediately above 60 centimeters must remain somewhat equivocal because of a scattered intrusion of later potsherds and some disturbed burials. The types of blades, microliths and obsidian artifacts and ground stone were in no way inconsistent with the foregoing materials but would not be normal in the Uruk or Ninevite V inventories to which the potsherds belonged. Howe and I are *not* among those archaeologists who announce "grain" because of the presence of milling stone fragments, but these were well represented here and one quern fragment from well below 1.0 meters has already been mentioned. There is one further determination (10,590 ± 95 B.P.) from this equivocal zone.

Howe's tentative conclusion in *Prehistoric Investigations* was that these higher materials in Palegawra perhaps represent a late subphase of the general Zarzian occurrence. Howe himself found Zarzian materials in three other shelters he tested. Solecki's Shanidar B yields Zarzian materials and Ghanim el-Wahida excavated unfinished portions of Zarzi itself in 1971. Thus, much information on the Zarzian phase, in its rock-shelter aspect, is well in hand even if it is not yet fully published. What is worrisome, however, is that we still have no firm notion as to the likelihood of an open-air settlement aspect of the Zarzian (or of a phase close to it, typologically and chronologically). In retrospect, I now feel especially sorry that excavation on at least one of two open sites near Jarmo—Turkaka and Kowri Khan—remained as unfinished business when the interruption came. Our surface survey yields were best for Turkaka, although Howe observed that ". . . the weight of evidence seems to favor aligning them [both] with the generalized Zarzian range." We were already worried over the proposition that if one *only* looked for traces of Paleolithic occupation in caves, one would only find such traces in caves! Had we returned after the 1955 season, we certainly would have tested Turkaka. Unfortunately, no open-air site of the approximate Zarzian range has yet been exposed along the Zagros.

We were even more predisposed to expect open sites for the next step upwards in time and development, as we conceived things within our general problem focus. Our surveys in the autumn of 1950 (while neither very intensive nor regionally exhaustive) turned up what we took to be a likely candidate for the range of incipient domestication and cultivation. This was Karim Shahir, less than 2 kilometers up wadi east of Jarmo. Howe excavated there for slightly over a month in the spring of 1951. The site was a pleasant, flat, grass covered field, high atop a silty bluff over the wadi bed, at an elevation of about 835.0 meters. Its present area of surface scatter is about 7700 square meters, i.e., about 1.9 acres. We do not have the staff geologist Herbert Wright's authoritative opinion in the matter, but I would guess that some of the southern portion of the original site has been eroded away by the wadi. Howe's exposures were fairly well placed for sampling different areas of the site, although they total to just under 7 percent of the present area of surface scatter. In the case of Karim Shahir, however, a greater proportion of exposed area would probably not have yielded much significant architectural or settlement plan information. The fact was that the matrix at Karim Shahir was a very thin layer, seldom over 25 centimeters in depth. At the base of this lay random broad scatters of fist-sized cracked limestone cobbles, with no hint of meaningful architectural plans. Given the very thin layer of matrix over these stones, even the simple plows used in subsequent millennia of cultivation of the site would have jumbled any original architectural arrangements. We reckon there must certainly have been architecture, as there is no natural reason for these cracked wadi cobbles to lie on top of a 50.0 meters high bluff of fine silt. At the same time, such structures as there were cannot have made much use of mud (either as formed sun-dried bricks or as *touf*), or the thickness of the present overburden would have been greater.

The Karim Shahir flint industry was of certain characteristic blade and microblade tools, knapped from skillfully prepared pyramidal cores. Obsidian was virtually absent and there was seldom trace of "sickle" sheen. Chipped celts with polished bits were characteristic. There were boulder mortar, quern, rubber and pestle fragments as well as finer ground stone objects—beads, pendants and bracelets or rings. Two small and lightly baked clay figurines also appeared. Howe's final report will describe a substantial, characteristic and evidently completely consistent small object inventory for Karim Shahir. In the *Prehistoric Investigations* he has already scouted the idea that it ". . . may have been a seasonal site marked by tool selectivity for periodically recurring jobs and representing but a portion of the total artifactual tradition of its horizon."

Nevertheless, while there were no significant signs of intrusion or of artifacts we could recognize as of later phases, the shallowness of the deposit makes us somewhat nervous about the non-artifactual categories. We have not felt justified in submitting radiocarbon samples. We feel that Solecki's two determinations (of 10,600 ± 300 and 10,800 ± 300 B.P.) on his similar inventory from upper Shanidar B and Zawi Chemi Shanidar probably suggest the approximate age of Karim Shahir as well. Helbaek has not reported any botanical evidence, but Barghoorn identified charcoal as being from elm-like, mesquite-like and tamarisk woods. There is some suspicion that not all of the animal bones classified in the field by Fredrik Barth finally reached the United States for study by Reed and Hans R. Stampfli. Stampfli lists sheep and goat as amounting to almost 50 percent of the total animal bones, with pig, deer, cattle, gazelle, fox and smaller forms making up the remainder. Stampfli is emphatic that there is no morphological trace of domestication, also no significant number of young sheep and goat, as at Zawi Chemi Shanidar. He concludes that domestication of sheep and goat cannot be denied but it is improbable.

In retrospect, it seems clear that the contextual situation at Karim Shahir was a mixed blessing. There is every evidence that it was occupied only in its single early period. However, as far as the niceties of archaeological excavation are concerned, we might as well have skimmed off the top 25 centimeters, sieved the resultant matrix and settled down to typological sorting of the artifacts.

From the point of view of our general problem focus and our heuristic conception of a range of incipient cultivation and domestication before the appearance of effective village-farming communities, Karim Shahir let us down. It must represent an even more interesting phase than does Jarmo, which appears to be well over the food-producing threshold. In late 1954 we briefly tested two other sites, M'lefaat and Gird Chai, which probably were occupied during the same general time range as Karim Shahir or slightly later. Gird Chai proved to have significant later disturbance and we quickly abandoned work there, but M'lefaat would certainly have been reopened had we returned for further Iraqi seasons of work. It is a small mound, about 1.25 acres in area, on the right bank of the Khazir river just north of the Erbil-Mosul road, and about 300.0 meters above sea level. We tested it in six days with three small squares, exposing slightly under 1 percent of its probable total area, and to a depth of only 1.5 meters; we do not know its full depth of deposit. We did encounter portions of round and oval stone-founded structures, and the yield in coarse ground stone—boulder mortars, querns, rubbers, pestles and full ground celts—was considerable. The chipped flint industry was similar to that of Karim Shahir. M'lefaat is certainly worth full excavation but, as matters stand now, we still have too little evidence from it to allow it much place in generalizing.

Hence, our putative range of incipience remains very incompletely examined by our own Iraqi operations. The best case for incipience along the Iraqi Zagros, remains Dexter Perkins' proposition for the herding of still morphologically wild sheep at Zawi Chemi Shanidar. I would also still guess that we yet have phases or subphases to discover between the general Karim Shahir-M'lefaat-Zawi Chemi Shanidar range and that of Jarmo. I see no reason to believe that more intensive survey along the Zagros flanks and upper piedmont would not locate sites of pertinence.

The Site of Jarmo

As we first saw it, the site of Jarmo (about 800.0 meters above sea level) was a grassy knoll on the top of a bluff above the left (south) bank of the Cham Gowra wadi, a tributary of the Basira-Tauq Chai. Its present overall size of surface scatter is about 3.7 acres, its depth

FIGURE 1
Air view of Jarmo, as seen from the west-northwest. The wadi (not shown) runs at the bottom of the northern and western bluff faces in the foreground. Virgin soil appears at the bottom of the operation at the apex of the two bluffs. The badly dissected surface of the valley plain shows clearly in the background.

of deposit almost 7.0 meters. The Chemchemal Valley plain, in which Jarmo (and Karim Shahir, Kowri Khan and Turkaka) lies, is very seriously dissected. Herbert Wright reckons that at least a third of the northern portion of the original site has already been eroded away by the wadi since the site's occupation. If we assume the original size of the site was about 2 hectares, our total exposures (including 153 2.0 meter × 2.0 meter test squares) amounted to slightly over 7 percent, but the exposure area which showed comprehensible architectural remains was only 2.4 percent and the area exposed to virgin soil was only 0.8 percent of the probable original settlement size.

During our 1948 and 1950-51 field seasons, we opened the two largest of our trenches. Operation One was eventually expanded to about 10.0 meters × 15.0 meters in size and taken to virgin soil. Operation Two was extended to about 15.0 meters × 30.0 meters but cut back as it was deepened and did not reach below its 6th floor. These operations yielded our only really significant evidence of house plans and sizes, structural practices, orientation and degree of proximity of buildings. We also learned that the normal *touf* (walling used by the Jarmo people) was only preserved at depths of somewhat over 1.0 meter below the surface. Wright's (1952: 11) geological description of the Chemchemal Valley notes the tendency for the silty surface soil to leach and to develop calcium carbonate nodules from the surface downwards. On Jarmo itself these concretions extended downwards to a half meter's depth or more. The leaching itself extended below that for another half meter, altering the silty matrix to a granular form and obliterating the original nature of *touf* wall remains within this entire upper zone. It was fortunate for us that the Jarmo structures tended (in the upper building levels, at least) to have single course foundations of cobblestones. These gave us indications of orientations and several-roomed rectilinear plans, but no sense of original living circulation, as the foundations appear to have been no higher than floor line. At depths of below 1.0 meter, the *touf* walls were preserved and we could trace and clear them, along with certain secondary features of loaded mud such as ovens. In retrospect the matrix below the leached zone was relatively soft (not so soft as that of Sarab in Iran but much softer than the tough compacted matrix we now face at Çayönü in Turkey). The reason I go into the above details is to suggest the background of our thinking in attempting an overall testing of the site by a checkerboard of 2.0 meter × 2.0 meter tests. We hoped we might find some section of the site where the leaching effect was not so pronounced. We sought broad areas of well preserved architectural concentration. Most of all, we believed we might possibly extrapolate something in the way of an overall village plan from such a grid of test pits. It has always seemed to us rather fruitless to generalize very far about village-farming communities without getting some substantial evidence of what such communities looked like. In fact, however, our attempt to get a village plan was not very successful. The leaching effect went well down below the surface everywhere and this meant that we had not the staff, workmen or resources to take all of the approximately 200 squares we projected to fruitful depths. In fact, we only managed to open about 160 squares, seven of which were later subsumed within one broader operation. Also, to our disappointment, it did not prove possible to extrapolate effectively from square to square so that we might draw profiles along the axes of the grid. Jarmo, at least, does not have the neat horizontal stratification of a cake! It is not that we did not gain information from the squares but rather that we gained far less information than we had hoped for.

With a single exception (which one of the 2.0 meter × 2.0 meter squares exposed) the structural remains we encountered at Jarmo were of small several-roomed rectilinear buildings, undoubtedly of *touf* walled houses. Unfortunately, we cannot claim to have a single completely intact overall floor plan, although two or three examples were so nearly complete that we feel we may with some confidence suggest a restored house plan of about 36 square meters roofed area and possibly a small open court. Under these circumstances, however, we would feel it unwise to speak of a "typical" Jarmo house plan. In at least one case, two houses appear to have been built abutting each other; in other cases, the houses seem to have stood in open spaces. The exception I note above is of our clearance (near the last season's end) of a "T" shaped portion of *touf* walling of monumental thickness, but to what sort of building it pertains remains unfinished business at Jarmo. Allowing for the fact that plans of structural remains in the uppermost meter exist only as stone foundations, I see no reason—in the available traces of domestic structures from bottom to top at Jarmo—to see more than one generally developing phase of occupation.

In our thickest sectional exposure to virgin soil, we could account for sixteen "floors" at Jarmo, but some of these "floors" were more ephemeral than real. In the nearby Operation Two, our largest, there were potsherds only as low as the fifth "floor" and in other operations, including many of the 2.0 meter × 2.0 meter squares, there were no potsherds at all. Hence, in retrospect, I am embarrassed that earlier easy generalizations of my own have left the impression that the inhabitants of the entire "upper third" of Jarmo were pot makers. This impression, taken together with the conventional tendency to see the appearance of pottery as necessarily a horizon marker has led some colleagues to believe that there were two distinct phases at Jarmo.

The situation is certainly not that simple. The most competently made pots are represented by those few sherds which came at the deepest appearance of pottery (e.g., in Operation Two, 5th floor), in those restricted areas of the site where potsherds actually occurred. Presumably these examples were not home-town products. They were presently succeeded, and in increasingly impressive numbers (in the areas where sherds occurred) by a rather wretched soft simple-surfaced coarse ware. There is, of course, some reason to suppose that the present wretchedness of this lightly fired pottery may be due to the effect of leaching.

The remainder of the Jarmo inventory (already described in some detail in our preliminary report) has, from bottom to top, an essential typological uniformity and consistence. This does not mean that we cannot see developmental trends in one category or another or that some new types of artifacts do not appear. Any assessment of "typological uniformity" or "inventory consistency" in a case like this is bound to be frankly subjective. My judgment is based on some familiarity with the contents of most of the other southwestern Asiatic inventories of this general range of time, and on due respect for the imbalanced proportions of the Jarmo exposures, bottom to top.

I noted above that once through the leached zone, we found the Jarmo matrix relatively soft and workable. This may account in part for our ability to recover numbers of lightly-baked or simply sun-dried clay objects and fragments, especially of figurines. The final report on these will add significantly to the corpus of early plastic art of this time range. The Jarmo chipped stone tool kit was a fairly simple one, based on blades and microblades in both flint and obsidian. The proportion of obsidian to flint increased as time went on, although obsidian tended to be used mainly for tools of microlithic scale throughout. In flint, retouched and used blades and "sickle" blades were most common and both often showed traces of bitumen (as an adhesive for hafting). There was considerable variety in the category of larger ground milling stones (boulder mortars, querns, pestles and rubbing stones) but this lack of standardization may have depended on the supply of hard raw materials. The yield in finer ground stone objects—marble bowls, "bracelets," pendants and beads—was both large and impressive from the point of view of workmanship. I realize there is a tendency at present to stress the ease and leisure supposedly available to hunter-collectors and to assume that food-producers had lives of relative drudgery. *If* such was indeed the case, the objects of the finer ground stone category of Jarmo, hardly immediately utilitarian to our eyes, must have had weighty culturally-imposed functions which still escape us. Certainly a heavy investment of man-hours was involved in their production.

Unfortunately, we encountered little in the way of caches or "activity clusters" and the few human skeletons we uncovered were hardly proper burials but rather apparently the contorted remains left by roof or wall cave-ins. Possibly there is a still undiscovered cemetery somewhere adjacent to the site.

The non-artifactual yield at Jarmo, also indicated in some detail in our preliminary report, leaves no question that both plant and animal domesticates were present. Stampfli's final report on the animal bones is now with the editor but it does not seem likely that Helbaek's health will allow him to add much to his already substantial description in our preliminary report. Helbaek's (1966: 350) general paper naturally shows certain changes in emphasis in his account of the history of wheat and barley domestication, due to subsequent finds, but he maintains his positive identifications regarding the Jarmo materials. How much less we would have known, early on, had not Hans Helbaek written me in 1949 (completely out of the blue) of his interest in early Old World plant domesticates, adding a plea for samples. Helbaek's role in making this research focus a weighty one has been considerable. Stampfli's report confirms Reed's preliminary identifications of goat and probably sheep as domesticates throughout and Flannery's opinion on domesticated pigs only in the upper levels of Jarmo. Stampfli also notes that the percentage of wild animals was larger than previously assumed. This touches the point that our evidence for assessing dietary balance, i.e., wild vs. produced food, is not impressive.

No aspect of Jarmo has been as exasperating as the results of radiocarbon age determinations made on samples from the site. There are now fifteen assays, with several still pending. Six different laboratories have been involved and the samples have included shell, potsherds and bone collagen, although most were of charcoal. The assays run (in Libby half-life terms) from 5,266 ± 450 B.P. (C-744) to 11,240 ± 300 B.P. (W-657), a completely unrealistic span by any reckoning. I would certainly agree with H. T. Waterbolk's (1971: 15) opinion, which he has reaffirmed in more recent private correspondence, that the best possible estimation, based on the nature of the samples and their assays, would be about 8,000 B.P. At the same time, with respect to other available early village inventories with radiocarbon age determinations in southwestern Asia, an age of about a millennium earlier would make much more comparative archaeological sense. To cite an example I know well at first hand, I simply cannot believe that the Jarmo inventory represents a time a thousand years in retard of Çayönü, which is rather comfortably fixed by radiocarbon at about 7000 B.C. (Libby). With Waterbolk, I rather strongly suspect that bitumen contamination of the Jarmo samples may account for part of our trouble on the early side. There is still a bitumen flow in the southern end of the Chemchemal Valley; much bitumen was used by the Jarmo people, and it was doubtless softened up for use as an adhesive or as water-proofing over household hearths. The sources of later contamination are unclear. As to Protsch and Berger's (1973: 235) brave but very muddled attempt to hang everything on bone collagen based assays, done by themselves, this is not the place to take detailed notice. They propose a duration for Jarmo of almost two thousand years. In my opinion, 500 years would be an outside limit.

In this connection, it is wryly amusing to recall the so-called Jericho-Jarmo controversy. Five out of six of our first radiocarbon samples assayed by the early dry carbon method to about 4750 B.C. (the sixth was the 5,266 ± 450 B.P. assay, or about 3316 B.C.!). Although our pre-radiocarbon guess dates for Jarmo had been for at least 6000 B.C., I was fascinated with the 4750 B.C. determinations. Given so late a date for the appearance of effective food-production, I reasoned, the rate of the resultant cultural acceleration was excitingly fast—only 1750 years from village-farmers to literate urban centers! Then came Professor Kathleen Kenyon's first report on the British work in basal Jericho, with radiocarbon assays which approached 7000 B.C., her claims for a preliterate urbanity at Jericho and my own outraged response! Before too long, however, it became clear that the first five Jarmo radiocarbon assays were too late by a couple of millennia, and much of that academic storm lost its force.

Now, how to face Jarmo in retrospect? Were it suddenly to become possible for us to return there (supposing also we had no firm commitments to Çayönü, and that a shift to areas other than the Chemchemal region were not at issue), how would we react in the matter? Certain strong sentimental and logistical factors—friendly villagers who knew and had worked for us, good water and access to the site, etc.—would pull us towards resumption of work at Jarmo. The advantage of already knowing at least something of the nature and peculiarities of the site, curiosity concerning unfinished matters (such as the monumental *touf* wall) and fascination with what new techniques of reclamation might yield would all be weighty factors. On the other hand, there are the restrictions on the preservation of above-floor *touf* walls in the upper levels (due to the leaching effect) to consider. As to Jarmo's apparent lack of caches or "activity clusters" of artifacts, one can, of course, never predict either the accidents of original deposition or the fortunate or unfortunate locations of subsequent archaeological exposures on many-layered mounds. At the same time, our recent good fortune in finding a number of impressive "activity clusters" at Çayönü seems to have been a function of a rather widespread number of burned buildings in one subphase of that site. At Jarmo, on the contrary, there were no clear traces of building fires in any of our exposures. Finally, we would have to consider the high probability that much of the northern portion of Jarmo is eroded away, so that an overall village plan will never be reclaimable.

All things considered, my hunch is that were a hypothetical opportunity to arise, we would probably opt for some site other than Jarmo (with a few tears shed for an old love lost!). Of the sites we know in the more immediate vicinity of Jarmo, a strong candidate would be Kharaba Qara Chiwar. It is adjacent to, but evidently not eroded by, the Tauq Chai just above that stream's mouth onto the piedmont plain. Qara Chiwar's surface yield hints at a typologically very early Jarmo-like inventory, and the fact that it is near the plain should add to its interest.

Our preliminary report included some description of the test operations and yields of four post-Jarmo phase sites. Gird Ali Agha may not, in fact, have been occupied much later than Jarmo, but its exposure and yield was very restricted. El Khan, with its Hassunan yield, was also a small operation, but at Matarrah—where we excavated for over a month—we made a reasonably impressive Hassunan exposure. A Banahilk, well to the northeast in a valley near Ruwanduz, Patty Jo Watson's brief tests yielded a significant amount of Halafian material. However, since each of these yields belong to inventories well over the threshold of food production, and hence not at the center of our present problem focus, I will not give them more attention here.

Retrospective Overview

In the immediately preceding section, I have tried to keep my remarks restricted to the actualities of the Iraq Jarmo Project's field efforts. In an earlier section, I suggested that the choice of Jarmo and the immediate Chemchemal-Kirkuk region as the center of most of our operations was itself something of a fluke of the immediately post-war political climate of southwestern Asia. In fact, our own first post-war proposal was for a reexamination of Baghouz, a Samarran phase site on the middle Euphrates in Syria, with the intent of moving northward from there once we had cleared up questions concerning the whole spectrum of the Samarran inventory. Had the Syrians agreed to this proposal, we probably would have eventually stumbled upon something like Mureybit. Again, I am haunted by the specter of how for years afterwards quite accidental priorities of discovery may influence culture-historical generalizations!

Our interest in working at least as far east as the Euphrates depended on the fact that by the end of the period between the two World Wars, much more had already been learned of the beginnings of later prehistory in the Syro-Palestinian littoral and its immediate hinterland than in the trans-Euphrates regions. The cave Natufian had been well explored, Garstang's work at Jericho had already established the presence of substantial Pre-ceramic horizons, and a deep test pit of Schaeffer's at Ras Shamra suggested the same for the north Syrian coast. East of the Euphrates, there was the long gap in knowledge of cultural development and change between the Zarzian blade tool industry and full-fledged village assemblages such as the Hassunan and Sialk I. To the north, in the upper Euphrates-Tigris headwaters in Turkey, there was essentially zero pertinent knowledge (which is, of course, why we always kept that region in our minds and eventually went to Çayönü).

Given this background, my notion is still that while the Iraqi Directorate of Antiquities' suggestion of Jarmo was a very lucky break for us, we probably could have—with a more orderly effort in surface survey—found some dozens of sites approximating Jarmo along the Zagros flanks. Our preliminary report suggests two sites found by Stuart Harris, Urwell and Rasein, down on the piedmont plain near Tauq, while Joan Oates's Tamarkhan near Mandali and the lower Ali Kosh horizons in Khuzestan also show strong Jarmo-like elements. Shimshara, Guran and Sarab, in higher intermontane valleys, also have Jarmo-like elements, as perhaps do some items in Ganj Dareh, high and east of Kermanshah in Iran. Thus, more than ten years ago, I was forced to relax my earlier ideas about a rather restricted elevational band along the Zagros as a "hilly flanks" optimal zone.

How far west and south of the Zagros piedmont may sites of a generalized Jarmo type inventory exist? The exact consequences, for lower elevations, of the Zagros vegetational history established by Wright and van Zeist, are not yet clear. Did the same general trend towards climatic amelioration in the Zagros, following after 14,000 B.P., mean a consequent slow trend toward desiccation in the now desert portions of Iraq, and beyond to the south? Diana Kirkbride Helbaek's new site, Umm Dabaghiyah, west of the Tigris and of Hatra, although probably later than the Jarmo range, suggests an economy which could barely persist there at the present. Masry and Zarins have begun to establish substantive understanding of at least Ubaid and immediately pre-Ubaid settlements along the gulf-littoral of Saudi Arabia. I am now suspicious that we may have thrown out every element of "climatic determinism" too soon in our preliminary report, and Wright's (1968: 334) generalizations certainly suggest his agreement with this.

Clearly, our investigations of the Jarmo-Karim Shahir-Palegawra range of time began in a somewhat disorderly catch-as-catch-can way. Would it not have been much better to commit a preliminary field season or two to surveys, of which Adams's *Land Behind Baghdad* (1965) is an excellent example for later time ranges? There are, to my mind, two difficulties in this suggestion. First, I would take it to be somewhat inefficient to begin any very intensive survey as the first step, for ranges of time and places for which a time-space systematics has not yet been worked out. I know such surveys have been brought to success, but I wonder about their immediate efficiency. My second difficulty is even more serious. The various national governments in the Near East tend to hold to the conventional image of the archaeologist as one who goes to a specific mound and digs a hole in it. Requests for permission to do wide-ranging surface surveys and for the maps and air photos to facilitate them—especially if minority groups happen to live within the regions requested—often tend to get lost. We ourselves did propose and receive permission for general survey in the greater Zab basin during our third field season in Iraq. By that time, however, we had some sense of our range's time-space situation *and* officialdom had had time to size us up and to decide we were what we claimed to be. Had we been able to persist in the Chemchemal Valley, an intensive surface survey would certainly have been undertaken.

That southwestern Asia's claim to priority for the appearance of food-production is being challenged from almost every Old World quarter does not concern me much. Claims for Europe, northeast Africa, southeast Africa and southeast Asia are all being vigorously pushed—in most cases on so far rather flimsy evidence to my way of thinking. My own fascination with southwestern Asia is with the developments and processes which brought about a way of life upon which, after a few millennia, a certain pristine, literate, urban way of life could arise.

It also seems to me that there has been a good deal of recent armchair theorizing about how food production was achieved in southwestern Asia. The breadth of the theories seem to me to correlate negatively with their authors' familiarity with the region and its evidence! During the last dozen years, British, Canadian, Danish, Dutch, French, Israeli, Iraqi, Japanese, Russian, Spanish and Turkish as well as American (and most recently, German) colleagues have become involved in the search for evidence of the phases from just before to immediately following the achievement of effective village farming communities in southwestern Asia. Some of these colleagues mistakenly neglect to write in English! It is not always clear that some of the generalists know of their existence or their evidence. Nor does it usually seem possible for generalists to write with due regard to the still very incomplete state of our knowledge of the potential evidence.

I think my final retrospective thought would be that if I had to begin all over again, I would still choose the same region and problem focus. For such a reincarnation, I would, of course, request escape from the many mistakes and oversights on my present record. In that way, I would only find myself guilty of the mistakes and oversights of archaeologists of the generation of my reincarnation! Most of all, I would try for something in the general range of Karim Shahir.

References

ADAMS, ROBERT MC C.

1965 Land Behind Baghdad. A History of Settlement on the Diyala Plains. Chicago, University of Chicago Press.

1968 Archaeological Research Strategies: Past and Present. Science 160: 1187–92.

BRAIDWOOD, ROBERT J.

1959 Correspondance. Kush 7: 236–7.

1972 Prehistoric Investigations in Southwestern Asia. Proceedings American Philosophical Society 116: 310–20.

BRAIDWOOD, ROBERT J. AND BRAIDWOOD, L. S.

1950 Jarmo: A Village of Early Farmers in Iraq. Antiquity 24: 189–95.

1953 The Earliest Village Communities of Southwestern Asia. Journal of World History 1: 278–310.

1960 Excavations in the Plain of Antioch, I. Oriental Institute Publications, Vol. 61. Chicago, University of Chicago Press.

BRAIDWOOD, ROBERT J.; BRAIDWOOD, L. S.; TULANE, EDNA AND PERKINS, ANN L.

1944 New Chalcolithic Material of Samavan Type. Journal of Near East Studies 3: 48–72.

BRAIDWOOD, ROBERT J.; BRUCE HOWE, ET AL.

1960 Prehistoric Investigations in Iraqi Kurdistan. Studies in Ancient Oriental Civilization, Vol. 31. Chicago, University of Chicago Press.

GARROD, DOROTHY A. E.

1930 The Palaeolithic of southern Kurdistan. Bulletin American School of Prehistoric Research 6: 8–43.

HELBAEK, H.

1966 1966: Commentary on the Phylogenesis of *Triticum* and *Hordeum*. Economic Botany 20: 350–60.

PERKINS, D., JR.

1964 Prehistoric Fauna From Shanidar, Iraq. Science 144: 1565–6.

PROTSCH, R. AND BERGER R.

1973 Earliest Radiocarbon Dates for Domesticated Animals. Science 179: 235–39.

TURNBULL, PRISCILLA
1967 Bones of Palegawra. Bulletin Field Museum of Natural History 38; 9: 4–5.

WATERBOLK, H. T.
1971 Working With Radiocarbon Dates. Proceedings Prehistoric Society 37: 15–33.

WRIGHT, H. E., JR.
1952 Geologic Setting of Four Prehistoric Sites in northeastern Iraq. Bulletin American School of Oriental Research 128: 11–24.

1968 Natural Environment of Early Food Production North of Mesopotamia. Science 161: 334–9.

PALEOLITHIC EUROPE

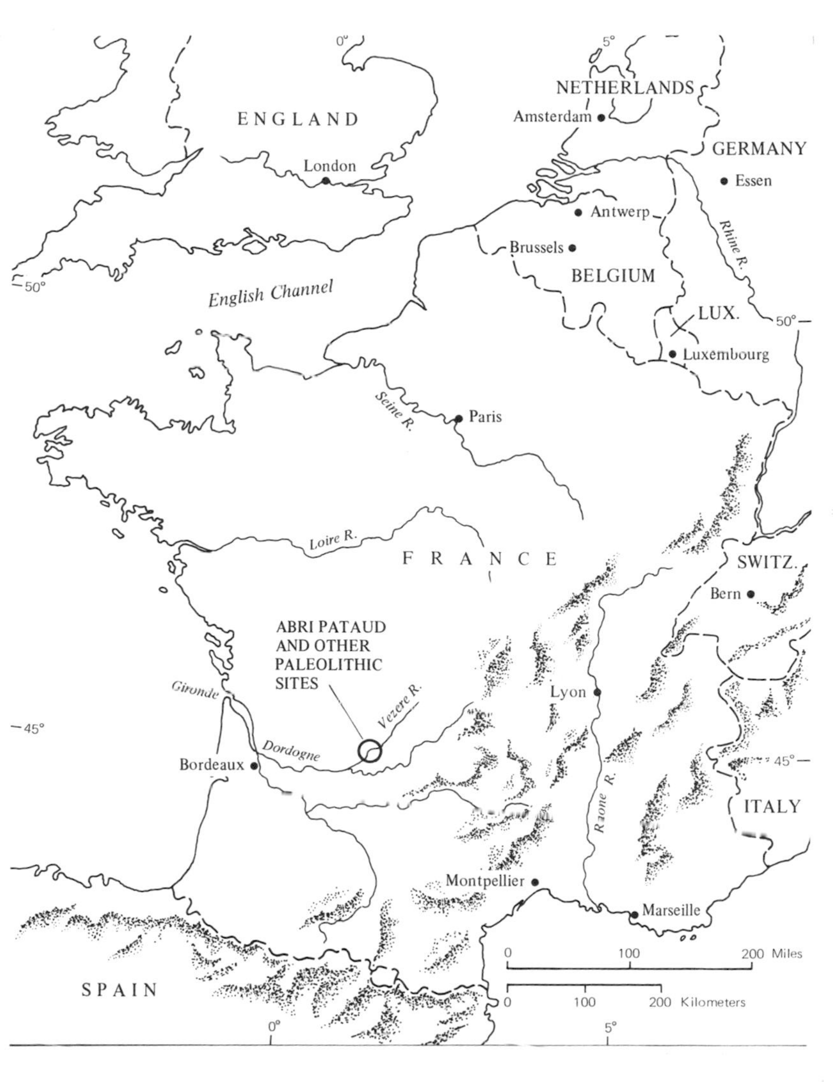

(preceding page)

Map of France showing location of the Abri Pataud and other famous Paleolithic sites. These sites are situated in or near the little town of Les Eyzies (Dordogne), on the Vézère River, and include, in addition to the Abri Pataud, such well-known stations as Cro-Magnon, Laugerie-Haute, and La Ferrassie.

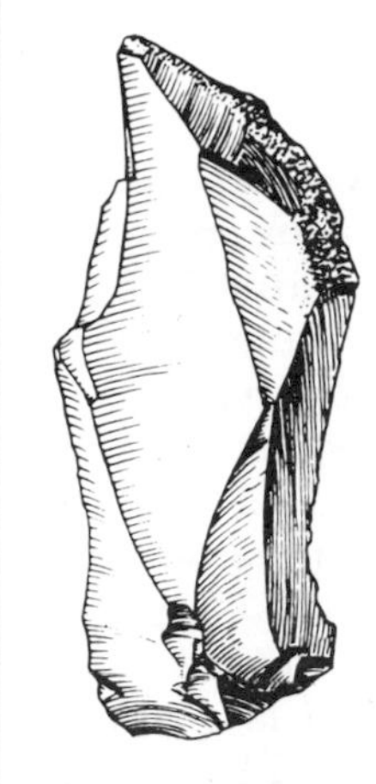

The Abri Pataud Program of the French Upper Paleolithic in Retrospect

HALLAM L. MOVIUS, JR.

Introduction

I visited post-World War Two France in 1948 to attempt to organize an excavation program. At that time the major problem in Upper Paleolithic archaeology under discussion was a then relatively new concept concerning the validity, or non-validity, of the Périgordian archaeological culture, or tool-making tradition, in western Europe, which the famous French archaeologist, Denis Peyrony, had originally propounded in 1933. This concept represented a modification of the accepted and widely employed notion of a unitary Aurignacian culture established by the Abbé H. Breuil in 1905–1906, and later subdivided by him into the three-fold succession of Lower, Middle and Upper Aurignacian. Although the importance of Breuil's work on the Aurignacian cannot be overestimated, Peyrony propounded the view that the Lower and Upper Aurignacian should henceforth be included together in a complex which he proposed to call Périgordian, thereby destroying the unity of Breuil's original Aurignacian, a term limited by Peyrony to the Middle subdivision of the abbé's formulation. But certain of the basic concepts that Breuil had developed were too deeply ingrained in the thinking of many leading Paleolithic archaeologists for them to be discarded even in 1948. Despite the change in terminology, much of recent thinking about the Périgordian is still based on what Breuil had

Headpiece: Flint instrument, known as a burin, representative of those found at the Abri Pataud in the European Upper Paleolithic. From Movius, David, Brickner, and Clay, *The Analyses of Certain Major Classes of Upper Paleolithic Tools* (American School of Prehistoric Research, No. 26, Peabody Museum, Harvard University, Cambridge, Mass., 1968).

originally said with reference to the various subdivisions of the Aurignacian. Indeed, it is quite clear that many of the current problems relative to the Upper Périgordian have stemmed directly from the results of the poorly excavated sites that were available to Breuil for study during the early decades of the twentieth century.

As the result of his own considerable and extensive excavations at the sites of Laugerie-Haute and La Ferrassie in the Dordogne region of southwestern France, Peyrony suggested in the early 1930's that the Périgord region had been occupied during the early part of the Upper Paleolithic by two separate groups of people using two separate and unrelated tool-making traditions. He claimed that each of these traditions, or "cultures," was characterized by a process of typological development which permitted clear periodization. Furthermore, he considered that these traditions were contemporaneous, each developing in a parallel but separate fashion for a long period of time. One of these, his Périgordian, was characterized most notably by the use of abrupt retouch, or backing; this was broadly the equivalent of Breuil's Lower and Upper Aurignacian. For the second tradition, which was characterized by split-base bone points, busked burins, carinate scrapers and "strangled," or doubly notched, blades, he proposed retention of Breuil's original name Aurignacian—actually the Middle Aurignacian in terms of Breuil's scheme. In other words, Peyrony suggested that Breuil's terminology was no longer applicable, and, in addition to typology, he documented his reconstruction with data from comparative stratigraphy and human paleontology.

Fundamentally, as stated above, it was the various categories of backed blade tools that tied the Périgordian tradition together. There is admittedly a rather long list of characteristic Périgordian tool types, but the relevant facts pertaining to each of the major subdivisions may be summarized as follows:

Périgordian I—Châtelperron points and blades representing a wide range of morphological variation, end-scrapers on both flakes and blades, occasional burins, a few truncated blades, and a variable component of Mousterian-type tools consisting mainly of points and side-scrapers.

Périgordian II—Small bladelets with fine, abrupt marginal retouch (either alternate, normal, or inverse) called *lamelles Dufour* (or Dufour bladelets), carinate and nose-ended scrapers, blades with heavy marginal retouch, a few truncated blades, thick end-scrapers, and a small series of burins.

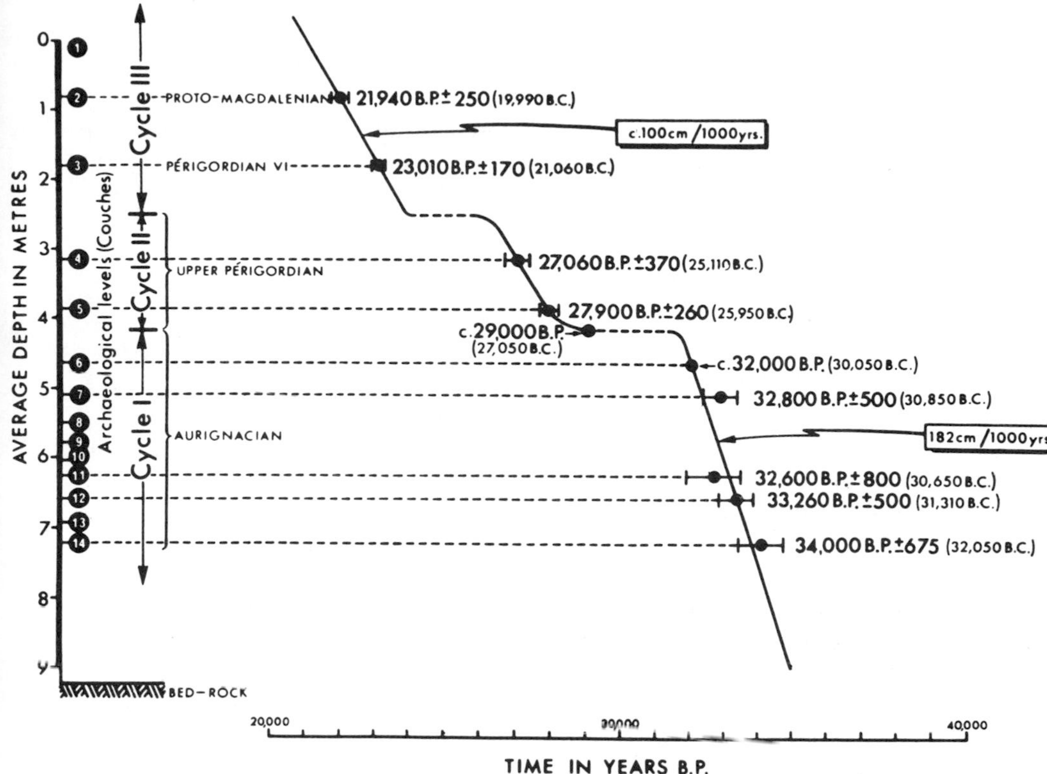

FIGURE 1
Diagrammatic representation of deposition at the Abri Pataud, Les Eyzies (Dordogne), plotted with respect to time as determined by radiocarbon measurements. Note the two stages of non-deposition at about 31,500 to about 29,000 B.P. and about 26,000 to about 24,000 B.P., respectively. An approximate figure in centimeters per thousand years has been computed for the deposits of Cycles I and II. (After William R. Farrand.)

Périgordian III—Peyrony considered that certain of the backed or truncated pieces in this assemblage were analogous to Châtelperron point or blade variants of the Périgordian I. But at the same time the occurrence of Gravette and micro-Gravette points indicated close affinities with the Périgordian IV of the classic site of La Gravette. There also occurred a wide range and variety of end-scrapers on blades, truncation burins and dihedral burins. Accordingly, Peyrony considered his Périgordian III to be transitional between the Lower Périgordian (Phases I and II) and the Upper Périgordian (Phases IV and V).

Périgordian IV—On the basis of the evidence of the type site of La

Gravette (Dordogne), Peyrony stated that this phase was characterized by a wide range and variety of Gravette and micro-Gravette points, end-scrapers on blades, truncation and dihedral burins, truncated pieces, and armatures of both bone and antler.

Périgordian V—This phase consisted of three subdivisions:
(a) the level with tanged points of Font-Robert type;
(b) the level with numerous truncated elements (*éléments tronqués*); and
(c) the level with Noailles burins.

On the basis of the very sketchy summary presented above, it will be noted that it was Peyrony's conviction that the Périgordian consisted of five successive assemblages, each of which he considered to be clearly separate and independent of the Aurignacian insofar as the Périgord region of southwestern France was concerned. He further believed that human paleontology supported this concept: (a) the Combe-Capelle race, found at Combe-Capelle (Dordogne) with a Périgordian I assemblage was responsible for the Périgordian tradition, and (b) the Cro-Magnon race, found at the Abri de Cro-Magnon (Les Eyzies, Dordogne) had introduced the Aurignacian tradition. However this may or may not be, the most important facet of Peyrony's hypothesis was that these two totally different and independent traditions had existed contemporaneously in southwestern France, and that they had developed in parallel fashion. But his evidence in support of the latter view was based on a completely mistaken interpretation of the placing of the vast site of Laugerie-Haute in the sequence of the Fourth Glaciation. This interpretation was later discarded.

By the end of World War Two Peyrony had come to recognize that the Aurignacian constituted a single, linear or monolithic sequence. On the other hand, the Périgordian tradition was far more complicated, mainly due to the fact that in his Périgordian II abruptly and semi-abruptly retouched backed blades and bladelets (*lamelles Dufour*) apparently occurred in intimate and direct association with typical Aurignacian tools (carinate scrapers, nose-ended scrapers, etc.). This anomaly was explained by Peyrony as due to an "Aurignacian influence," but even this interpretation was destroyed in 1955 by Mme. de Sonneville-Bordes, wife of Professor Bordes of the University of Bordeaux. She applied her "statistical method" (based on the newly developed 92-type list) to three Périgordian II assemblages, two Aurignacian ones, and a sixth referable to the Périgordian III of Peyrony. She concluded that not one

FIGURE 2
General view of the Abri Pataud, Les Eyzies (Dordogne). Photograph taken in July 1958 from near the railway bridge over the Vézère River.

of the Périgordian II assemblages contained a single element which permitted their assignment to the Périgordian. On the other hand, each of them presented all the qualitative and statistical characteristics of the Aurignacian, and she proposed that henceforth they should be so considered. Although the continuum between the Lower and the Upper Périgordian no longer existed, Peyrony's 1933 publication was a very considerable contribution to our understanding of Upper Paleolithic culture-history.

The Abri Pataud Project

Following extensive reconnaissance and a test excavation, the Abri Pataud, a large rock-shelter in the village of Les Eyzies (Dordogne), was chosen in 1953 as a site that offered the maximum potential for an investigation of the Périgordian problem. Although the trial dig yielded no indication of the existence of an Early Périgordian horizon there, evidence of a fairly long series of Aurignacian occupations overlain by the Périgordian IV, Vc (the Noailles burin horizon), VI (formerly the Périgordian III of Peyrony's original scheme), and the Proto-Magdalenian, an assemblage previously reported only from Laugerie-Haute, came to light. But the scope and aim of the Abri Pataud Project was conceived of on an even broader base including the relative geologic age, associated fauna, typological range of the flint, bone, antler and ivory implements associated with the oldest Upper Paleolithic cultures of western Europe, using modern archaeological, ecological, geological, paleontological and paleobotanical procedures. The older excavation and classificatory techniques had produced very little in the way of evidence of ideas concerning the layout of living-floors, or even an appreciation of the total typological range of the several industrial assemblages, the prevailing environmental conditions at the time of the successive occupations, or the daily economy of these early hunting groups. The data recovered have shed new light on each of these areas of knowledge, and the overall results have provided us with a very badly needed revision of our understanding of and concepts pertaining to the history of man and his culture in western Europe between about 33,000 and 18,000 B.C.

A total of six field seasons, each generously funded by the National Science Foundation, were required to attain bed-rock at the base of the deposits at the Abri Pataud, some 9.25 meters below datum. The results of this research program, which are as yet unpublished, have been extremely impressive. They involve the following:

1. *Stratigraphic Sequence*—The deposits at the Abri Pataud have revealed a sequence of some fourteen (14) occupations that took place during the first half of the Upper Paleolithic in western Europe. These: (a) confirm the complete independence of the Aurignacian and the Périgordian traditions, as maintained by D. Peyrony; (b) demonstrate that the Périgordian is even more complex than had originally been conceived; and (c) confirm the reality of the Proto-Magdalenian occupation of the area that had previously only been reported from the nearby site of Laugerie-Haute.

2. *Excavation Techniques*—At the outset of the program it was recognized that, if certain important data were to be forthcoming, it would be necessary to develop a new and more precise excavation technique in order to make possible the recognition of micro-stratigraphic units—*i.e.*, to isolate the assemblages found in association with specific occupation "floors." Such a technique was ultimately developed, and, as explained

below, the results proved to be invaluable in connection with the analysis and study of the material.

3. *Ecological/Environmental Studies*—In a very real sense certain of the major issues on which the Abri Pataud research project was primarily focused can only be understood as involving a series of events in both natural and cultural history. Since the highly specialized hunters and gatherers of the Upper Paleolithic were closely adjusted to their successive environments, the compilation of as complete data as possible bearing on contemporary natural conditions is of primary importance. Hence the cooperation of an outstandingly able team of natural scientists working on problems, not only of a cross-disciplinary nature, but also of importance for dating purposes, was a vital necessity.

4. *Classificatory Procedures*—The typological approach to the study of Upper Paleolithic assemblages, currently utilized by Paleolithic archaeologists, is far too broad and comprehensive to permit a study of the very marked stylistic differences which characterize a given phase, or sub-phase, of any single one of the Upper Paleolithic assemblages under discussion. This aspect of the Abri Pataud research program certainly represents a major "break-through" in knowledge relative to the study of blade tool assemblages.

In retrospect let us examine each of the major results outlined above and attempt to assess the contribution to knowledge of each.

Stratigraphic Sequence

Comprehensive summaries of the results achieved during each field season at the Abri Pataud are set forth in a series of Progress Reports submitted annually to the National Science Foundation covering the work of each field season. The significant facts presented in these reports is as follows:

Level 1–Lower Solutrean

The existence of this Level was established in 1958 and further confirmed in 1963. But it yielded only a very small handful of artifacts —actually too few for accurate attribution. One very typical unifacial point (*pointe à face plane*) suggests that the horizon in question may perhaps be assigned to the Lower Solutrean.

At the Abri Pataud no C-14 samples were recovered in Level 1. What is believed to be the corresponding Level (Couche 31) at Laugerie-Haute: Ouest has been dated to 20,890 B.P. ± 300 years, or about 18,940 B.C. (GrN-1888), which suggests that the Level 1 occupation is some 1,000 years younger than the underlying Proto-Magdalenian.

FIGURE 3
Proto-Magdalenian. Skull and mandible of adolescent female *in situ*. These remains were found directly below a large fallen limestone block on 2 July 1958. No traces of any vertebratae came to light.

Level 2—Proto-Magdalenian

The great importance of the discovery of this occupation layer, which yielded an assemblage of just under 2,000 artifacts that are very similar to those originally described by D. Peyrony from Couche F at the nearby site of Laugerie-Haute: Est, can scarcely be overstressed. Preliminary reports on the Proto-Magdalenian assemblage from the Abri Pataud have been published elsewhere, together with a summary description of the adolescent female skull and mandible found during the 1958 season (Movius and Vallois 1960; Movius 1961). The evidence of the fauna and the sediments themselves demonstrate that at the time of this occupation, cold and somewhat moist climatic conditions prevailed in the Les Eyzies region. In addition to the local material, imported flint was also employed for implement manufac-

FIGURE 4
Périgordian VI. Large rock engraved with "serpentine" decoration found in Trench IV, Square F.

ture. Radiocarbon measurements of a series of samples from this Level demonstrate that the Proto-Magdalenian of the Abri Pataud may be dated to 21,940 B.P. ± 250 years, or about 19,990 B.C. (GrN-1862). This is in excellent agreement with the results of measurements of a sample (GrN-1876) from the corresponding Level at Laugerie-Haute, which has been dated to 21,980 B.P. ± 250 years, or, 20,030 B.C. From a typological point of view the Level 2 assemblage constitutes a very distinctive and interesting entity (cf. Movius 1961), which in no way whatsoever is related to either the Périgordian, the Aurignacian, or even the Magdalenian, for that matter. For it the name *LAUGERIAN* has been proposed (Clay, unpub.)

Level 3—Périgordian VI

As in the case of the Proto-Magdalenian, or Laugerian, this occupation has also been documented at Laugerie-Haute: Est (Couches B and B′), where in the absence of correct stratigraphic data, it was originally described as Périgordian III by Peyrony, as stated above. Level 3 at the Abri Pataud contains high concentrations of red ochre, or hematite, a series of clearly defined hearths, as well as evidence suggesting a long-house type of occupation (Movius 1966). The characteristic features of the industrial assemblage (total: about 1,860 catalogued pieces) from this assemblage have been summarized elsewhere (Movius, with Vallois 1960). The faunal remains and the geological evidence indicate that the prevailing climate was somewhat less severe and drier than was the case during Level 2 (Proto-Magdalenian, or Laugerian) times. One of four C-14 measurements of a sample of unburned bone from this stratum indicates a date or 23,010 B.P. ± 170 years, or about 21,060 B.C. (GrN-4721) for the Périgordian VI in the Les Eyzies region. A small bas-relief carving of a female figure that is considered to represent a very fine example of an Upper Périgordian "Venus" was found in Level 3 (Movius, with Vallois, 1960). A detailed study of the Périgordian VI assemblage from the Abri Pataud (David and Bricker, unpub.) demonstrates that it was directly derived from the Périgordian IV tradition of Level 5.

Level 4–Noaillian (Formerly Périgordian Vc)

A total of almost 8,000 catalogued specimens was recovered from the twelve lenses that comprise Level 4, and it is felt that this total has provided a reliable series for statistical processing and analysis. Not only is there a significant typological change between the three major stratigraphic subdivisions of this Level—Raysse burins (Movius and David 1970) become very common in the Upper unit, whereas Noailles examples are particularly numerous in the Lower subdivision—but also from a quantitative point of view the assemblages from the front of the site differ significantly from those of the rear. Furthermore, the virtual absence of Gravette points (less than 2 percent), and the evidence of attribute analysis, support the view that this assemblage does not belong in the Périgordian tradition. In the rear portion of the site an extensive "bonfire" type Hearth Complex occurred, indicating occupation by a fairly large social unit in contrast to the "lineage" type of community suggested by the presumed long-house types of dwelling revealed in the overlying Level 3 mentioned above. In the basal portion of the Lower subdivision of Level 4, a semi-circular arrangement of stones came to light delimiting the areal extent of six small, semi-basin shaped hearths. During much of the interval represented by this occupation, the climate was fairly cold and relatively moist, although the faunal and geological evidence indicate that milder conditions were beginning to prevail during the interval of the uppermost subdivision of the Level. It is virtually certain that more precise information bearing on the whole problem of the climatic sequence at the Abri Pataud will be forthcoming when the results of detailed paleobotanical investigations, which are now in progress, become available. In the meantime, only one of a large series of C-14 samples from Level 4 has been measured; it was collected in the Middle subdivision of the layer, and it indicates an age of about 27,060 ± 370 years B.P., or about 25,100 B.C. (GrN-4280), which is somewhat earlier than expected on the basis of the figures for the underlying Level 5 samples.

Dr. Nicholas David, who conducted the attribute study of the Level 4 assemblage at the Abri Pataud, as well as a large number of other sites in France, Spain and Italy where Noailles burins have been reported, concludes his monograph as follows:

> The participation of the Noaillian in the Upper Périgordian cultural tradition can no longer be maintained. Differentiation of the Noaillian has been conclusively demonstrated at the Abri Pataud, Isturitz (a large site in the western Pyrénées), and numerous sites, including all those excavated by modern techniques that have been fully published. Attributal and quantitative analyses combine to show that the Noaillian industry expresses technologically, functionally and stylistically distinctive manufacturing norms. In such a case, where a tradition has flourished in an area for a period that can scarcely be less than a millennium and where another suddenly appears to displace it and truncate its local development, it is appropriate to identify them with separate peoples. Peyrony's Upper Périgordian theory must then be modified to admit the intrusive element. (David, unpub.)

Recognition of this fact is certainly one of the most significant contributions of the Abri Pataud research project.

Level 5—Périgordian IV (Level with Gravette Points)

Only the uppermost subdivision of this horizon belongs to the classic La Gravette Stage of the Upper Périgordian, according to Dr. Harvey M. Bricker (unpub. thesis). At the type site, however, the middle and the lower units (except for a thin, isolated workshop area) are not represented. At the Abri Pataud, Level 5 occurs as two major disconnected deposits—one in the front and one in the rear of the site. Over 11,000 catalogued pieces were found in this very thick (thickness: up to 70 centimeters) and prolific level. In

FIGURE 5
Périgordian IV. General view of Trenches III and IV, Squares E and F, showing the excavation of the "bonfire" type hearth area in Lens H-3 in progress.

the front portion of the deposit, a total of five major subdivisions was recognized; most of these in turn consist of three or more lenses, of which a total of twenty-three was recognized. In the rear of the site, two major subdivisions, made up of ten lenses, were identified. As in the overlying horizon (Level 4), a series of superimposed "bonfire" type hearths occurred in the rear sector. In addition to Gravette points, the major components of this assemblage include: fléchettes, truncation, dihedral and break burins, end-scrapers on well-struck blades, truncated blades (rare), a few perforators and some retouched blades. The faunal evidence, together with the results of an analysis of the soils, suggest that relatively cool, temperate conditions prevailed in the Les Eyzies region during the time interval represented by this occupation. Several C-14 dates are available for Level 5—average: about 27,900 B.P. ± 225 years, or 25,950 B.C.—which is manifestly "too young" on the basis of the figure obtained for a sample from the overlying Level.

FIGURE 6
Intermediate Aurignacian B. Excavation of the Hearth Complex shown above revealed that each hearth had been placed in a shallow pit or basin. The X and Y units were the oldest; Hearth W, which was 1.50 meters in diameter, consisted of three distinct levels, designated W-1 and W-2 (a and b) and W-3, respectively. A sample of ash from Hearth W has been given a C-14 date of 32,800 B.P. ± 450 years, or about 30,850 B.C. for this occupation.

Level 6—Evolved Aurignacian

Only a small series of about 200 artifacts were recovered in the two main subdivisions of this relatively thin remnant of a once more extensive Level, for the major portion of Level 6 had been removed by the Level 5 occupants of the site in order to provide additional head room in the rear portion of the shelter. The assemblage includes retouched blades, often with an end-scraper at one extremity, Dufour bladelets, steep scrapers on thick flakes, carinate and nose-ended scrapers, and truncation and dihedral burins. Both the fauna and the nature of the sediments themselves indicate that the climate was cold and somewhat moist—similar to the conditions that prevailed during the interval of the Level 3 (Périgordian VI) settlement.

Although none of the radiocarbon samples from this Level has yet been measured, it is very unlikely that the Evolved Aurignacian horizon is younger than about 30,000 B.P., or 28,050 B.C.

Level 7—Intermediate Aurignacian B

In this Level a flattened, losangic-shaped bone sagaie, which is the type implement of D. Peyrony's Aurignacian II, came to light. This was a fairly rich stratum (total: about 450 catalogued pieces), which filled a large, roughly oval and basin-shaped depression with a complex series of hearths near its northern end. Each of these hearths, designated W, X and Y, respectively, rested in a specially prepared shallow basin, and each was associated with a layer of purposely selected river-stones. In addition to the losangic-shaped bone sagaie, mentioned above, this Level produced numerous retouched blades, end-scrapers on blades that are often retouched, busked and carinate burins, as well as truncation and dihedral burins. Radiocarbon determinations of several very homogeneous ash samples from the uppermost of the three main subdivisions of Hearth W indicate an approximate date of 32,800 B.P. ± 450 yrs., or about 30,850 B.C., for this occupation. But this figure may be as much as one millennium "too old" on the basis of comparison with the dates for comparable occupations from other sites in France. A cold and somewhat moist climate prevailed at this time in the Dordogne, just as elsewhere in southwestern France.

Level 8—Intermediate Aurignacian A

A considerable portion of this horizon was removed when the Level 7 basin was excavated during prehistoric times. In the middle subdivision in the front portion of the site a hearth was found in a circular basin 52 centimeters in diameter and 15 centimeters deep. As in the case of the Level 7 hearths, this feature contained a large number of water-rolled stones from the river. A second small hearth occurred in the lower subdivision of Level 8 in the rear of the site directly below one of those associated with the overlying occupation. In Level 8, which yielded an approximate total of 250 catalogued pieces, numerous micro-blades with steep, obverse/inverse retouch (Dufour bladelets) were found. In addition to a large number of retouched blades, often with one extremity worked into an end-scraper, Level 8 yielded truncation and dihedral burins, but busked burins, very characteristic of the Level 7 assemblage, were rare. In addition, an interesting series of carinate, nose-ended and steep-ended scrapers also came to light. At the time of this occupation—for which no C–14 date has yet been announced—cold, rigorous, albeit somewhat moist, conditions prevailed in the Dordogne.

Level 9—Intermediate (?) Aurignacian

This level, which yielded an approximate total of only thirty five artifacts, appears to represent a very minor but nevertheless definitely Aurignacian occupation of the Abri Pataud.

Level 10—Intermediate (?) Aurignacian

Very similar to Level 9 in all essential respects, Level 10 likewise represents a thin, minor occupation. In this horizon a total of fifty catalogued pieces, all of Aurignacian type, came to light.

Level 11—Early Aurignacian B

In this level several cleft-base bone points were recovered. At the base of this stratum an impressive group of structural features occurred, consisting of no less than seven hearths and two shallow pits. Each of the latter was associated with a series of large-to-medium-sized stones. In marked contrast to the hearths of Levels 7 and 8, river-stones were exceedingly rare throughout Level 11, including the hearths. Furthermore, the ash content of the latter, shallow, basin-shaped depressions indicates that bone was now extensively used as a source of fuel. The almost regular arrangement of these interesting features across the back of the site, in two lines roughly parallel to the line of the former rear wall of the shelter, suggests that their positioning was not random, but that in a sense they form a patterned series. Only two of a large number of C–14 samples from this horizon have been measured, the results being 32,000 B.P. ± 800 years and 32,600 B.P. ± 550 years. Although the Groningen laboratory has accepted a central date of about 33,000 B.P. (31,050 B.C.) for both Levels 12 and 11, it is apparent, on the basis of the stratigraphic evidence, that Level 12 must be slightly older than 33,000 and Level 11 must be slightly younger. One may conclude, therefore, that the two occupations were very close to one another in time, and that C–14 was unable to separate them successfully.

Including flint implements, stone, bone, antler and ivory objects, as well as a few fragments of hematite and manganese, a total of approximately 820 catalogued pieces came to light in this Level. In addition to numerous blades with medium to heavy marginal retouch, many with one extremity worked into an end-scraper, there is an interesting series of steep scrapers on thick flakes, carinate

FIGURE 7
Early Aurignacian A. Hearth complex P, Q, R and S. General view of Trenches II and III in the front of the site showing excavation of the four hearths in progress. Note how the basin of R truncates that of Q.

scrapers and nose-ended scrapers, but blunt points are rare. There are a few perforators, and, as in the underlying Levels 12, 13 and 14, burins are absent. Objects of bone and antler include sagaies and awls. In the rear of the site this horizon rested directly on bed-rock, and in front on Éboulis 11–12. Indeed, at several points, Level 11 actually overlies Level 12 unconformably, and along the southern edge of both pits the truncated surface of the underlying horizon could be discerned. At the time of this occupation, cold and rigorous, but somewhat moist climatic conditions prevailed in the Dordogne.

Level 12—Early Aurignacian A

The original extent of this Level toward the rear of the site is unknown, since it had been removed in this sector when the Level

11 settlers cleared and leveled the area prior to their occupation. This horizon, which yielded an approximate total of 160 artifacts, attained a maximum thickness of 15 centimeters. The archaeological assemblage from Level 12 includes blades with medium to heavy marginal retouch, end-scrapers on Aurignacian blades, blunt points, carinate scrapers and a few Dufour bladelets; burins are absent. Associated with this occupation four hearths were found. All of them lay in clearly defined basins in the southern portion of the excavated area. In each case these basins were filled with burned bone and ash; a few river-stones also occurred. The evidence of the fauna and the sediments indicate that very cold, humid conditions prevailed in the region during the time interval represented by this occupation. It is hoped that detailed pollen studies will throw additional light on this matter. One very tentative, and certainly "too young" radiocarbon date has been announced by the Groningen laboratory for the Level 12 occupation. Just as in the case of certain other figures for the Abri Pataud samples, this result should very definitely be checked.

Level 13— Basal Aurignacian B

This is a doubly truncated remnant of a formerly more extensive deposit. Along its eastern margin it abuts against the sharply sloping bedrock of the shelter, and a portion of it was cut across at the time of the levelling of the shelter's floor prior to the Level 11 occupation. Of a dark reddish-yellow color, this horizon averages 8 centimeters to 10 centimeters thick, its maximum thickness being 15 centimeters. The western limit of Level 13, apparently artificial, was formed either by erosion or, more likely, by human activities during the time of the occupation. It extended further toward the west than either the underlying Éboulis 13–14 or Level 14; in fact, it rested on a surface that obliquely truncated the latter units. This presumably resulted from excavation in antiquity. Level 13, which yielded only fifty seven catalogued pieces, was manifestly not rich; furthermore, no hearths were found in the excavated area. The assemblage includes Aurignacian blades some of which have end-scrapers at one extremity, strangulated (or doubly notched) blades, and carinate scrapers (including several pointed examples), but no burins. Since the quantity of cultural material increases markedly from north to south, it is very probable that this occupation lies in the latter direction. Pit I and one of the hearths (M) of Level 11 were actually cut down into the surface of this horizon. During this interval of time very cold and fairly humid climatic conditions prevailed in the Les Eyzies region.

Level 14—Basal Aurignacian A

This is the earliest occupation layer at the Abri Pataud; quite possibly it is as much as 34,000 years old (about 32,050 B.C.) on the basis of several recent radiocarbon measurements. The Level increases markedly in thickness in the direction of the main hearth complex in the southern sector of the excavated area where it attains a thickness of about 25 centimeters. Toward the north it thins down to 12 centimeters thick or less. In this Level three major and two minor hearths occurred, all lying in shallow, sub-oval to circular basins. A total of 290 catalogued artifacts of flint, bone and stone, including blades with medium to heavy marginal retouch, end-scrapers on Aurignacian blades, blunt points, carinate scrapers, and a few teeth perforated for suspension. As in the case of the overlying Levels 13–9, burins were absent.

In and immediately adjacent to the hearth area, a large, irregular pit came to light. It is believed that this shallow feature is in part artificial and in part due to the occupants having taken advantage of a natural depression in the Basal Éboulis. The apparently artificial and more regular portion of this pit is in the eastern area of the site where it was excavated to a total depth of about 25 centimeters. In this pit Level 14 attained its maximum thickness.

The results of the excavation of the Abri Pataud have contributed very important data bearing on knowledge of the culture-history in the Dordogne. This new information may be summarized as follows:

a. The existence of the Proto-Magdalenian, or Laugerian, as a discrete tradition separate and independent of either the Aurignacian or the Périgordian has been confirmed. Previously recognized only at Laugerie-Haute: Est, this very distinctive development has recently been reported from the site of the Abri du Blot in the Allier Valley some 125 miles due east of Les Eyzies.

b. The fact that the assemblages from Couches B and B′ at Laugerie Haute: Ouest, originally described by D. Peyrony as Périgordian III, in reality belong to the final phase (VI) of the Périgordian sequence has been demonstrated by the evidence of Level 3 at the Abri Pataud.

c. The evidence of Level 4 which has proved that the Noaillian (formerly called Périgordian Vc by Peyrony) does not in fact belong to the Upper Périgordian cultural tradition. Both quantitative and attributal analyses have been combined to show that the Noaillian industry expresses distinctive technological and stylistical manufacturing norms.

d. The occurrence of nine separate and distinct horizons of Aurignacian occupation in contrast to the four levels reported by Peyrony at La Ferrassie (Dordogne) clearly demonstrates that the development of this tradition is far more complex than had previously been suspected.

Thus, from the point of view of the Upper Paleolithic sequence in southwestern France the major advances in knowledge which have resulted from the Abri Pataud excavation program are by no means insignificant. But perhaps of even greater importance and interest for Paleolithic archaeology as a whole were: (a) the new excavation techniques developed at this very extensive and rich site; (b) the overall conclusions based on the results of the ecological/environmental studies; and (c) the development of completely new and revolutionary classificatory procedures. Each of these is briefly summarized on the following pages.

Excavation Techniques

New and improved excavation techniques, developed and employed at the Abri Pataud for the first time in 1959–1960, are now widely used in western Europe. In the first instance, the working area was controlled throughout by a 2.0 meter grid, consisting of a series of parallel north-south and east-west pipes. These pipes intersected at 2.0 meter intervals, and from the intersections, plumbs were suspended. Thus, each set of four plumbs defined a grid square consistently and accurately throughout the depth of the rocky deposits.

On either side of the 4.0 meter wide main excavation area, test trenches 1.0 meter wide were dug in accordance with an arbitrary 10 centimeter system of vertical units in order to determine the real stratigraphy, or actual subdivisions (micro-stratigraphic units), or lenses, which collectively comprise each occupation layer. There is good reason to believe that each of these lenses represents an occupation "floor," but the actual duration of the occupation in question cannot be determined on the basis of any dating method developed thus far. Next, the 4.0 meter wide central area of the site was excavated by following these lenses, a procedure which makes possible the exposure of a single extensive horizontal surface, or contemporary occupation at one time. In terms of the north-south and east-west coordinates, the location of each artifact was thus accurately plotted within a given 2.0 meter square, in relation to a given specific feature—*e.g.*, a hearth, or a series of hearths—and a study made of its actual association with other artifacts of the same or comparable

FIGURE 8
Abri Pataud. General view of the excavated areas showing the installation of the 2.00 meter grid system. The six west-east units (left right) designate Trenches I-VI, those at a right angle to the latter are the Squares A-F, G being located under the existing overhang of the shelter.

types. A third measurement—*i.e.,* depth below datum—was also recorded for each object. The results of preliminary investigations along these lines have revealed that major quantitative differences in the artifactual materials do in fact occur, not only vertically throughout the thickness of a given occupation layer, but also horizontally from the front of the shelter toward the rear wall. Indeed, rather marked typological changes exist between the materials from the front of the site as compared with those of the area in the rear, where the large hearth complexes normally occur.

This new and improved excavation procedure has led to the formulation of an interesting hypothesis concerning the social organization of the Upper Périgordian and the Aurignacian peoples who occupied the Abri Pataud during early Upper Paleolithic times. Indeed, the evidence of the hearths and associated living floors ex-

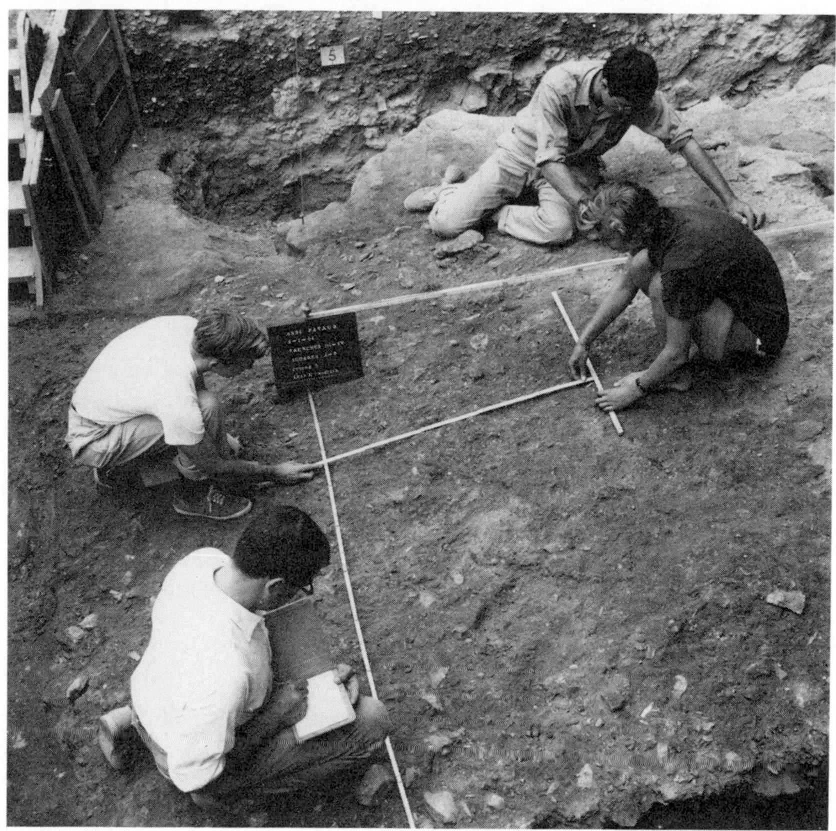

FIGURE 9
Front (Périgordian IV). The surface of Lens U in Trenches III and IV, Squares A and B. The excavators are measuring and recording the horizontal coordinates of each individual object.

posed at the site suggests that there very probably was a basic and fundamental difference in the social structure of these two groups (cf. Movius 1966). For the characteristics of these features indicate that in the case of the Level 3 (Périgordian VI) one is dealing with the so-called "longhouse" type of the "lineage" category of kinship organization. Furthermore, it seems apparent on the basis of ethnological parallels that one may justifiably presume that the large "bonfire" type of hearths in Level 4 (Noaillian) and Level 5 (Périgordian IV) likewise imply occupations by fairly large social units in both cases. At the base of Level 4 the concentration of small hearths, briefly mentioned above, presumably resulted from a temporary settlement by a relatively small group which later expanded and occupied a larger area of the site. Admittedly this is pure speculation. On the other hand, an entirely different type of social structure is suggested by the evidence of the hearths and associated features found in Levels 7 and 8 (Intermediate Aurignacian A and B) and in Levels 12 and 14 (Early and Basal Aurignacian). The evidence on which this statement is based has been more fully discussed elsewhere (Movius 1966), the essential facts being that the hearths found in each of these horizons have been placed in clearly defined basins which occur in association with a concentrated area of limited occupation. It has been suggested that a much smaller residence unit, perhaps limited to one expanded nuclear family, or a series of such units extending along the cliff, is indicated on the basis of this evidence. In the final analysis, however, one must confess that the possible significance of the multi-hearth-cum-pit arrangement found in Level 11 (Early Aurignacian B) remains obscure. Insofar as the writer is aware, no such complex arrangement has ever been previously reported from an Upper Paleolithic site in western Europe.

Ecological/Environmental Studies

During the last fifty years or so, there have been rapid changes in the intellectual framework of those disciplines of the natural sciences which deal with Pleistocene ecology. If one considers the reindeer *(Rangifer tarandus)* as a case in point, its presence in considerable quantity at various sites in southwestern France formerly was considered to be indicative of a characteristic mossy, wet tundra environment, reminiscent of that of contemporary northern Eurasia and North America. But recent studies in both Scandinavia and Canada have shown that the southern limit of this herd animal borders on the July isotherm of 15° C. (59° F.), which is the upper limit of the cool, wet summer climatic zone found today at an approximate elevation of 1,000 meters (3,250 feet) on the slopes of the extinct volcanoes of the Massif Central, some 100 kilometers (62.5 miles) to 150 kilometers (94.25 miles) east and northeast of Les Eyzies. Now the essential requirement for the reindeer is a certain species of lichen *(Cladonia rangiferensis),* a form which survives almost anywhere in the Northern Hemisphere wherever competition is at a minimum. Since it grows today in the Dordogne, its climatic significance is only very limited.

Recently a herd of reindeer was successfully introduced into the Cairngorm area of Scotland, and in European Russia until the seventeenth century (when the last remnants of the herds were killed off by commercial hunters) great numbers of these animals are stated to have migrated annually as far south as the Caucasus. In other words, the alleged axiom that the presence of substantial numbers of reindeer was indicative of an arctic/sub-arctic environment is a complete myth. Admittedly this animal is cold-adapted, but one can go no further, except to point out that apparently it cannot survive in an area where the July temperature mean exceeds 15° C. (59° F.). Therefore, the concept that the prevalence of reindeer in the various Upper Paleolithic levels at the Abri Pataud is indicative of a Last Glacial habitat in the Les Eyzies region of southwestern France which was in any way similar to that of northern Eurasia and northern North America at the present time is completely erroneous. Indeed, on the basis of the sum total of the available evidence, one may conclude that those climatic oscillations which did occur during about the 15,000-year interval represented by the sediments at the site were of a relatively minor ecological order. A similarly varied vegetation is in fact extant today near tree-line in the Massif Central. Furthermore, the total faunal assemblage represented is tolerant of a wide range of climatic variation.

The continuous and apparently intensive occupation of the river valleys of the Dordogne region of southwestern France during Upper Paleolithic implies that these areas must have been dependable places for human occupation. Indeed, with its abundant flint deposits, numerous caves and rock-shelters at the base of south-facing Cretaceous limestone slopes, and its consistently abundant and varied supply of game during all twelve months of the year, the Dordogne must have been a very attractive region—one which would be difficult, if not impossible, to duplicate at present. Certainly there is absolutely *no* evidence in support of the concept advocated by the proponents of the classical notion that the environment and ecological conditions in the Les Eyzies region during Last Glacial times were in any respect comparable with those now prevailing in either the taïga (sub-arctic) or the tundra (arctic) regions in comtemporary Eurasia and North America. Even the vegetation on the wind-swept upland plateau areas between the valleys must have closely resembled that which occurs at present within about 300 meters or so of tree-line on the slopes of the ancient volcanoes of the Massif Central. In such an environment the reindeer would certainly thrive.

The evidence of the invertebrate fauna found in the various occupation horizons of the site leads to a similar conclusion. Indeed, the eleven species of non-marine mollusca found at the Abri Pataud all thrive today in the Les Eyzies vicinity, and they demonstrate that the climate has remained basically unchanged for an exceedingly long interval of time. Especially common in the Noaillian (Level 4; formerly Périgordian Vc) horizon, a total of twenty-two recent marine mollusca was recovered. Of these, four forms, all of which are common at present in the Mediterranean, were apparently obtained either in trade, or as exchange commodities of some sort. Of the balance, *i.e.*, eighteen species, all are living today in Aquitania and Poitou on the Atlantic shores of France. This evidence provides no support for the contention that the then-prevailing climate was substantially more rigorous than it is at present. For it is a self-evident fact that, if the composition of the invertebrates in southwestern France is still basically the same today as it was during early Upper Paleolithic times, even the remote possibility that tundra or taïga-forest conditions could have prevailed in this region during Last Glacial times is automatically ruled out.

Palynological studies have shown that, in addition to three shrubs (juniper, willow and hazel), the pollen composition of the Abri Pataud samples includes some twelve trees (birch, pine, oak and alder, together with sporadic grains of elm, beech, maple, lime, ash, fir, hornbeam and walnut). Some twenty-three non-tree pollen types were also identified, and these predominate in almost all the samples. In general, the relative amount of trees and shrubs is below 50 percent of all the pollen counted, and in some cases it drops down to 20-30 percent. The trees most strongly represented—birch, pine, oak and alder—almost certainly grew in the immediate vicinity of the site, where the shrubs—juniper, willow and hazel—were also present. One likewise finds sporadic grains of elm, beech, maple, lime, ash, fir, hornbeam and walnut. It is likely that the Upper Paleolithic park-like forests persisted in sheltered areas in the valleys, often protected by high cliffs, whereas the upland plateau between the water courses apparently supported a more open, steppe-like vegetation. Although it is difficult to trace any significant changes in the vegetational history of the vicinity of the site on the basis of the pollen diagram, such an assemblage of deciduous trees (with the exception of pine and fir) as that listed above is manifestly *not* representative of a forest vegetation in the present taïga zones.

On the basis of the data summarized above, it is clear that the whole problem of the biological and/or ecological order of the climatic changes that did occur in this sector of the Dordogne during early Upper Paleolithic is in urgent need of further intensive investigation. In the first place, it is evident that both the vertebrate and the invertebrate faunas are capable of a rather wide range of climatic variation. Certainly it is apparent that the existence of warmth-loving components in the Last Glacial flora of the Abri Pataud demonstrates that the then-existing climate of this area of the Vézère Valley was even less rigorous than that which now prevails in the Massif Central at an elevation of about 1,000 meters (3,250 feet), except during certain intervals of maximum cold. But the mean daily summer temperature range at this elevation of south-facing slopes is normally between 7° and 15° C. (45° to 59° F.), although there are very few nights without some frost. One vital fact is now abundantly clear: the classic notion that Last Glacial conditions comparable in any manner to those now obtaining in northern Eurasia or northern North America ever prevailed in this refuge area is not only misleading but also completely untrue. Therefore, since we are dealing with a region where a far less severe and harsh environment prevailed than what one has heretofore been led to believe, no group of living reindeer-hunting peoples—Esquimo, Athabascan or Paleosiberian—can serve as a model in an effort to reconstruct by analogy the hunting patterns, social organization, demography, etc., of our Upper Paleolithic forebears in southwestern France. Indeed, the ecological conditions of Last Glacial times in the Les Eyzies region of the Dordogne have only been reported from a few limited present-day sectors of the globe, and in none of them is the reindeer still extant.

Classificatory Procedures

For just over ten years now it has been apparent to the author that in the broad field of Old World Paleolithic research, the development and employment of modern field methods have progressed a great deal faster than have the introduction and use of precise analytical and descriptive procedures for processing the excavated materials. In other words, the design of new excavation methods has outstripped the capacity of the archaeologist to study and describe accurately the material finds brought to light during the course of a given research program. A complete description of the significant results of this work—regarded as a major "break through" in the field of Paleolithic studies—has been published (Movius, *et al.* 1968; with Brooks 1971). A summary of the fundamental procedure(s) underlying the research is set forth below.

For the past century Paleolithic archaeologists have stressed the importance of the "type fossil concept," of which the finished artifact is the material expression. This approach, which is by no means confined to Paleolithic archaeology, is based to a greater or lesser extent on a relatively few "type fossils," the distinguishing features of which have been defined and imposed on the material by the prehistoric archaeologists themselves. Not only does this result in confining the analytical procedures to the strictures of a taxonomic discipline, but also the very rigidity of the systematics involved obscures the true significance of the artifactual materials in question. It completely disregards the basic and fundamental point at issue, namely, the "constructional idea" that underlies the tool itself—*i.e.,* in the first instance what was the artificer actually trying to produce? For this reason none of the common types of artifacts—burins of all categories, end-of-blade scrapers, etc.—found in Upper Paleolithic sites have ever been adequately studied.

During the past decade a series of new techniques have been developed for obtaining empirical data to serve as a basis for analyzing the assemblages from the extremely rich occupation levels at the Abri Pataud. Indeed, the Abri Pataud team believes it is beginning to understand certain of the "constructional ideas" expressed in the various groups of tools constituting these assemblages. We are convinced that detailed attribute analysis procedures along the lines that have been developed at the Abri Pataud will make it possible to define true clusterings, or real types, within a given assemblage, and to establish the norm and range of the variations within the materials from the various subdivisions of the stratigraphic units in question. Finally, these results can be used as the basis for establishing refined criteria of cultural likenesses between the several horizons of a given locality, *i.e.,* in the study of temporal, or synchronic, variation. Before such results can be used, however, as the basis for spacial, or diachronic, studies—*i.e.,* comparing one site with another in the same or contiguous region(s)—archaeologists must agree on what are the significant attributes and how these should be measured and expressed within a given tool group. For, in the final analysis, it is only in terms of a standardized methodology that the data from any two localities can be compared.

In a very real sense, therefore, the ultimate major scientific contribution of the Abri Pataud Project to the field of Upper Paleolithic archaeology unquestionably lies in the area of methodological procedures involving the application of statistical analysis to the elucidation of problems in prehistory. In his attempt to understand the past, the prehistoric archaeologist makes use of a series of fundamental hypotheses. First, he defines as artifacts those objects that have been deliberately altered by human labor. These in turn are resolved into categories of tools each of which can be distinguished as possessing one particular range of consistently recurrent humanly imposed traits. Finally, human cultures, or social traditions, can be recognized as consistently and, within certain limits, concomitantly recurrent assemblages of categories of tools found in definite geographic areas. In other words, the prehistoric archaeologist is constantly scanning the ever-increasing mass of data for consistently recurring groupings of interrelated characteristics which should reflect the very social alignments that he is trying to isolate. In all of these concepts there occurs the condition that the attributes should be "consistently recurrent," or some such alternative, thereby preventing rare or chance characteristics from assuming undue importance. Thus, in essence, the term "consistently recurrent" is a statistical definition, directly related to the number of times a group of traits occurs together within a specified statistically reliable sample of traits. In other words, the prehistorian's attempt to understand ancient material culture and social traditions is based in part on statistical assumptions. Therefore, statistical methods are not just peripheral aids to archaeology; they are vital to its very basis.

Retrospect and Lines of Future Development

During the period of the Abri Pataud excavations from 1958 to 1964, it must be admitted that the field work as a whole marked a considerable advance over that of any other comparable program ever attempted in the field of Old World Paleolithic archaeology. In retrospect, however, one may state that what one may perhaps refer to as "the lens system of excavation" was the one basic advance or contribution to excavation technique that emerged from our program. In any case, the system of examining in detail the distribution of cultural debris on a given occupation floor had not yet been developed. This system is both extremely time-consuming and almost prohibitively costly. Yet it was very successfully employed by Professor André Leroi-Gourhan of the College de France in Paris, at the huge Magdalenian open air hunting campsite of Pincevent (Leroi-Gourhan and Brézillon 1966), a single occupation site near Montereau (Seine-et-Marne), and by Dr. Henry de Lumley of the Université de Marseilles and his collaborators at the Grotte du Lazeret, an Acheulian site near Nice on the French Riviera (de Lumley 1969). In both instances the grid system was used, and the position of each object was plotted on a three dimensional coordinate system as at the Abri Pataud. Before a given living floor was removed, however, a vertical photo of it was taken, and at Pincevent a latex mold was made as well. Samples for sedimentary and pollen analysis were, of course, extracted, and in many cases analyzed while the work was proceeding. Good organization, good working conditions, a laboratory of sorts near the excavation to allow simultaneous examination and study, and, by implication, plenty of money to make it all possible permitted an almost unbelievably rewarding recovery of data in both instances.

The author does not believe that in the study of the actual tools the attribute analysis system developed by us at the Abri Pataud will be substantially modified in the foreseeable future. As the result of the detailed study of the waste flakes recovered at Pincevent, however, many spalls were found which could be fitted back onto a specific burin. As an offshoot of this painstaking analysis many nuclei were also reconstituted, thereby permitting a study of the actual knapping technique employed by the various prehistoric craftsmen. But no one has as yet attempted a detailed study of the waste material itself with a view to determining changing techniques employed in the process of blank production. It is hoped that a project along these lines will be developed and implemented at the Abri Pataud during the next few years. Finally, a microscopic study of traces of wear and use in an effort to determine what work may have been done with a given tool still remains to be organized. This latter approach, which was very sketchily attempted at Pincevent, was developed by the Russian archaeologist, S. A. Semenov (1964). Finally, there remains the whole problem of the normally broken faunal remains to be investigated. Along these lines we know very little concerning either the actual breakage itself—believed to have been for the purpose of extracting the marrow—or prehistoric cooking methods. Manifestly if the meat was boiled then a container of some sort would have been necessary. And no such object has ever come to light. Thus it seems inevitable that the major lines of future research in Upper Paleolithic archaeology will involve a very considerable amount of careful and painstaking field research. But there is *no* short-cut: if one wants to obtain information bearing on the way of life and activities of our prehistoric forebears there is *no* alternative to constant, detailed and unbiased research.

References

BRICKER, HARVEY M.

The Périgordian IV (Level 5) Assemblage from the Abri Pataud and Other Localities in France. In press.

CLAY, R. BERLE

The Proto-Magdalenian (Level 2) Assemblage from the Abri Pataud, Les Eyzies (Dordogne). In press.

DAVID, NICHOLAS C.
The Noaillian (Level 4) Assemblage from the Abri Pataud, Les Eyzies (Dordogne): Part I; The Noaillian in Aquitania and Other Areas: Part II. In press.

DAVID, NICHOLAS C. AND BRICKER, HARVEY M.
The Périgordian VI (Level 3) Assemblage from the Abri Pataud, Les Eyzies (Dordogne). In press.

LEROI-GOURHAN, ANDRÉ AND BRÉZILLON, MICHEL
1966 L'Hebitation Magdalénienne N. 1 de Pincevent, près Montereau (Seine-et-Marne). Gallia Préhistoire 9; 2: 263–385.

LUMLEY, HENRY DE
1969 Une Cabane Acheuléenne dans la Grotte du Lazaret (Nice). Mémoires de la Société Préhistorique Française 7: 235.

MOVIUS, H. L., JR.
1954 Les Eyzies: A Test Excavation. Archaeology 7; 2: 82–90.

1960 Bas-Relief Carving of a Female Figure Recently Discovered in the Final Périgordian Horizon at the Abri Pataud, Les Eyzies (Dordogne). Festschrift für Lothar Zotz: Steinzeitfragen der Alten und Neuen Welt. Bonn, L. Röhrscheid, 377–387.

1961 The Proto-Magdalenian of the Abri Pataud, Les Eyzies (Dordogne). Berich Über den V Internationalen Kongress für Vorund Frühgeschichte, Hamburg, 561–566.

1966 The Hearths of the Upper Périgordian and Aurignacian Horizons at the Abri Pataud, Les Eyzies (Dordogne) and their possible significance. American Anthropologist (Special Issue) 68; 2: 296–325.

MOVIUS, H. L., JR. AND BROOKS, ALISON S.
1971 The Analysis of Certain Major Classes of Upper Palaeolithic Tools: Aurignacian Scrapers. Proceedings of the Prehistoric Society 37: 253–273.

MOVIUS, H. L., JR. AND DAVID, NICHOLAS C.
1970 Burins avec modification tertiaire du Biseau, Burins-points et Burins du Raysse à l'Abri Pataud, Les Eyzies (Dordogne). Bulletin de la Société Préhistorique Française, Études et Traveaux 67; 2: 445–455.

MOVIUS, H. L., JR.; DAVID, NICHOLAS C.; BRICKER, HARVEY M. AND CLAY, R. BERLE
1968 The Analysis of Certain Major Classes of Upper Palaeolithic Tools. Bulletin of the American School of Prehistoric Research 26: 1–58.

MOVIUS, H. L., JR. AND VALLOIS, HENRI-V
1960 Crâne Proto-Magdalénien et Vénus du Périgordien Final trouvés

dans l'Abri Pataud, Les Eyzies (Dordogne). L'Anthropologie 63; 3–4: 213–232.

SEMENOV, S. A.
1970 Prehistoric Technology. M. W. Thompson, trans. Bath, England, Adams & Dart.

THE EASTERN UNITED STATES

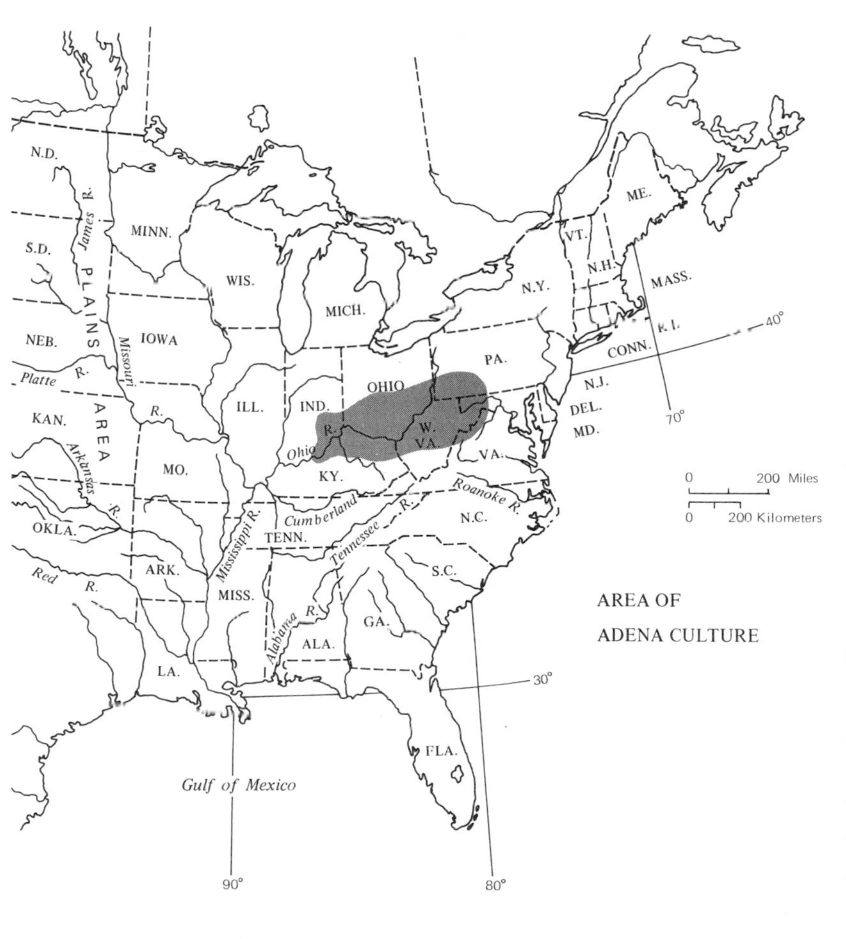

(preceding page)

Map of eastern United States showing area of the Adena culture in the Ohio Valley and adjacent terrain.

The Adena Culture

WILLIAM G. HAAG

Introduction

There are no practicing archaeologists today who ever use the expression "Mound Builders." Yet a few decades ago all professional archaeologists and serious amateurs considered the mounds that dotted the Mississippi Valley and its tributaries to have been the work of a mysterious race of people who preceded the American Indian. Nowhere was this concept better fed than in the middle reaches of the Ohio Valley where a number of large mounds in Ohio, Indiana, and Kentucky had disclosed the presence of peoples of a higher culture than that represented by the Indian of historic contact times. The acceptance of this idea by an older generation of archaeologists is by no means unique in its quaintness and is paralleled in a variety of other sciences. Hardly four decades ago, physical scientists were certain we could never attain the escape velocity necessary to get a rocket off the surface of the earth and out of its gravitational influence. Certainly early American archaeologists were not lacking in judgment nor were they dependent wholly upon intuitive interpretations of what they saw. Rather, the content of the archaeological picture in the Ohio Valley was such that the material found was far more impressive than anything that could be historically documented. I might point out that, for some time, archaeologists considered the Fort Ancient culture, which had no spectacular metal or stone artifact assemblage, to be older than the Hopewell and the Adena cultures, which were very rich in both metallic and fancy stone work.

It is not necessary at this point to rehash the old theories about the origins of the people who built the large mounds that dotted the Ohio River drainage, for this has been done in a number of studies. Nonetheless, it is important to recall how fixed some of the interpretations of archaeologists were about the origins of the

Headpiece: Vessel of Montgomery Incised type from Morgan Stone Site, Bath County #15, Kentucky. (Courtesy, University of Kentucky Museum of Anthropology.)

Ohio River Valley cultures. For example, at the beginning of the nineteenth century, there was a concensus of opinion that the peoples who had built the great mounds and earthworks of the Ohio River Valley were quite different and quite superior to the Indians who were known to the first frontiersmen and later settlers who crossed the Appalachian Mountains. This differentiation between the "Mound Builders" and the Indians became even more greatly emphasized when such learned men as Thomas Jefferson and William Henry Harrison wrote about the superior and different qualities of these peoples. Another speculation was that the mound building Indians were descendants of the lost tribes of Israel who had managed to make their way into the New World and spread throughout that area, populating some regions to a greater extent than others. The discovery of Bering Strait more or less convinced early archaeologists that the people responsible for the construction of earth-mounds, as well as those that became the predecessors of the historic contact Indians, had crossed from Asia into America and diffused throughout both continents in a relatively leisurely manner. This migration was thought to have taken place only a few thousand years before the arrival of Europeans in the sixteenth century.

Adena Diagnostic Traits

Just how did the concept of a distinct culture, now labelled the Adena culture, come about? In the first year after the turn of the century William C. Mills, who was then the most active excavator in the Ohio Valley, dug a relatively large mound on the estate of a former governor of Ohio. The estate was called Adena. Mills immediately recognized that the contents of this mound constituted a number of relatively unique finds which had not been discovered in any previous excavations—even though there were very few scientifically conducted excavations up to 1900. Although we might deplore some of the techniques utilized by Mills, we may at least be assured that what he did in 1901 was looked upon as very scientific and certainly adequate to the times for the recovery of a great deal of factual information. Mills immediately recognized that other conical mounds that dotted the landscape of southern Ohio might prove to be similar to the mound excavated on the Adena estate. Thus, he began to refer to an Adena "culture" and began to specify some of the traits that he thought to be related to that culture. Most obvious, of course, were the large conical mounds that in each instance of excavation proved to be burial mounds that contained the remains of only a relatively few persons—individuals that must

FIGURE 1

Chronological chart of the cultures in the eastern United States. The position of the Adena culture (in the Ohio Valley column) is placed at an inception of about 1000 B.C. with an implied continuity up until about 300 B.C.

MAJOR PERIODS	DATES	UPPER MISSISSIPPI-GREAT LAKES (Illinois-Missouri / North)	CENTRAL MISSISSIPPI VALLEY	SOUTHEAST (Tennessee)	OHIO VALLEY	NORTHEAST
Temple Mound II	1700 1500	(Historic Tribes) Keshena; Oneota, Black Duck	Trappist, Walls	Mouse Creek; Duck River, Dallas	Shawnee-Siouan(?) ↑ Fort Ancient	Iroquois + Algonquin ↑ Iroquoian
Temple Mound I	1200 1000	Maples Mills, Aztalan ?	Old Village, Obion; Early Cahokia, Late Baytown	Hiwassee Island		↑
Burial Mound II	700 500 A.D. / B.C.	Effigy Mound ↕ ? Hopewellian; Illinois Hopewell	Early Baytown	Hamilton	Intrusive Mound Culture; Hopewell	Owasca; Hopewellian
Burial Mound I	300	Red Ocher	Tchula; Baumer	Candy Creek; Watts Bar	Adena	Middlesex
Late Archaic	1000 2000	↑ ↑	↑	Big Sandy	Parrish-Ward	Brewerton
Middle Archaic	3000	Old Copper Culture ↓ ?	Faulkner	Three Mile; Eva	Indian Knoll	Lamoka; Boreal Archaic; Coastal Archaic
Early Archaic	5000 7000	Dalton, Graham Cave, Plano	Modoc	Nuckolls (Dalton)	Plano	↑
Paleo-Indian	8000 9000	←	Clovis Points	→	Cumberland	Cumberland / Bull Brook

From Gordon R. Willey, *An Introduction to American Archaeology*, Vol. I. (Englewood Cliffs, N.J.: Prentice-Hall, 1966), p. 251.

have represented a select group. The burials obviously received considerable attention and, in most instances, the people were interred in tombs that consisted of log construction that produced a relatively shallow pit. In addition to the log tombs, the use of copper for effigies, pendants, and ornaments was almost as great as that of any other culture then known for the Ohio Valley. A particularly impressive object was the tubular pipe—specifically the unique anthropomorphic form of a squat-legged figure—perhaps a representation of one suffering from cretinism—that Mills found in the Adena mound.

CONICAL MOUNDS

Mills' work established without doubt that the Adena culture was largely responsible for the numerous conical burial mounds in southern Ohio. The discoveries of other archaeologists after Mills' 1901 excavation of the Adena mound contributed to a slow jelling of other ideas about an Adena culture. Thirty years after Mills' 1901 work, Emerson Greenman drew the information then known about this culture into a single fairly comprehensive report. This was in 1932. In 1932, when I received my bachelor of science degree from the University of Kentucky, it seemed to me then that the work of a number of archaeologists including Greenman was of a high scientific order. Greenman's "trait list" approach seemed the most appropriate to the solution of problems about the Adena culture.

We have already noted that two outstanding traits seemed to distinguish the Adena culture from its inception, even though these were by no means diagnostic traits—the conical mound and the log tomb. The conical mounds were of considerable range in size but all those recognized as belonging to the Adena were relatively large mounds. At the time that archaeologists in the central Ohio Valley were recognizing that the Adena culture was largely responsible for the mound construction in that area, neighboring archaeologists in the northeastern part of the country were recognizing a Woodland culture, which also was characterized by burial mounds. The burial mounds of the Woodland culture were, however, much smaller than those which distinguished the Adena. Even in the eastern part of the United States archaeologists were just beginning to be able to define certain of these cultures on the basis of their distinctive trait content. The spectacularness of the burial complexes of the middle Ohio Valley Adena culture was such as to demonstrate more or less that it was an independent manifestation.

It is certainly appropriate at this point to mention the fact that there was a recognition of a separate but closely related culture, the Hopewell, that seemed to coincide with the area of concentration of the Adena culture but still could be separated on the basis of its quite distinctive traits. The Hopewell culture is a nuclear development in the heart of the Adena distribution but its earliest antecedents appear to have been in Illinois. Before 300 B.C. it had diffused to southern Ohio and modified some Adena traits to an impressive degree. The cultural emphasis was still on mortuary practices, earthworks, and ceremonial artifacts. Hopewell crematory basins and submound tombs are more elaborate than Adena tombs and the burial furniture includes many exotic objects such as cut grizzly bear mandibles, numerous copper objects, and carved zoomorphic stone pipes. The Hopewell evolved a characteristic ceramic assemblage that remained peculiar to the culture and distinguishable from the contemporary Adena.

At the time that Greenman was preparing his analysis of the Adena culture, the conical mounds were an impressive part of the Adena but by no means diagnostic. On the other hand, the log tombs were considered to be an integral part of the Adena culture. These structures were quite variable but generally were rectangular, or even circular or polygonal, and they seemed to have been prepared with a great deal of care. They seemed directed also to the production of an enclosure which could contain anywhere from one to three bodies. The process of construction seemed to involve a hole dug into the old ground surface with logs surrounding this hole and perhaps covering it; eventually the hole was covered by earth. In practically all examples of the Adena burial mounds there seemed to have been this central theme of an initial construction that launched the construction of the mound. Afterwards, there may have been any number of tombs added, but invariably there seems to have been some initial impetus for the beginning of the accumulation of the earth mound.

It is also a trait or characteristic of the Adena that the mounds were located on relatively prominent elevations. Adena mounds were never to be found in bottom lands where agricultural peoples or maize raisers were commonly found. This fact indicated that Adena burial mounds were undoubtedly memorials to the dead; that is, these mounds were monuments directed to signal the presence of the interred. Hence, an Adena mound might have contained any number of burials with perhaps thirty-five to fifty people being the maximum. Today we may use the expression such as "cult of the dead" to indicate that there was considerable preoccupation of these people with the proper disposal of the dead. It may be warranted to repeat that these dead constituted a very small percentage of the population. They certainly must have been a select group to receive this kind of individualistic treatment. It was early recognized that one aspect of this interment was the incasing of burials in a shroud of bark. This may have been an unfortunate characteristic from the viewpoint of an archaeologist, as the presence of bark contributes to the deterioration of bone. Consequently, the skeleton material recovered from Adena sites rarely is of very good preservation.

Tubular Pipes

We have already noted that tubular pipes constituted another of the rather diagnostic traits of the Adena culture. These pipes were manufactured from very fine grained silt stone that seems to have been the choice material everywhere that the Adena occur. These were approximately one inch or less in diameter, thin-walled, and about six to seven inches in length,with the mouth end flattened and with a small hole. These pipes were without any decoration except for the single example that occurred in the original Adena mound excavation where the squat-legged figure previously mentioned was found. Some years later a different kind of pipe was discovered that belongs in the Adena culture, the modified tubular pipe with a mouthpiece on the side rather than the end.

Graves or tombs were the most central or initial feature that lay beneath every Adena mound, although Greenman recognized that there were other submound graves that were not the central feature of the mound but some kind of a peripheral or marginal structure that perhaps may even have preceded the erection of the mound. A further indication of the care with which the sub-floor tombs were constructed by the Adena was revealed by the discovery that gravel was sometimes used as a symmetrical wall around the tomb. This trait was substantiated time and time again in later excavations.

However, Adena peoples did not confine their efforts to the construction of mounds for the purpose of interring special dead persons. They also engaged in considerable earthworks construction like the earth walls that frequently enclosed the mounds. Although the dimensions and configuration of these walls vary considerably, they almost without exception have some kind of a gateway or gateways that suggests that the walls were used to demarcate a sacred enclosure of some kind, possibly a mound being the central feature.

Engraved Tablets

Another highly diagnostic Adena trait is the use of engraved tablets. Perhaps the great concern with engraved tablets is a carryover from the old idea that the builders of these conical mounds and other structures were a highly intelligent, mysterious race that had been wiped out by the American Indian. In Greenman's 1932 analysis of the Adena culture he refers to these tablets as "stones with incised characters." There has been some speculation about the possibility that these tablets were some form of writing. As inevitably happens in instances of this kind, several of the tablets were considered to be frauds. Later studies of additional tablets from Adena mounds have tended to authenticate many of these suspected tablets. Several specimens are undoubtedly conventionalizations of some animal form and most suggest a raptorial bird. There was no adequate treatment and analysis of these stone tablets until fifteen years later when W. S. Webb and C. E. Snow of the Museum of Anthropology, University of Kentucky, began their analysis of the Adena culture.

The Adena peoples are notable workers in a variety of other stone objects. The stone pipes and stone tablets are undoubtedly confined to the Adena, but in some other objects a great deal of ingenuity as well as skill and artistry has been demonstrated. Among these stone traits probably most notable and early recognized was the expanded center bar gorget. These are about six inches long, flat on one side and convex on the other. Two holes perforated the bar which, in its center portion, was expanded to about three or four times the width of the ends of the bar. In the early 1930's this gorget was considered to be one of the diagnostic traits of Adena. It was further distinguished by the fact that the two holes drilled through it were conically drilled from the flat side only. A second type of gorget was one to which the name bow-tie gorget was often given because it was concave on the sides so that its narrowest dimension was in the middle. The ends were convex so that it somewhat resembled a formal bow-tie.

The bow-tie gorget is now known to be not confined to Adena alone; these are found in other Woodland sites. Yet their occurrence in Adena was enough to label them as important Adena artifacts. There were other Adena gorgets of a variety of shapes—some perfectly rectangular with two holes perforating them. A few other gorget types also occurred in Adena, but these are not very commonplace.

Copper Artifacts

Another whole class of objects characteristic of the Adena was made of copper. Again, copper is not a diagnostic trait of Adena and, in fact, copper occurs in ornaments and other objects at a much earlier time and in many other places in North America. Nonetheless, there is a notable use of copper for the manufacture of ornaments as well as a few other things, but copper was used principally for ornaments in the Adena. These objects consist of bracelets, rings, and beads which are manufactured by pounding nuggets of native copper into flat sheets. These sheets then are rolled into the desired object, whether it be a bracelet or ring or something else. One of the more common objects made from copper were celts or axe blades which often were of considerable size. Such celts were relatively common in Adena but in some related cultures they were even more numerous.

A variety of other substances were utilized by the Adena peoples. One was the mineral mica that was cut into a variety of shapes such as a crescent that undoubtedly was a headdress. Sometimes these objects were made of small pieces of mica that had been sewn together to manufacture a much larger object.

An artifact that was early associated with the Adena was one classed as "pitted stones." These are relatively large stones, one foot by two feet by one half foot or so, that are covered by a number of small pits, each about an inch in diameter and a half inch deep, relatively uniform in size. These stones almost invariably have small pits on all surfaces, not just on one side. The function of these objects is still unknown and they are frequently referred to as "nut stones" because it is hypothesized that they were used to crush a number of nuts at the same time by placing nuts in these holes and smashing them with another object.

The Adena unique burial and mound construction traits plus a number of distinctive artifacts, tended in the 1930's to characterize the Adena as a distinct culture. The work of the next two decades expanded upon this same concept. Most archaeologists were convinced that several distinctive, wholly diagnostic, artifacts would identify Adena wherever it might be found.

The people who were principally important in this new evaluation and expansion of ideas on the Adena were workers at the University of Kentucky and at the Ohio Archaeological and Historical Museum in Columbus. After 1934 I first became personally involved in some of the Adena excavations and the productions of the Museum of Anthropology at the University of Kentucky were those largely instrumental in modifying and elucidating the Adena culture. In retrospect, the 1932 description and analyses of the Adena culture by Greenman show that there is not one archaeological site of the Adena culture attributed to Kentucky. Twenty years later, however,

FIGURE 2
Robbins Mounds, Boone County #3, Kentucky. Tomb 36, left, and another. Burial #61 in Tomb 36. (Courtesy, University of Kentucky Museum of Anthropology.)

all the new sites that illuminated the culture were those from the University of Kentucky excavations.

The Adena Sites

RICKETTS SITE

The first of these sites was excavated in the summer of 1934. It was the Ricketts site in Montgomery County, Kentucky, a project on which I constituted one third of the work force. The site was of particular importance because of the fact that trait after trait that appeared in the course of its excavation fitted neatly into the already known Adena situation in Ohio. However, the description of the Adena culture had appeared only two years prior to the excavation of this site.

Some previous amateur archaeological investigations in the same county in which the Ricketts site occurred—Montgomery County—had revealed some stone tablets in local collections. These tablets were recognized as bearing some resemblance to stone tablets that had been attributed to the Hopewell culture in Ohio. However, at that time the authors of the *Kentucky Archaeological Survey* (Webb and Funkhouser 1940) had noted resemblances between these tablets and objects at Moundville, Alabama, and inferred some Middle American origins for these motifs.

Prior to 1934 some excavations had been conducted in central Kentucky into mounds which subsequently were realized to be Adena, but nothing at that time could be related to any other known manifestations. As a consequence, it was not until there was a much greater awareness of the nature of the Adena culture as indicated by Greenman in 1932, that association of this Ricketts' material with other cultures was possible. By 1935 archaeologists in Kentucky and Ohio generally conceded that the Adena was a distinctive culture form, consisting of a group of people who shared the same kind of ideas about mounds and construction, burial disposal, and artifact manufacture. It is noteworthy that we simply did not think very much beyond that point and yet no one doubted but that Adena was a highly stylized and distinctive kind of culture. During this time of the mid-30's there was something rather exciting about being in the middle of the development of these new ideas that were to culminate in the description of a distinct kind of culture. I later felt the same elation when we were becoming aware of the Poverty Point culture in the early 1950's.

In Kentucky, as has been mentioned above, our first contributions to the notion of an Adena culture stem from these excavations at the Ricketts site. In the summer of 1934 we partially excavated the site and then returned to complete the study of this site in 1939. Although we had learned a great deal about the Adena culture in that five-year period it must be confessed that our techniques of excavation had hardly improved during the time. This is not wholly true as an examination of the 1934 report and the 1939 report of the Ricketts site would reveal. Yet it is fairly obvious that our *objectives* had not changed very much. We still were carefully excavating with the view of associating a variety of artifacts with the burials and of comparing these with other sites.

In 1935 the archaeological work in Kentucky was and had been for some decades shared by W. D. Funkhouser and W. S. Webb. But beginning in 1934, Professor Webb had begun the conduct of the Tennessee Valley Archaeological Program which had obviously elevated his sights to a considerable degree and made his awareness of archaeological manifestations much broader than had been his scope prior to that time. When Funkhouser and Webb worked as an archaeological team in the 1920's and early '30's, it is hard to imagine two more disparate personalities than were represented here. Both men were scientists, both had international reputations in their respective fields, and both were prodigious workers. Dr.

Funkhouser was then Chairman of the Department of Zoology at the University of Kentucky, Dean of the Graduate School, and Secretary of the old Southern Football Conference. He was a tremendously charismatic, outgoing personality who was well-known thoughout the state of Kentucky; he lectured widely throughout the state and the United States, frequently talking about the prehistory of one area or another.

I had just returned from my initial archaeological experience with the TVA in eastern Tennessee, where I was exposed to such qualified archaeologists as Tom Lewis and Charles Wilder, not to mention Professor Webb in his new role of Director of the Archaeological Excavations for the Tennessee Valley Authority. Hence, I was strongly imbued with a drive for extreme accuracy in the recovery of archaeological materials. I consider that most of that stemmed from the training in physical sciences that characterized Professor Webb. Although at that time he was not a broadly experienced field archaeologist and had a great deal to learn himself, he certainly learned in the way that he had been trained, mainly to strive for great accuracy in reporting any kind of phenomena. I am happy to say that most of the young archaeologists who worked under Professor Webb were equally imbued with that paramount idea. Although many of us were influenced by our exposure to a variety of archaeologists we certainly never lost anything by having had this early contact with Webb.

These excavations at the Ricketts site in Montgomery County in the summer of 1934 represented the first excavations in the state in which Federal Emergency Relief Administration (FERA) labor was used. At this time the Works Progress Administration was still in the offing and this use of Federal Relief labor enabled a much greater excavation than would otherwise have been possible. The FERA was interested in supplying free labor, and archaeology was ideally adapted to this program in that it needed a lot of free labor and virtually no expenditures for materials or for supervision. This opened a vista which was destined to be expanded to a considerable extent in the ensuing years. However, several years were to elapse before this relief labor program was to be capitalized upon in Kentucky. The delay, however, was not a period of quiescence but rather of furious activity in eastern Tennessee and northern Alabama. This activity absorbed just about all of the available young archaeologists in the eastern United States at that time. Actually, it utilized a great many young non-archaeologists who were simply available and willing to do archaeological research under the guidance of a few trained individuals.

The partial excavation in 1934 of the Ricketts mound was the first excavation conducted in Kentucky in which it was realized that some of the artifacts indicated affinities with either the Hopewell site or the Adena site in Ohio. The expanded bar gorgets, the use of copper bracelets, were the two artifacts noted by Dr. Funkhouser as indicating some kind of affinity with the Adena mound. The numerous other artifacts, the celts and the variety of projectile points that were found at the site, could hardly be distinguished from similar objects which had been found in other localities in Kentucky. But nonetheless, the straw was already cast in the wind that indicated the affinities with the Adena Culture. Certainly no strong case was made for the simple reason that the concept about the kinds of assemblages that went to make up distinct cultures were not really a guiding principle to Dr. Funkhouser or Professor Webb at that time.

For me the fall of 1934 was occupied with the laboratory analyses of the artifact material from the Ricketts site as well as the restoration of skeletal materials recovered from the Norris Reservoir in east Tennessee. This latter work continued throughout the spring of 1935 and early that summer I went to Alabama to work with David DeJarnette and others in the Pickwick Reservoir. These were truly halcyon days for me. My feet became firmly planted in the direction of archaeology and I easily turned my back on my earlier commitment —vertebrate paleontology. It is a remembered thrill when discussions with Jimmy Griffin, of the Museum of Anthropology at the University of Michigan, visiting among us, opened our eyes to the fact that the great shell middens that we were excavating were southern reflections of the Kentucky Indian Knoll culture. On that same visit we invented the name Copena, derived from the "copper and galena"—artifacts that characterized a burial mound complex in the Pickwick basin. Copena was chosen to rhyme with Adena, for even then we thought that there must be some kind of connection between that Ohio manifestation and north Alabama. The fact of the matter is we simply did not know anything else with which to compare it at that time. I think that the excavations of Copena sites in north Alabama laid the foundation for ideas that Adena must have exerted widespread influence in the southern United States. The Ohio Valley may have seemed relatively remote at the time we were digging in north Alabama but we were beginning to draw larger regional connections, perhaps much larger than we now know to be justified.

By the summer of 1937 the excavation program in north Alabama and east Tennessee had reached truly phenomenal proportions.

There may have been as many as ten archaeological excavations underway at the same time. The richness of the archaeological materials throughout the whole Tennessee Valley clearly indicated to us that we would never be able to excavate everything and our programs became more and more selective in order that we might be assured of getting a sampling of everything that was available.

It was at this time that Professor Webb decided to open a similar program in the state of Kentucky and, as a consequence, I returned to Kentucky in the late summer of 1937 to take over as Curator of the Museum of Anthropology and to serve as Webb's ramrod for the state program in Works Progress Administration (WPA) archaeology. It was at this time that our attentions returned to the Adena culture.

Today much of the archaeology which is undertaken is not problem oriented but rather is emergency or salvage archaeology. In other words, we frequently make studies of archaeological sites which are destined soon to be destroyed by an encroaching highway or some other construction. We simply do not have the luxury of choosing the sites that we would like to excavate but rather we choose the sites we *have* to excavate. Similarly, when we returned to Kentucky in 1937, much of the direction of the archaeology was also somewhat out of our hands, in that we could do archaeology only in those areas where an abundance of WPA labor was available. Thus, much of the concentration of our archaeological research during the next five years was in areas where we could get the labor rather than in areas where we wanted to do the work.

Fortunately, central Kentucky was filled with a number of different kinds of archaeological sites. Earthworks, mounds, and villages were not commonplace, but at least there was a number of each in that immediate vicinity. It is because of the facts that there were available sites, available labor, and the staff at the University of Kentucky close to home that we began early to concentrate some efforts in that region. It was because of these circumstances that again the efforts in Kentucky archaeology turned to the Adena culture.

The Wright Mounds

In the fall of 1937, excavation was begun on two mounds in Montgomery County not far from the Ricketts site. The Wright mounds were a group of three or possibly four, the largest being thirty feet in height and nearly 200 feet in diameter at the base. Excavation on this large mound continued for a period of about a year and a half, during which time it was studied in its entirety. Finally, a fragment of the village area upon which the mound had been built that was preserved by the construction of the mound was reached and studied. It was this fragment of preserved village that first disclosed the large circular house patterns that were characterized by paired postmolds, i.e., the wall poles were set in holes in pairs. The size of these circular structures was such as to almost preclude the possibility that they could have been roofed. Several of the circles of postmolds were just over 100 feet in diameter. Another very interesting feature about this preserved piece of village was that it stood about four feet higher than the surrounding terrain, a clear indication that much of the land had been reduced since the time of the construction of the mound. It should be noted at this point that nearly all Adena mounds are located on high ground, not necessarily promontories (although this was sometimes the case) but invariably on higher ground than bottomland.

The number of major artifact types that came from the Wright site clearly related it to the Adena. There was no doubt but that the numerous mounds that dotted the area of central Kentucky must all be part and parcel of this great Adena culture. In fact, subsequent excavations proved that the mounds of Adena culture were not confined to just central Kentucky but were amply represented in northern Kentucky as well. In Boone County, just across the Ohio River from Cincinnati, several large mounds were excavated under the supervision of John B. Elliott (who today combines innovative mixed farming with teaching anthropology at the University of Indiana in Evansville). Other mounds in that vicinity were excavated under the direction of Claude Johnston—a successful civil engineer in Washington, D. C. today. Adena mounds extended all the way to the extreme eastern border of Kentucky where again the paired postmold structures appeared along with some diverse and anomalous artifacts. This extent of the Adena mounds in Kentucky disclosed some other interesting things not the least of which was the pottery assemblage. Heretofore, the identification of specific pottery types with the Adena culture had not been established. Professor Webb had noted earlier that most of the Adena mounds were made from relatively sterile material and not a great deal of pottery was included in the mound fill, nor had much been found in the preserved remnants of old villages beneath mounds, such as the Wright mounds in Montgomery County. The so-called C & O mounds in Johnson County, Kentucky, did have a considerable complement of potsherds that could be identified with the pre-mound village and with the mound fill as well. This enabled the recognition of two or three different kinds of pottery which, before that time, had not been pinned down to any kind of Adena manifestation.

In 1939, the same year that the C & O mounds were being excavated by Jim Greenacre, a small mound was excavated in Bath County, Kentucky, about halfway between Lexington and Johnson County to the east. This was a small mound known as the Morgan Stone mound. Perhaps this name is unfortunate, for Morgan Stone was the name of the property-owner rather than stone being one of the ingredients that made up the mound. The reason for the prehistoric construction of the mound was to cover a single circular house which obviously had been ceremoniously burned to the ground and covered immediately. Hence, there was preserved a single burial in the center of the floor of the house, a burial that had been covered by the burning structure. Since it was immediately covered with earth, much of the wood support had been preserved as charcoal. Two large pots were either a part of the dwelling or ceremonial chamber whatever it might have been or they were accompanying furniture for the burial. These two pots enabled us to extend further our description of the Adena pottery assemblage. Thus, by 1939 we were increasingly convinced that Adena was a burial cult or a burial complex, at least.

MT. HOREB EARTHWORKS

In that same year the concept that Adena was the burial practices of a relatively widespread cultural manifestation was strengthened by investigations that were conducted in Fayette County, central Kentucky. One of these Fayette sites was a circular earthworks which had been known for many years as a fort. Back in the nineteenth century it was recognized that there were many of these circular earthworks that consisted of a circular ditch or moat with a causeway at one side. It was realized that the Fayette "fort" was surely related to some cultural manifestation of southern and central Ohio. This site was known as the Mt. Horeb earthworks and was the first piece of archaeological property ever acquired for preservation by the Kentucky Archaeological Society.

Later it became apparent that the Mt. Horeb earthworks was associated with some other earthworks. A nearby hilltop was completely enclosed by a low earth wall and within that enclosure was a village midden which eventually was tied in quite closely with the Adena culture. In 1939 it was decided to investigate the Mt. Horeb earthworks and a series of trenches was excavated across

FIGURE 3
Robbins Mound, Boone #3, Kentucky. Tomb #9 with Burials 64, 65, 66. (Courtesy, University of Kentucky Museum of Anthropology.)

various parts of the earthworks. The net result of this was to disclose that around the margin of the central unmodified portion of the earthworks there was a paired postmold pattern. This postmold pattern was unique in that it had no evident opening anywhere. The pairs of postmolds were unbroken in their continuity which, of course, led to the inevitable conclusion that the earthwork was indeed a sacred enclosure. Before 1850, Squire and Davis had concluded that similar earthworks were sacred enclosures. So perhaps we added nothing to our knowledge of Adena except to prove that the sacred enclosure was a part of the entire Adena manifestation.

Drake Mound

A second site in Fayette County was the Drake mound located about eight miles west of Lexington on the Old Frankfort pike. Like other Adena mounds, the Drake mound was a monument to a single central feature. In the case of the Drake mound it was a deep central pit. The pit had been dug in such a way that the earth from the pit was built up as a slight ridge around the lip of the pit. There was again the suggestion of a relatively ceremonious disposal of a single person or personage in the mound. At the very bottom of the pit there were the cremated remains of a single individual. There was a number of typical Adena artifacts deposited with this cremation including a copper dagger with a preserved wooden handle. The walls of this pit gave every evidence of an extremely intensive fire which probably lasted for only a relatively short time, for the burning did not penetrate the clay walls very deeply. Obviously this and other spectacular discoveries contributed to our growing commitment that the Adena was a burial cult that clearly rivaled Hopewell in Ohio.

From the fall of 1937 to the spring of 1940 a whole series of excavations compounded and extended the scope of the Adena culture. All of these discoveries, however, only increased our knowledge of the artifact content and, to a limited degree, extended our capacity to reconstruct dwellings and sacred structures. That latter term is used in a very loose sense, but the implication is that these were something other than common dwellings and that they were preserved or memorialized by the erection of earth mounds over these building remains.

With this increased activity in Kentucky, Dr. Funkhouser decided to return to the Ricketts mound and finish its excavation. In the summer of 1939, this excavation was completed and a whole series of new artifact traits was added to the Adena list. As in most of the other known Adena sites the information gathered was largely that contributed by burials. Here, too, our convictions about the Adena seem to be again reinforced.

It was the bone artifacts found at Ricketts in 1939 that were most impressive to us at that time. The rather large number of artifacts that were included as burial furniture enabled a clear realization for the first time that the artifact correlation among Adena, Hopewell, and Copena was indeed very low. At this time we knew surprisingly little about any Adena village. At the Ricketts site a condition prevailed which was quite similar to that formerly found at the Wright mounds in the same county, namely, a fragment of the former village of these peoples was preserved by the erection of the mound. But the level at which the mound had been first begun stood as much as four and one-half feet above the existing surface of the ground at the time we began to excavate the mound. What this clearly implies, of course, is that the surrounding country was reduced by four and one-half feet through the continuous agricultural pursuits that may have gone on for something of the order of 2,000 years since the time of the erection of these mounds. This was actually not a new recognition, for as early as 1835 William Henry Harrison had noted that the trees that covered some of the mounds in Ohio were as old as any of the trees in virgin forest and that that area and therefore the mounds must be as old as the forest lands. Secondly, he pointed out that the mounds were not located on the modern floodplains and thus they had to be older than the present conditions of the river. Considering the time and considering the training of a man who later became U. S. President, this was rather an astute observation. It may, of course, suggest why such a militarily trained man would become the president.

THE CRIGLER MOUND

It is difficult to believe that some of these mounds were not located for purely aesthetic reasons. The Crigler mound is an example of the location of a memorial site. The Crigler mound was located in an absolutely beautiful portion of the Ohio River Valley. It is not generally known to the casual observer, of course, that the Ohio River Valley from just about the West Virginia line to the mouth of the Little Miami River is a rather young portion of the river valley. The last glacial advance covered the ancestral mouths of the Big Sandy and Monongahela Rivers, which were in Lake Erie and dammed the headwaters to such an extent that eventually a great lake in front of the glacial ice spilled over into a smaller stream valley that eventually emptied into the Mississippi River. This is now all a continuous Ohio River Valley, but the portion that was cut during Pleistocene time is obviously much younger, with steeper valley walls. The Crigler mound sits on the crest of one of these margins in such a way that one can look down a considerable reach of the Ohio River. It is difficult to believe that the location is mere coincidence. The mounds constructed by the Adena peoples appear to be without exception monuments to the dead, and obviously they would select a suitable site.

During the 1939 excavations of the Wright mounds we discovered the paired posthole pattern that was preserved by the erection of the mound. Although this was looked upon as unique and as something never before encountered in the literature or in the field, it was not impressed upon us as a truly Adena trait until subsequent excavations began to show the same trait. There were so many excavations going on at the time that we could not evaluate the importance of each new thing as it was discovered. And yet, the occurrence of paired postholes, that is, of a circular house pattern of individually dug holes that were in pairs, was so patently new that we could not but be impressed by it. It was enough to find several long arcs of these paired postholes beneath the Wright mounds but when a similar phenomenon was found beneath the C & O mounds in Johnson County in the same spring of 1939, then we were truly impressed. Finally, it was the Boone County excavations that brought home to us how distinctive this trait was. The Robbins mound and the Crigler mound both disclosed beautifully proportioned circular structures with paired postholes. Here a second revelation was forced upon us, namely, that in these ceremonial structures the postholes were not truly vertical but were inclined inward at the bottom, suggesting some kind of an outward sloping wall. The true nature of the construction remains today a matter of conjecture, but it has been rediscovered often enough to indicate that this is a diagnostic Adena trait. It was about this same time that we were excavating the Mt. Horeb earthworks, using the most sophisticated field work of the time. Only in this way was it revealed that, here too, a paired posthole pattern encircled the inner margin of the moat. Summer student archaeologists are inclined to be rather blasé about the archaeological material that they excavate. But one should remember that in 1939 we felt that we were not too far removed from Schliemann, the excavator of Troy, when he exclaimed, "I have looked upon the face of Agamemnon."

Rather than have one think that this Adena archaeological investigation was operating in a vacuum it is necessary to know that other archaeological operations were going on in the state. In western Kentucky, Albert Spaulding, Ralph Brown, and David Stout had begun some excavations that were concerned with later Mississippi occupations in those areas. We should not minimize the fact that having young men of the caliber of Spaulding, Brown and Stout associated with the development of archaeology in Kentucky undoubtedly led to a different kind of orientation of the thinking of Professor Webb at the time. There were all too few occasions where all these young archaeologists gathered at Lexington on the University of Kentucky campus. But, nonetheless, when these occasions did arise, it may be said that it was a revelation to Professor Webb to find that there were so many diverse opinions about the interpretation of the archaeological materials that were then being exposed. It was a source of great satisfaction to Professor Webb to see what subsequently happened to these numerous individuals—Brown, Cotter, Spaulding, Stout and others.

By the summer of 1940, WPA archaeology in the eastern United States was more than six years old, but in Kentucky only the last three years had been so occupied. When one realizes that there were a great many shell mound Archaic sites being excavated in western Kentucky at the same time that these numerous Adena sites were being studied in central Kentucky, then one can have some appreciation of the tremendous amount of archaeological work that was accomplished in so short a time. Further, as mentioned above, at the same time a much more extensive archaeological program was being conducted under the guidance of Professor Webb in northern Alabama and eastern Tennessee. During this three year span the excavation of a number of quite large sites of the Fort Ancient culture in northern Kentucky along the Ohio River was undertaken. Finally, in 1941, a large-scale operation was begun in western Kentucky on some sites of the Mississippian culture. But these sites—both Fort Ancient and Mississippian—with a barely prehistoric flavor, never really captured our interest as did the spectacular Adena culture.

By the summer of 1940, the economic recovery of the United States was so far advanced that the WPA program was being sharply modified. No longer was it an operation primarily designed to put as many men to work as possible. Rather, it became a bureaucratically top-heavy governmental operation that saw more money being spent for administration than for actual field operations. At this same time, too, there were some curtailments in the allowed time that an individual might work in each given two-weeks' period. I do not recall the exact number of hours per month, but it did approximate about forty hours out of two consecutive two-weeks' period.

Because of the limitations of work hours, all of the supervising archaeologists in the state decided to arrange their work schedule in such a way that all of the work allowed in one two-weeks' period was worked in the first of those weeks. All of the work allowed in our second weeks' period was confined to the second week. Thus, we had two whole weeks in between in which there would be no work operations going on in the field. As a consequence of this abiding interest in Adena, we arranged for a two-weeks' excavation to be conducted by the archaeology supervisors themselves. We selected a rock shelter in Powell County, Kentucky.

Hooton Hollow

Beginning earlier than 1930, Webb and Funkhouser had excavated a number of these sites and had taken students to work in these during some summer operations. But the quality of the field technique left quite a bit to be desired even though there were some very meticulously done jobs in these rock shelters. However, stratigraphic control was rarely perfect, so it was decided to excavate in one of these rock shelters to see what we might determine by way of stratigraphy. I had scouted around in the mountains and found what looked as though it might be a rock shelter with considerable depth of midden in it. Unfortunately, many of the rock shelters in eastern Kentucky had been very badly disturbed because their ash content was used as a source for the manufacture of black gun powder beginning in the early nineteenth century and continuing well up in the twentieth century. Many a shelter also had (or did) housed a still. Hence, we felt fortunate in having a site upon which we could lavish all of our professional attention. In honor of this occasion and our Harvard colleagues, the rock shelter was named Hooton Hollow.

This crew included John L. Cotter, James Greenacre, John D. Elliott, Ralph Brown, Ed Hertzberg, Henry Carey, Claude Johnston, Richard Von Schlicten, George Jackson (a WPA administrative supervisor), and myself. We were joined by Dr. Funkhouser in what was to prove to be his last field work before his death.

Of course, this particular project was designed to satisfy some of our answers about possible cultural successions in the rock shelters as well as possible cultural evolution. Our excavation certainly rewarded us to a great extent. We not only found what we concluded to be undoubted Adena burials but, from my viewpoint, one of the outstanding finds was a dog skeleton buried in a wooden slab-lined pit. If it had just had an expanded bar gorget around its neck we would have known that it was a true Adena dog. However, at that particular time in our archaeological careers we were terribly pottery conscious and we were rather delighted to find a good many potsherds. They diminished in frequency as we dug deeper into the site and disappeared completely in the lower levels of the midden. We felt we had some of the best field notes that had ever been acquired, for we certainly felt ourselves to be as experienced a group of young archaeologists as might be found anywhere in the United States. Yet, not all of our time was taken up in anything like the digging drudgery. We had some tremendously stimulating discussions and arguments about some of the things that we were seeing and certainly this was an opportunity for not only exchanging myriads of individual ideas but also for getting to know better men with whom one had already worked two or three years.

I should be able to report that the result of our excavation of this rock shelter revolutionized our information about the Adena culture, but unfortunately that is not the case. Some time during the war years when most of us were absent from our various campuses, a graduate student borrowed the Hooton Hollow notes and they were never seen again. We should like to repeat that experiment but the opportunity is gone forever. Nevertheless, it was undoubtedly demonstrated that a considerable portion of the content of the Hooton Hollow midden could be readily assigned to the Adena culture. Some Adena people were rock shelter dwellers.

During the remainder of 1940 and the first half of 1941, it was quite obvious that the whole WPA program was undergoing still further curtailment and modification. However, the excavation of Adena sites remained the central theme in the Kentucky operation with the exception of some large-scale late Mississippian sites in the Tennessee River area of western Kentucky.

In September of 1941, I returned to the University of Michigan to attempt to complete my doctoral work. I requested some assurance from my draft board that I would be able to complete at least one year but this was not forthcoming, as the chairman of the board told me it was quite possible that we would be in a shooting war sometime during that academic year and a shooting war we were in before the end of 1941. I was able to complete that academic year but the onset of the war spelled the end of the WPA program. It did hang on in a few isolated spots until some time in 1942. Long before that time, though, the program in Kentucky had begun to change greatly. Albert Spaulding had left two or three years before to finish his doctoral work at Columbia; John L. Cotter had gone to the University of Pennsylvania; Ralph Brown had moved up to an administrative position for the state of Kentucky; and so on down the line. Perhaps it is correct that John Elliott continued doing work on Adena sites longer than anyone else in the state. Yet finally that, too, came to an end in 1942.

Archaeological research anywhere in the United States was a bit slow in picking up after the conclusion of World War Two. When I returned to the University of Kentucky in the fall of 1945 there were so many loose ends to be caught up that it was the spring of 1946 before Professor Webb and I could begin to think about field work and, of course, it was some Adena site that crystallized our attention at that time. The Mt. Horeb earthworks, which had been excavated in 1939, was only a part of a larger earthworks and associated archaeological units. Professor Webb had been reading and researching everything he could about these other sites during the course of the war. As a part of the Mt. Horeb configuration a relatively small conical mound was chosen to be excavated—the Fisher site.

THE FISHER SITE

As almost anyone might know, Fayette County, Kentucky, is right in the heart of one of the great tobacco raising areas of the world. Prior to World War Two the planting and harvesting of tobacco was largely done by seasonal workers. But after the war there were very few seasonal workers available, there were so many other economic adjustments being made that the cost of field hand labor had skyrocketed. As a concomitant of this economic development, the cost of labor for archaeological excavations simply was so great that our departmental budget was not able to accommodate any such expenditures. As one might suspect, the result was that Professor Webb and I personally completely excavated this small mound, although at the time it did not seem small at all. Nonetheless, excavate it we did, and found that the Fisher site was a veritable treasure-house of Adena artifacts which had not been found in the central Kentucky area before.

It was during the excavation of Hooton Hollow that I felt that I got to know Dr. Funkhouser better than I had ever known him before. On the other hand, I think the excavation of the Fisher mound is the time at which I got to know Professor Webb better than I ever had. There were times, of course, when we were just simply moving a lot of dirt and during those times Professor Webb usually talked incessantly about something that was concerning him at the moment or reminisced about his early experiences. A curious aspect of this was the fact that the owner of the Fisher site lived only a few hundred yards from the mound and he frequently came out to watch us in our digging. Invariably during his visits we were digging in some sterile portion of the mound, just simply removing dirt. As a consequence, when we finally did have a public display of the artifact material that came from the site as well as the various burial configurations, and tombs, he was flabbergasted. He just could not believe that he could have visited the sites so often and never see us uncover any of that material. But such was the case.

In Retrospect

All of the foregoing largely expresses the limitations of our knowledge about the Adena culture, but more than anything it exemplifies how our attention was focused on artifacts. Our artifact list was almost exclusively confined to materials that were associated with burials. This is one of the reasons why Professor Webb's trait list for the Adena culture reached out, extended in every way possible, to encompass some traits which were not just other artifacts. It is pertinent to say something at this point about that Adena trait list which he published in 1945. It was one of the first attempts at seriation ever done in American archaeology and, like most attempts at seriation, it made just as much sense turned completely upside down as it did in the form that Professor Webb produced. The theoretical basis upon which he composed that trait list was that the scarcer items were the more recent and thus it was that the items that pertained to the Hopewell culture, such as gold, were so scarce that they obviously (he argued) were the most recent. Also it was axiomatic in Professor Webb's thinking that cruder, less well-done objects were older than some more finished product. Here again this made Adena older than Hopewell.

It is certainly true that up to this time our thinking about Adena had been almost completely material culture-oriented. Although we had made some rather fundamental contributions in terms of house patterns or settlement patterns, there was nothing beyond that. We still thought only in the framework of trait lists. The frequency of occurrence of things was about as far as statistical treatment was carried. We sometimes attempted to justify correlations of these occurrences from Kentucky to Ohio or from these two states to Indiana. Hence, when we look back on the sum and substance of all of the publications directly referring to the Adena culture that emanated from the University of Kentucky there really was a tantalizingly incomplete picture of what the Adena culture might have been like. There was not one blade of grass nor one grain of any kind of a food source that could have told us something about the actual subsistence base for the people who built these numerous mounds. In fact, the last really significant publication of Professor Webb that related to the Adena culture was an extension of the trait list that he had previously developed with Charles Snow, his colleague in the department, at the University of Kentucky. In this volume he collaborated with Ray S. Baby and again simply added whatever traits that might have been discovered in the years after the publication of his original 1945 trait list.

The static quality of these trait lists was not fully realized for some time. Dragoo's most recent comprehensive treatment of the Adena culture, even though an expansion of the trait list idea is one that for the first time goes considerably beyond that. In his book, *Mounds for the Dead* (1963), every implication is that the Adena culture is something far beyond just a series of associated burial traits or a series of cult activities that are concerned with disposal of the dead. We now are agreed that there is no evidence to derive Adena from Middle America. What had formerly been taken as such evidence may now be seen as superficial or more apparent than real. Adena developed *in situ* out of the Archaic, a phenomenon repeated numerous times in the case of other cultures in eastern North America. It is easy to overlook the fact that Adena was contemporary with Poverty Point culture. The latter was as vigorous in the Lower Mississippi River Valley as was Adena in the Ohio River Valley. The stone artifact resemblances between the two cultures are actually numerous, and such similarities are at once generic and genetic because both cultures are local florescences on an Archaic background.

In retrospect it seems as though a long period of time was devoted to these Adena excavations and we might wonder what we would have done differently. Before speculating on that thought, it is important to point out that even during the course of these numerous excavations in Kentucky the young archaeologists had a strong feeling that they would be doing things differently had they been in control. In other words, these "Young Turks" were not fully satisfied with the conduct of excavations, writeups, and conclusions. However, from this distant view I cannot imagine what we would have done differently. We were doing the "new archaeology" of that time. Every generation's new archaeology is destined to be replaced by an even newer new archaeology.

I think everyone who has worked with Adena materials in the past would agree that our over-emphasis of artifacts and trait lists obscured our knowledge, or at least our awareness, of a variety of other things that characterize the Adena culture. It is obvious that our techniques of the 1930's and 40's did not lead us to a particular emphasis upon the relationships of these cultures with their environment. This was simply not one of the aspects of the time. But now we would be much more inclined to approach our problems in a different sort of way. It may be surprising to some readers to know that even in the 1930's we were meticulously taking soil samples from each burial pit, although at the time we hardly knew what we expected to discern from that.

There is but little doubt that if we were approaching this Adena problem for the very first time today, as we are approaching the Poverty Point problems, we would have an entirely different mental attitude. We would be much more aware of settlement pattern and perhaps more than anything else we would try to discern what we could of the subsistence patterns. But through all the problems and our struggling over their solutions there does remain this feeling that we were really "doing archaeology" of the most important kind—a thought not always shared by others.

Not many months ago I was looking for a reported site in north Louisiana and asked permission of a local landowner to check for this site on his property. With some suspicion he asked why I wanted to know about that and I gave him my one-dollar lecture on the use of potsherds and arrowheads for relating one prehistoric people to another. At the conclusion of the erudite recital he asked with disdain, "Do you mean to tell me a grown man does that for a living?" Yes, and I would hate to think that I might have had to work for a living.

References

DRAGOO, DON W.
1963 Mounds for the Dead: An Analysis of the Adena Culture. Annals of Carnegie Museum 37.

FUNKHOUSER, W. D. AND WEBB, W. S.
1935 The Ricketts Site. University of Kentucky Reports in Archaeology and Anthropology III; 3: 67–100.

GREENMAN, EMERSON
1932 Excavation of the Coon Mound and an Analysis of the Adena Culture. Ohio State Archaeological and Historical Quarterly 41; 3: 366–523.

MILLS, WILLIAM C.
1902 Excavations of the Adena Mound. Ohio Archaeological and Historical Quarterly 10; 4: 452–79.

RITCHIE, WILLIAM A. AND DRAGOO, DON W.
1960 The Eastern Dispersal of Adena. New York State Museum and Science Service Bulletin, No. 379.

SPAULDING, ALBERT C.
1952 The Origin of the Adena Culture in the Ohio Valley. Southwestern Journal of Anthropology 8; 3: 260–268.

WEBB, WILLIAM S.
1941 Mt. Horeb Earthworks. Site 1, and the Drake Mound, Site 11, Fayette County, Kentucky. University of Kentucky Reports in Anthropology and Archaeology 5; 2: 135–218.

WEBB, WILLIAM S. AND BABY, RAYMOND S.
1957 The Adena People, No. 2. Ohio Historical Society.

WEBB, WILLIAM S. AND FUNKHOUSER, W. D.
1940 Ricketts Site Revisited, Site 3, Montgomery County, Kentucky. University of Kentucky Reports in Anthropology and Archaeology 3; 6: 209–378.

WEBB, WILLIAM S. AND HAAG, WILLIAM G.
1947 The Fisher Site, Fayette County, Kentucky. University of Kentucky Reports in Anthropology and Archaeology 7; 2: 47–104.

WEBB, WILLIAM S. AND SNOW, CHARLES E.
1945 The Adena People. University of Kentucky Reports in Anthropology and Archaeology 6: 1–369.

THE PERUVIAN COAST

The Peruvian Culture Area

(preceding page)

Map of the Peruvian archaeological culture area, with location of Virú Valley indicated (North Coast sector). From Gordon Willey, *An Introduction to American Archaeology*, Vol. 2 (Englewood Cliffs, N.J.: Prentice-Hall, 1971), p. 78.

The Virú Valley Settlement Pattern Study

GORDON R. WILLEY

The Virú Valley Program

The idea of a concentrated archaeological and anthropological study of a single Peruvian coastal valley, which led to the Virú Valley program, was first put forward by the late Wendell C. Bennett. He expounded his idea at a luncheon table conversation (which developed into a series of such conversations) with the late Julian H. Steward and myself, in Washington, D.C., in the fall of 1945. World War Two was just over, and archaeological field work was possible again. Bennett had long been associated with the Peruvian field, and I had had a single year's work there and wanted to return. Steward's interests were somewhat different. He was an ethnologist-social anthropologist who had acquired a knowledge of Andean prehistory in his editing of the *Handbook of South American Indians*, a task he had then just completed and in which I had served as his assistant. But, as is now well-known in the anthropological profession, he had a considerable theoretical concern with the rise of ancient Peruvian civilization and its implications. Bennett observed, quite rightly, that in spite of the wealth of Peruvian materials in the world's big museums—most of which had come from unreported grave-robbing over the past century—there had never been a truly "big dig" in Peru or Peru-Bolivia. Perhaps Hiram Bingham's clearings and excavations at Machu Picchu on the Andean edge of the montaña had been the closest thing to it, but this had been a rather specialized operation, confined to a single-occupation late Inca site. The great and complex multi-occupation sites—Tiahuanaco in

Headpiece: A modeled head-and-spout jar in the negative or resist-painted style of the Gallinazo culture. The Gallinazo phase or culture (about A.D. 100) of the Virú Valley marked the first maximization of valley irrigation and the first great population concentrations. (Courtesy, Museum of Archaeology and Ethnology, Cambridge University, Cambridge, England.)

Bolivia, Pachacámac on the Peruvian central coast, or the huge north coastal ruins—were really only known from test digging. Not that such digging, which had been begun back in Max Uhle's time and before, was not important. It had given Peruvian archaeologists a sound working spatial-temporal frame of reference as a guide for future research; but, as Bennett argued, we should now go beyond that.

One way to have gone beyond strati-pit sampling would have been to launch a truly "big dig" in Peru, an operation on the scale of what had been done in the ancient Near East or even in the Central American Maya area under the Carnegie Institution's sponsorship. But excavations on such a scale presented a great many problems, not the least of which was expense. No single American university or museum at that time could have funded such an expedition. A multi-institutional effort would be a possibility, but the complications of direction, control, and other matters would not have appealed to university or museum administrators. There were also other considerations about a "big dig" that gave us pause. Were we experienced enough in this kind of large-scale excavation, with all of its attendant administrative and technical difficulties? And, on a more theoretical level, did we really know enough about what we wanted to do, what kind of questions we wanted to ask, to pursue such an undertaking over a period of several years?

An alternative way to go beyond the limited kind of archaeology that had been traditional in Peru was to conduct an intensive regional survey. For this a natural valley of the Peruvian coast, linking mountains to coast and separated from similar valleys to the north and south by several kilometers of desert, seemed a logical unit. And for that reason Bennett suggested the Virú Valley. He was familiar with it, having done some rapid survey work and grave-digging there in the 1930's, and his published report (Bennett 1939) on the Peru north coast, which included a section on the valley, offered an outline of an archaeological sequence. We would not be going into archaeological *terra incognita* but could tie into some foreknowledge of Peruvian archaeology. Moreover, the valley was a relatively small one so that we could be reasonably thorough in our survey coverage. In Moche or Chicama, given our expected resources and available time, we would have felt lost, too limited in our sampling, and defeated in our objective of intensive coverage of the designated geographical region.

After our initial discussions, we proposed the general scheme of the Virú Valley intensive survey to various colleagues. Other archaeologists who agreed to take part were W. D. Strong (Columbia

Figure 1
Chronological chart of Peruvian coastal cultures.

Periods		Dates	Far North	North	North Central	Central	South Central	South	Far South
Late Horizon		1534–1476	Inca Influences	Inca-Chimú	Inca-Chimú	Inca Influences	Inca Influences	Inca Influences	Inca Influences
Late Intermediate Period		1476–1000	Chimu-Piura	Chimú	Chimú Santa	Chancay Huancho	Chincha	Ica	Ilo
Middle Horizon		1000–600	Piura	Tomaval	Pativilca	Epigonal Pachacamac Nieveria	Cerro de Oro	Epigonal Atarco Pacheco	Loreto
Early Intermediate Period		600 A.D. – 200 B.C.		Moche Gallinazo Salinar	Patazca	Lima Baños de Boza; Mira-Mar	Estrella Carmen	Nazca	San Benito Islay
Early Horizon		200–900	Sechura Paita	Cupisnique	Pallka	Colinas; Garagay	Topará Pozuelo	Paracas	Ichuña
Initial Period		900–1800	Negritos San Juan	Guañape	Cerro Sechin Haldas	Curayacu Florida Chira		Hacha	
Preceramic Periods	VI	1800–2500	?	Huaca Prieta	Culebras	Paraiso Rio Seco	Asia Unit I	Casavilca	Ocoña Toquepala III
	V	2500–4200	Honda			Encanto; Chilca Corbina		Cabezas Largas	
	IV	4200–6000	Siches	Paiján		Canario Luz			Toquepala II
	III	6000–8000				Chivateros II			Toquepala I
	II	8000–9500				Chivateros I			
	I	9500–				Oquendo Chivateros R.Z.			

From Gordon R. Willey, *An Introduction to American Archaeology*, Vol. 2 (Englewood Cliffs, N.J.: Prentice-Hall, 1971), p. 84.

University), Clifford Evans (Columbia University), James A. Ford (Columbia University and the American Museum of Natural History), Junius B. Bird (American Museum of Natural History), and Donald Collier (Field Museum of Natural History). Julian Steward was to be represented in the field by the cultural geographer, F. W. McBryde, and the social anthropologist, Allan R. Holmberg (both of the Smithsonian Institution), and the Peruvian Instituto de Estudio Etnológicos was to be represented by J. C. Muelle. The program, thus, as conceived, was to be not only archaeological but was to take into account cultural geography and modern community studies. A Virú Valley Program Committee was formed of Strong, Steward, Bennett, and myself, and this committee, under the aegis of the Institute of Andean Research, solicited and received funds from the Wenner-Gren Foundation in New York for the joint financing of various features of the project, such as vehicles and air photographs. The main financing of the program, however, was borne by the several participating institutions; and it was agreed at the outset that all participants would publish their own particular results under their respective institutional sponsorships.

Although we came together in the Virú project under the enthusiasm of the idea of a broad, coordinated valley approach, when we began to plan our actual operations we all tended to slide back into standard research behavior patterns. This was no indication of lack of cooperative good will among us; rather, it was that we had no very clear idea of just how this cooperation would proceed, either on an integrative intellectual level or a practical field level. It was, of course, obvious that we needed to know more about the relative archaeological chronology of the valley. There were some "kinks" in the sequence that wanted straightening out, and a greater refinement of phasing or periodization would be useful for whatever kind of problem might be envisaged. A number, in fact most, of the archaeologists opted for this kind of familiar work. Strong, with Evans as his assistant, wanted to attack this matter of chronology with stratigraphic digging, and so did Collier. Bird, in a determined search for "early man," or Preceramic levels, was really dedicated to the same approach. Ford, with his successful surface survey and pottery seriational studies of the southeastern United States, decided to conduct an archaeological surface survey of the entire valley in an attempt to surface-date as many sites as possible. My own predisposition was to work with Ford on this survey with stratigraphic pitting at selected sites. Clearly, the Virú Valley program, conceived so grandly as a broad-spectrum anthropo-geographic approach to the culture history of a single valley, was settling down into a "pottery chronology hunt" before its creators had even taken to the field.

It was at this point that Julian Steward stepped in and convinced me that it would be the better part of archaeological wisdom if I withdrew from the "stratigraphic race" and conducted what he referred to as a "settlement pattern survey." There were more than enough colleagues conducting on-site dating and chronology; I would be doing more for the project, myself, and archaeology, he argued, if I attempted to say something about the forms, settings, and spatial relationships of the sites themselves and what all this might imply about the societies which constructed and lived in them. Bennett, who up to that point had been uncertain as to just what his share of the research pie would be, also decided to move in this "functional" direction by making an architectural survey that would link to my settlement one. Eventually, after he joined me in the field, he felt that the architectural theme was too closely intertwined to that which I had done and was doing, so he generously withdrew from this study. Instead, he made a series of excavations into a single site (and phase) in an attempt to give us more cultural context as opposed to stratigraphic chronicle so that his work, as well as mine, was addressed primarily to context and function, rather than chronology.

The archaeologists of the Virú group took to the field in early 1946 and completed their work there before the year was out. The first of us arrived in early March; others came later. Some of us finished by July or August of that year while others stayed on longer. My own settlement survey lasted from March through July. During that time I worked closely on the actual survey with Ford and exchanged information with Strong and Evans, Bennett, Bird, and Collier. McBryde, the geographer, was with us intermittently; however, Holmberg and Muelle did not come to the valley to begin their social anthropological study until the following year. In the time at our disposal all members of the program made significant contributions. Bird disclosed the Peruvian coastal Preceramic for the first time. Strong and Evans placed the Gallinazo culture, with its negative-painted horizon pottery, as antecedent to the Moche style and culture, and also gave us considerable early ceramic sequence detail. Collier provided comparable detail for the later ceramic periods; and Ford synthesized the whole sequence with his seriational procedures in site-surface dating. Bennett provided various kinds of detail—ceramic, artifactual, and architectural—on the Gallinazo site and culture. McBryde made the excellent base map of the valley which was a boon to Ford and to me in our surveys; and the social anthropologists produced a good study of Virú Valley society as of the late 1940's. What was lacking, of course, was a better integration of all our efforts. Originally, in the planning stage of the Virú program, we had all tentatively agreed that once our individual research jobs had been completed and published or prepared for publication we would all sit down together and plan a joint summary monograph, one that would integrate and synthesize the Virú findings. This never came to pass; in a sense, however, my own settlement pattern survey did have this function to a very large degree. Unfortunately, I did not realize its centralizing, integrative potential then. In fact, in that 1946 field season, as I walked over the stony and seemingly endless remains of Virú prehistoric settlements, I felt I had been misled by Steward and dealt a marginal hand by my colleagues. The latter were getting tangible pottery sequences to delight the heart of any self-respecting archaeologist while I was chasing some kind of a wraith called "settlement patterns" that had been dreamed up by a social anthropologist.

Archaeological Background

The archaeological background into which the Virú studies, and particularly my settlement pattern study, were projected must be considered on the Peruvian scene and the wider American horizon. Peruvian archaeology had gotten off to a "fast start," relatively speaking, at the turn of the nineteenth to twentieth centuries. This was due to the diligence and scholarship of the remarkable German savant, Max Uhle, who worked in the Peru-Bolivian area in the decades just before and just after 1900. By that date Uhle had devised and demonstrated an effective archaeological area chronology, something no other New World area was to achieve for another twenty years or more. Uhle did this by noting grave and architectural superpositions, by a close study of ceramic styles and some seriations of these styles, and by combining these findings with a knowledge of ethno-historical events. With reference to the last, he knew that the Inca Empire had dominated the Peruvian area at the end of the Pre-Columbian period. Its styles and artifacts provided a terminal horizon to an area sequence. A comparable, but earlier Pre-Columbian horizon, the Tiahuanaco, preceded that of the Inca. Various more localized or regionally restricted styles could be seriated to a position chronologically intermediate between Inca and Tiahuanaco, and other regional styles were similarly seriated to a position prior to Tiahuanaco. The result was the four period se-

FIGURE 2
An air photo of an archaeological ruin in a Peruvian north coastal valley. The adobe-walled outlines of the Huaca de la Luna, at Moche, can be seen in the desert sands at the foot of a rocky outcrop and not far from the cultivated lands of the valley bottom. The great pyramid mound of the Huaca del Sol, a part of which has been cut away by ancient river action, can be seen on the immediate edge of the cultivated lands. Air photos similar to this one were used in the survey of the nearby Virú Valley. (Courtesy, Servicio Areofotográfico Nacional del Peru.)

quence which forms the basis of modern Peruvian archaeological chronology.

A. L. Kroeber and his students gave all of this greater systematization in the 1920's, with the publication of Uhle's collections and data. P. A. Means and J. C. Tello, in their writings, diverged somewhat from this chronological interpretation, although Tello intuitively sensed the presence of a still earlier broad horizon to be added onto the bottom of such a scheme, the Chavín. Work in the 1930's by Bennett and by Larco Hoyle added more to the emerging picture, so that when Kroeber published a long survey article entitled "Peruvian Archaeology in 1942" (Kroeber 1944) archaeologists familiar with the area were operating with a time structure that ran, from earliest to latest, as : Chavín Horizon; Early Period; Tiahuanaco Horizon; Late Period; Inca Horizon.

This was the general state of knowledge when we began work in Virú. The north coast and the Virú Valley could be fitted into this frame of reference, although there were still problems about some of the "fits." It was, however, largely an archaeology of grave or mortuary pottery. In spite of its precocity of chronological development, Peruvian archaeology had lagged behind in many respects. Certainly, in 1946 no Peruvian archaeologist could tell you as much about the cultural content of any of his periods or phases (with the possible exception of the Inca, which was reinforced by ethnohistoric information) as a North American Southwesternist or a Middle Americanist could have told you about his. As a result, when we began the Virú digging and the site surface collecting, about 98 percent of the pottery that we found meant little or nothing to us. No one had ever truly looked at north coastal Peruvian refuse sherds; only the grave ceramics were recognizable. Several months elapsed before we could fit a proper sequence of our refuse potsherd, or "plain ware" phases onto a mortuary ceramic sequence. In other words, much of the Virú archaeology had to be built from the ground up, and what we would now call the "data base" of north coast Peruvian archaeology was hardly secure enough to bear a superstructure of cultural reconstruction and interpretation.

To take a wider perspective, it is fair to say that not only in Peru, but everywhere else in the Americas, archaeology as of 1946 was only just beginning to emerge from its over-riding concern with chronology building. This had been the great preoccupation since about 1914, when Gamio's Mexican and Nelson's Southwestern United States stratigraphic studies turned American archaeologists in this direction. It was not until the late 1930's and early 1940's that some archaeologists, stimulated by social anthropologists such as Steward and C. K. Kluckhohn, began to ask if this, in itself, constituted a fully satisfactory goal. By 1946 there was a little dissatisfaction and ferment. Walter Taylor, a student of Kluckhohn's, was to give voice to it in a long critical review (Taylor 1948). There was talk of "functional interpretation" and of "process," although the distinction between the two never quite came clear in some of this exploratory archaeological writing. We wanted to "recover" more of the past, to understand it better, to explain it; but just how we were going to do this was not explicit. This, as I recall it, was the intellectual climate of American archaeology at the time we began the Virú program.

My own archaeological background and experience was a reflection of this time of transition. I had been an undergraduate and a first year graduate student of Byron Cummings, at the University of Arizona, from 1931 to 1936. Here my training had been heavily descriptive, historical, and chronologically oriented. I took these attitudes to Georgia when I worked with Arthur R. Kelly as his assistant from 1936 to 1938; and my concern with stratigraphy, seriation, and pottery typology was given continued emphasis when I joined James A. Ford in Louisiana in 1938-39. As a graduate student at Columbia, my outlook was broadened by W. D. Strong. Strong, although staunchly historical, was one of the archaeologists in the 1930's who had expressed dissatisfaction with the narrowness of the prevailing archaeological goals in a trenchant article, "Anthropological Theory and Archaeological Fact" (Strong 1936). Still, my Florida research of 1940 and my Peruvian excavations of the following year remained heavily in the vein of ceramic typology and sequence building. At the Smithsonian, Julian Steward began to convince me that archaeology should be something more than potsherd chronicle, and his settlement pattern suggestion showed me a way in which it might be done.

Operations and Results of the Virú Settlement Study

When Steward first suggested the idea of a settlement pattern survey, and the potential in such a study for cultural-ecological and social interpretation, I recalled some of his works I had read as a graduate student, including his monograph on Great Basin ethnology and his now famous article, "Ecological Aspects of Southwestern Society" (Steward 1937). I went back to these, particularly the latter, and noted that he was talking about the kinds of constraints which natural environmental and subsistence adaptations placed on socio-economic forms. In Steward's view, these environmental-cultural-social relationships were revealed in settlement distributions over the wider landscape (macro-settlement) as well as the settlement arrangements of a single community (micro-pattern). In his 1937 article Steward had drawn on archaeology, ethnohistory, ethnology, and environmental considerations to piece together a highly convincing reconstruction of how and why aboriginal Southwestern society happened to be as it was. I had a good many reservations about a similar research for the Virú Valley. I had no real ethnographic or ethnohistoric base upon which to draw—or so I thought. The Virú populations impressed me as being thoroughly "mestizo-ized," a part of a national Peruvian culture, with its cash economy and the related agricultural and settlement patterns that would go with it. What help could any of this give us in interpreting the settlements of their Pre-Columbian predecessors in the valley? The Peruvian highlands, with their Quechua-speaking populations, did have an on-the-ground continuity from Inca times to the present so that there was a possibility there for Steward's kind of settlement-and-society reconstruction; but for the coast, and for Virú, this struck me as an unlikely line of approach. Steward conceded some but not all of this. He still felt that what Holmberg might do with the modern Viruñeros would have relevance to my study although not knowing the immediate situation himself he could not tell me quite how. I was convinced otherwise, and, as is obvious from my report, I followed through and finished up in this frame of mind. My study might now be called "archaeologically self-contained." But I know now that I missed some opportunities by being so restrictively archaeological. Perhaps if Holmberg had been working in Virú when I was there, and we had had day-to-day contact, I would have become alerted to what I was missing. As it was, I did not realize that the Virú farmers of 1946 could have given me considerable instruction in canal irrigation in the valley—with its pertinence for archaeological interpretation—until Holmberg's monograph came out in 1950. Moreover, I was surprised to learn that the Viruñeros of 1946–47 still maintained considerable ritual and lore about canal irrigation, with special ceremonies still being held at the time of cleaning of the canals before the descent of the waters of the first mountain rains and so forth. In other words, the links with the past had not all been severed, even though the Pan-American Highway passed through the valley.

Part of the failure here could be attributed to overall program planning, which didn't bring archaeologist and ethnologist together in time, but much of it must be laid on my own attitudes. I had the academic interest in ethnology-social anthropology required of most young Ph.D.'s, but my archaeological orientation was strongly humanistic. In my case this meant that I came to archaeology with an historical and literary background. I had had little or no natural science curiosity of the boyhood birds' eggs-collecting sort that for many of my colleagues led on to archaeology. While I had read some ethnology, I had no experience in interviewing informants, nor much desire to do so. These attitudes and this background were limiting for me in the intended settlement pattern study. This was not only true for the ethnological or social anthropological side of things but for the needed alliances with the natural sciences. Although I saw the necessity for help from agronomy and soil science, I did not make positive moves in this direction. McBryde offered some suggestions here, but these were not his specialties and what we needed was specialized advice. Part of the fault, again, was institutional; we were not financed nor set up to take care of these things in the Virú program. Part of the blame, however, can be placed on my own lack of initiative.

My conception of the settlement pattern study, as I say, was almost wholly archaeological. I described the objectives of the Virú settlement pattern study as:

> First, to describe a series of prehistoric sites with reference to geographic and chronologic position; second, to outline a developmental reconstruction of these prehistoric settlements with relation to function as well as sequence; third, to reconstruct cultural institutions insofar as these may be reflected in settlement configurations; and, fourth, to compare the settlement story of Virú with other regions of Peru. (Willey 1953: 1)

And I defined settlement patterns as:

> . . . . the way in which man disposed himself over the landscape on which he lived. It refers to dwellings, to their arrangement, and to the nature and disposition of other buildings pertaining to community life. These settlements reflect the natural environment, the level of technology on which the builders operated, and the various institutions of social interaction and control which the culture maintained. Because settlement patterns are, to a large extent, directly shaped by widely held cultural needs, they offer a strategic starting point for the functional interpretation of archaeological cultures. (Willey 1953: 1)

As I read over these passages now I see that they are admirably broad-gauged. The objectives and the definition leave little to be desired. They were dominated by the then new concern for function in archaeology, and they even went beyond this for in writing that settlement patterns were "directly shaped by widely held cultural needs" I was trying to say that I thought there was a basis for cross-cultural and causal generalization in the study of settlement forms.

I realized then that the whole idea was over-ambitious, and I labelled it as "experimental," with many difficulties attendant upon it; but I wanted to make a beginning. It was over-ambitious, of course, because I had nothing like a proper methodology to come to grips with the "admirably broad-gauged" objectives. There were no precedents for this kind of study. Steward's Southwestern model could not give me much help, and I had no other model clearly in mind and certainly not overtly stated. My approach was to be heavily inductive. I was going to map and record "everything" in the way of a human settlement feature that related to the Pre-Columbian past. I was then going to look at this map, or these series of maps representing sequent phases of occupation in the valley's prehistory, and come up with patterns that would be meaningful in terms of human behavior. And this was, in effect, the way I followed through on the project.

To be sure, there were little short-term shifts to deduction, as there always are in any archaeology. In the course of the field work I naturally began to conceive of functionally differentiated types of settlement. Clusters of small room foundations were formally different than a wall-encircled hilltop; a cemetery could be distinguished from a pyramid; and function could be imputed to these different formal types on the basis of general comparative analogy. As the survey developed further, I then began to look for certain types of constructions or settlements in certain locations. There were some types, for example, that would be situated closer to canals; or some kinds of fortifications would be on a certain kind of hill or natural terrain. The deduction, however, was piecemeal.

The only model I really carried in my head—and this is not indicated in the report—was a kind of large-scale developmental and diachronic one. Settlements, I reasoned, almost subconsciously, would reflect valley population increases through time and would grow larger and more complex in pattern. Also, for some reason which I do not now quite understand—although it may reflect some evolutionary bias—this model had another dimension: the settlement development through time would reflect a steady increase in formal planning, so that the ancient Viruñeros would be seen as moving from small and randomly arranged dwellings into something like planned cities. Curiously, though, in view of my stoutly stated functional concern, I never had anything resembling a synchronic model of how all of the valley settlements would be integrated at any one period or point in time. At least I did not have this before or during the actual field work. My attempts to look at the data in this way, which are incorporated into the monograph, did not begin until I was in the final stages of analysis and writing.

The actual field operations of the survey were quite straightforward. These are detailed in the 1953 monograph but can be summarized as follows. Site maps were prepared from air photos. Owing to the lack of vegetation on the valley margin, such features as stone and adobe-walled building foundations showed up very clearly. In many instances the walls of structures were preserved to remarkable heights. This is because on the rainless Peruvian coast there has been relatively little erosion or weather damage to sites over the centuries, and the historic and modern period populations have not been large enough to do them serious damage. Even in the cultivated area of the valley, where there had been more obliteration of site features through agricultural activities, sites could be spotted on

FIGURE 3
Area of garden plots or irrigated grid system of Pre-Columbian date in the Virú Valley.

the air photos. I made working maps from these photos with the aid of an epidiascopic projector. These maps were then taken into the field and checked with a compass and chain measurements, and at this time various setting and architectural detail features were recorded in the notes. Sites were numbered serially (V-1, V-2, etc.) and, eventually, all located on McBryde's master map. Individual site maps were, in most cases, later redrawn and were published, along with the big map, in the Virú settlement monograph. Site sampling was met in no formal way. Survey was pursued to some extent by convenience and to some extent with an eye to covering all portions of the valley, all types of terrain, and all of the functional categories which began to emerge in the course of the work. Ford and I travelled together in a Jeep or on foot, accompanied by two workmen. One of these workmen helped me in taking measurements of rooms and features; the other aided Ford in making the potsherd collections from the site surface. In all, we worked out of three base camps in the valley, and some of the survey was done driving out to Virú each day from Trujillo where the expedition had its principal headquarters. In all of this I give great credit to Ford. It was his ingenuity that devised the air photo-epidiascopic mapping system, and it was his pioneering spirit that forced me up on many of the mountain tops to visit fortifications and other sites, that I might have been inclined to slight if I had been left entirely to my own devices. By the end of the survey we had visited, mapped, taken notes on, and collected pottery from over 300 site locations. In our estimate, made from studying the air photographs, this was believed to be about one-quarter of the prehistoric sites of the valley. Subsequent archaeological survey in Virú suggests that this was probably about right. However, our sample was slanted on the side of large and imposing sites, including big pyramidal complexes, fortifications, and the like, and probably on the side of marginal or valley edge locations where sites were more readily seen than in the cultivated valley flats. In fact, in the latter I was always uncomfortably aware that there were many sites that had been destroyed, buried, or otherwise obscured by alluvium or by modern agriculture.

Besides dwelling sites, forts, cemeteries, and pyramids, I also mapped roads, cultivation plots that were still visible, and canal systems. The latter were picked up in the site maps where a canal had passed nearby, and I also had a very large-scale appreciation of the location of the major canal lines in the valley from the air photos; however, and regrettably I did not study and map these canals on what could be considered a "middle level" of detail. This would have been by means of maps which plotted canal system segments in sizable sections of the valley. Such could have been done—and should have been done—for a half-dozen or so sectors of the valley. Each such map would have extended over a few kilometers of the valley's total of 22 (length) by 7 (greatest width) kilometers. This kind of "intermediate" detail would have given us a much better understanding of ancient irrigation and agriculture.

One problem throughout was what really composed a site? In a valley as small as Virú there was no site unit that was more than a few hundred meters from another; often they were much closer than this. Our field decision was to treat this matter somewhat arbitrarily, making a pottery collection and assigning a site number to what appeared to be spatially distinct features or building units. But from the standpoint of function, one might ask: are two dwelling clusters, 200.0 meters apart and located on the same canal, two sites or one? It was from such questions as these that I gradually began to realize that any functional interpretation of Virú settlement patterns would have to be projected on a scale larger than what is usually called a site.

Obviously, the survey was closely bound up with the matter of archaeological dating. When we began the Virú survey, as I have said, there was no Peruvian "potsherd archaeology." The predominantly plain ware sherds which we picked up on the surfaces of the sites meant nothing to us. Occasionally, and usually in collections from the surface of a looted cemetery, there would be a few decorated pieces which I could place as belonging to one of the recognized north coast styles, and this gave Ford some clues in dating associated plain wares. Ford was carrying out some informal sherd analysis as the survey progressed, however, and these suggested a working sequence or seriation to him which aided us considerably in starting to identify sites by periods or phases. I was also further aided in this regard by the excavations of Strong and Evans, Bennett, and Collier which, early on, came up with pottery stratigraphy dating results from a number of sites. Their stratigraphies also enabled Ford to verify or correct his tentative seriations. The resultant Virú Valley chronology is subsumed under the North Coast subareal column in the accompanying chart (Figure 1). In the Virú settlement study the local Guañape phase is the chronological equivalent to both Guañape and Cupisnique on this chart; the Virú Puerto Moorin phase corresponds to the Salinar; Gallinazo is Gallinazo (named from the Virú Valley); the Virú Huancaco corresponds to Moche; Tomaval equates with Tomaval (the Black-White-Red Geometric Horizon); Virú La Plata corresponds to Chimú; and Virú Estero is the local Inca-Chimú phase.

The greater problem in site dating, though, was not the development of a "potsherd chronology" but the matter of the nature of the associations of sherd collections with individual sites or features. In the small Virú Valley, with its relatively dense populations from many periods of the past, there was some sherd debris scattered around almost everywhere. In a collection made around the slopes and the foot of a pyramid mound, for example, we might have several ceramic phases represented. Which one dated the construction of the pyramid? Had the pyramid been constructed over several phases? Or were pre- and post-construction sherds the results of incidental fill inclusions at the time of construction or during later superficial occupations and intrusions? These and many questions like them could never be settled satisfactorily, and to my way of thinking (although less so to Ford's) the ceramic associational problem plagued us throughout. This handicap was overcome, to a degree, by our luck in isolating some single phase sites and pottery collections; but, in my opinion, there is no real way around it short of excavation.

My own functional site classification, as I have noted, began to develop during the survey but did not take its final form until the post-field work analyses of the data. It was based upon what I considered to be the four most readily recognized functional categories for the Virú sites. These, in turn, were subdivided into types and sub-types based on form.

I. Living Sites:
  - Scattered Small-House Village
  - Agglutinated Village:
    - Irregular
    - Regular
    - Semi-isolated Large House
    - Compound Village:
      - Rectangular Enclosure
      - Great Rectangular Enclosure
      - Rambling Enclosure

II. Community and Ceremonial Structures
  - Community Building
  - Pyramid Mound
  - Pyramid-Dwelling-Construction Complex

III. Fortified Strongholds or Places of Refuge
  - Hilltop Redoubt
  - Hilltop Platform
  - Hilltop Village (Agglutinated)
  - Castillo Fortification Complex

IV. Cemeteries

As stated, these functional categories are broad ones and they are drawn not from any specific Peruvian ethnographical analogies but from more general cross-cultural observations. Thus, Living Sites were so classified on the basis of their appearance and great frequency in the valley; but even here there were problems of functional identification. Were the Semi-isolated Large Houses ordinary dwelling homesteads or did they serve, perhaps, for some more public functions?

Cemeteries and Fortified Strongholds or Places of Refuge are reasonably self-defining from their construction or situation; however, it is also probable that some sites of the latter category in Virú also served other than defensive functions. The Virú buildings that we called Castillo Fortification Complexes would be a good

FIGURE 4
Ruins of huge adobe pyramidal structure of the type designated as "Castillo Fortification Complex." This particular Virú Valley ruin is known as the Castillo de Tomaval.

example. There were also questions about segregating the Compound Village type (of the Living Site category) from Community Buildings (of the Community or Ceremonial Structures category). In each instance I had to make an *ad hoc* judgment on the basis of not very well-defined criteria.

All such individual classifications have been argued out in the Virú settlement monograph, site by site, but it was not an easy task nor one that left me with any great feeling of assurance about what I had done. The great weakness was that I had to make the judgments on too little evidence—and virtually always on superficial evidence. One can conceive of a procedure now where a simple functional hypothesis would be advanced, for example, the idea that all rectangular flat-topped mounds in the Virú had some sort of ceremonial, civic, or community functions. This hypothesis could then be examined by the detailed excavation of a selected sample of such structures. Unfortunately, I did not operate this way in 1946. I simply classed such mounds under my Community and Ceremonial Structures category by general comparative analogy with what we know of such mounds in other places in the New World. Even as of today, we know very little about the ones in Virú.

The descriptions of the Virú Valley sites ran to something over 300 pages in the 1953 monograph while my conclusions, the essence of my results, comprised only about fifty pages. Most of these conclusions were in a section entitled: "The Development of Virú Settlements: A Reconstruction." This was a summary organized by the four functional categories of the site classification, plus two additional headings, one on Public Works (canals, roads, great walls, etc.) and the other on what I called The Community Pattern. This last was my attempt to draw together the component parts of the Virú Valley communities at each phase of the archaeological sequence and to arrive at synchronic, valley-wide settlement patterns. As I have remarked, this type of synthesis was made only in the later stages of data analysis. Each of my headings was treated chronologically, beginning with the earliest phases of the Virú Valley occupation and running upward in time through the Inca Horizon.

For Dwelling Sites I had a fairly well-dated sequence which began with Scattered Small-House Villages in the Preceramic Cerro Prieto phase, with this form carrying into the succeeding Guañape phase. This Guañape phase was correlated with the Chavín Horizon level although it probably subsumed a time range of both pre-Chavín ceramics. These Scattered Small-House villages also continued into the post-Chavín Puerto Moorin phase although by this time there was good evidence for the appearance of what I called Irregular Agglutinated villages. The Gallinazo phase saw the Agglutinated village, either Regular or Irregular, as the principal village type, although some Rectangular Enclosure compounds occurred as did some Semi-Isolated Large Houses. For the Huancaco phase (Moche type culture) the situation remained about the same. What appeared to be significant changes came about in the Tomaval phase (the Tiahuanaco-Huari Horizon and later) and continued into the La Plata (Chimú) and Estero (Inca) phases. While some Irregular Agglutinated villages persisted, the Compound villages became much more important, particularly with the appearance of the Great Rectangular Enclosure form. These last are much more symmetrically planned layouts than anything that had been seen previously in Virú. In viewing the sequence as a whole I was struck by the notable changes which were concurrent with the Tiahuanaco Horizon, and, while seeing an evolution of settlement size and form in Virú up to that time, I interpreted this point of change as the result of foreign influence most probably accompanied by military might. I would still adhere to this interpretation.

My dating of Community and Ceremonial Structures was much

FIGURE 5
Weathered adobe ruins of the Gallinazo site, Virú Valley. This structure was classed as a "Pyramid Dwelling Construction Complex."

less secure than that for the Living Sites. According to Ford's and my ceramic dating, there were no mound structures in Guañape. Since such mounds are known elsewhere on the Peruvian north coast at this time this finding was suspect then and still is. Quite possibly, some of my Puerto Moorin, and even later phase mounds had Guañape beginnings. Mound construction was elaborated upon in the Gallinazo and Huancaco phases and included the large Pyramid-Dwelling-Construction Complexes; but with Tomaval there was a decline in mound building activity with a new kind of platform mound, one made within a Rectangular Enclosure, being the principal type, and these trends continued through the later phases of the sequence.

My dating of Fortified sites was probably better than that for the Mound constructions. Hilltop Platforms, on high ridges surrounding the valley, usually had sherds of all periods, including the Guañape phase; but the first large-scale forts were the Hilltop Redoubts which almost certainly came into being in Puerto Moorin. There were not many of these, and they were placed on isolated hills rising out of the valley floor. Later, in Gallinazo times, the much more elaborate Castillo Fortification Complexes, on valley side spurs, replaced the Hilltop Redoubts, and these remained in vogue for that period and the Huancaco period. They were abandoned, or nearly so, in subsequent periods, beginning with the Tiahuanacoid-Tomaval phase. Perhaps in these later phases the Great Rectangular Enclosure Compounds, the largest of which were located in the central parts of the lower valley, served as strong points or barracks. Again, we see a continuity of development that appears local, interrupted and changed at the time of the Tiahuanaco Horizon.

My Cemetery trends were summed up in my brief statement that there:

> . . . . is a mounting complexity and refinement of tombs and tomb goods, climaxing with the Huancaco Period. With this climax, the cemetery is often found near an important politico-religious building. Subsequent periods show less elaboration, but old cemetery sites continue in use. (Willey 1953: 361)

When this was written I was, of course, well aware of the fabled tombs of Chimú times (equivalent of La Plata phase) that had been found at Chanchan in the Moche Valley immediately to the north of Virú; and I reasoned then, as I would now, that Virú had become a province in what was probably the Chimú kingdom and that great riches in burials were reserved for the potentates of the capital alone. In this, as in other matters, I don't think I was ever guilty of believing that Virú was a microcosm of the whole Peruvian north coast for all periods.

Walls, canals, and related features are often difficult to date archaeologically, and this was the case for Virú. I attempted to place them as to phase by various *ad hoc* means, chiefly those of location associations with dated sites. Much more certainly remains to be done on the dating of such public work features in Virú. It was my conclusion at the time that there were no such features, at least of any consequence, in Virú in Preceramic or Guañape times. Since then we have had indications that this is not the case for other Peruvian coastal valleys and that such public works activities may have been begun by the Chavín Horizon, if not before. So my Virú conclusion needs more investigation. Actually, I then had little sure evidence for canal building even in Puerto Moorin times although overall settlement distribution for this phase strongly implied canal irrigation. By Gallinazo times there was indisputable large-scale canal digging and extensive defense wall construction in Virú. These systems continued in use through the Huancaco phase and, I thought, through Tomaval and La Plata. However, there were complications with these interpretations, as I detailed at length in the monograph. For example, there are hints, especially for La Plata, that large sections of the valley, formerly irrigated, were abandoned by this time. This may have been related to salinization of the soils through excessive and prolonged irrigation; or it may have been related to political and military difficulties. For roads, my most interesting assertion, which needs much further testing, was that the great inter-valley or trans-valley roads—that is, the type of Peruvian coastal road known from the Inca empire—first crossed Virú in the Tomaval phase or at the time of the Tiahuanaco Horizon.

Under my final sub-head—that of the Community Pattern—I attempted to diagram overall valley settlement or what was, in effect, the "settlement system" for each phase of the valley's prehistory. To do this I prepared a series of valley site maps, with differing symbols for different functional classes of sites, on which I postulated the small interaction spheres of Living Sites surrounding and supporting, and also being dependent upon, central features such as Community and Ceremonial Structures or Fortified places. I operated on the basis of site proximities, one to another, and on a vague "sustaining area" principle as to why village inhabitants would owe allegiance to or depend upon a center of some kind. There is little to recommend this section of the monograph now except as a document of historical interest in the development of American archaeology. The best that can be said about it is that it showed an awareness of an important kind of a problem for settlement study.

The other main part of the Virú conclusions was a section of only ten pages which I called "Settlements and Society" and which marked my furthest excursion into interpretation. I had written two preliminary papers after the Virú field work, but before I had completed the Virú monograph. And in these I had shown some disposition for "free-swinging" socio-political and socio-economic interpretations of the Virú findings (Willey 1948, 1951). However, by the time I wrote this concluding portion of the monograph I had grown more cautious. I suppose I was becoming more wary of criticism from my colleagues, some of whom had expressed negative opinions about the turn my archaeology had taken in the aforementioned preliminary papers. These criticisms had come largely by word of mouth, but I was sensitive to them and undoubtedly trimmed my sails a bit in the Virú settlement finale. At the time I justified this to myself by rationalizing that the whole settlement pattern approach was new and experimental and that I did not want to jeopardize its acceptance by other Peruvian archaeologists by linking it with unwarranted or "wild" speculation. However, I doubt if this really had as much to do with my "pulling my punches" as the fear of offending the archaeological "guild" with its dictum of "clean digging" and "sober thinking." I now look upon my timidity as a mistake. After almost six months of field work, wearing out three pairs of boots walking over the rocky surface of the Virú Valley, and after the writing of several hundred pages of archaeological description, I was entitled to a spree of interpretation and speculation and I should have taken it.

What I did was to devote five of my pages to population size estimates and their changes through time. The remaining five pages, addressed to "Socio-political Organization," were the net of my inferences, drawing from settlement patterns and from other aspects of archaeology, such as ceramics and art. In making these inferences I had reference not only to Virú alone, but to the wider Peruvian scene as a whole. I interpreted the early Viruñeros as simple villagers, first fishermen, then farmers. Although I did not use the word, I was thinking about an egalitarian society. The Chavín Horizon marked the dissemination of a religious cult, spreading in a peaceful context. However, even at this time, the communities of Virú and the architecture of the period remained small, in spite of more impressive contemporary sites in other valleys. In the succeeding Puerto Moorin phase, populations were larger and there was more corporate organization, as seen in the construction of defensive redoubts and, probably, the first canal systems. Although I was uncertain if all of the valley's population had been under a single political system in the Puerto Moorin phase, I was sure that it had been in the Gallinazo phase. This speculation was attested to by the definite valley-wide irrigation systems, by coordinated defensive works in the middle and upper valley, and by what appeared to be an incipient urban "capital" in the lower valley. This kind of a system remained for the Huancaco phase which, from its ceramic introductions, appeared to represent the taking over of the Virú Gallinazo state into the expanding Moche or Mochica kingdom. The radical settlement and other changes of the Tomaval phase were interpreted, again, as conquest, this time by the pan-Peruvian Tiahuanaco Horizon political entity which has since been interpreted as emanating from the site of Huari in the central Peruvian highlands. The new Tomaval settlement styles continued in La Plata

(Chimú) and Inca times. In both of these periods Virú was seen as a minor province in a much larger kingdom or empire. In general, none of these findings contradicted the then emerging larger synthesis of Peruvian prehistory. Rather, they consolidated it with particulars and, I think, significantly did so in the realm of architecture and settlement. But, all in all, my "social reconstruction" was very sketchy—even parsimonious as one reviewer remarked.

There were still twenty pages to go to the end of the Virú monograph. These were devoted to a standard comparative treatment of the Virú data with the rest of Peru. Because settlement data elsewhere was minimal or non-existent, such a section had to be rather limited. It did, however, point out various monumental architectural similarities and differences between Virú and other north coast valleys and then swept more widely over the rest of the Peru-Bolivian area.

The response to the Virú settlement study was generally favorable. The idea was considered a good one even though other "Peruvianists" might quarrel with certain particulars of interpretation. As it happened, most of the immediate quarrels were on matters of sequence arrangement and ceramic styles and focused more on Ford and the stratigraphers and their monographs than on mine. Eventually, these quarrels turned out to be insignificant. There was little criticism of my socio-political interpretations. Perhaps my caution had forestalled them, or, perhaps, the whole settlement pattern idea, while generally approved of, had not yet really caught on.

"Second-Guessing" on Virú

To conclude, there are two ways to "second-guess" the Virú settlement study, and both have their uses as providing guides for the future. The first way is to look at the original operation, insofar as this is possible, in the context of its times, and ask "What might have been done differently and better, even as of 1946?" The other way is to view the work from the standpoint of present knowledge and attitudes, and ask "If one were formulating a Virú-type settlement pattern investigation how would one go about it?"

In the context of 1946 I see the greatest weakness not in the basic concept of a functional attack but in the operations of carrying it out. Superficial surveys of site features, surface morphology alone, are insufficient to arrive at function. They are a good beginning, but after making a trial functional classification one should go to detailed excavation of some sites to check what are, in effect, the trial functional hypotheses. This course is more easily said now than done in 1946. At that time there was both a lack of funds and time to pursue my investigation. Looking at the project as a whole, it could be argued that the several Virú excavating parties should have directed their attention to such "functional" digging, rather than being almost wholly concerned with chronology. But they had not joined up on this basis, and I could hardly call upon them to do my work for me. From an "if I had it to do over" stance, I would argue for a much more tightly controlled and coordinated project than the one we ran in Virú in 1946. Centralized direction is necessary, a point which may have been better emphasized if we had attempted to write the combined Virú report that we once tentatively planned. This point was made most clear to me when I wrote my monograph.

There are, of course, other weaknesses in the Virú study which could have been corrected as of 1946. I have mentioned some of them. I could have informed myself more about the methods and technicalities of canal irrigation and hydrology by consulting with local farmers, with government officials, and by reading. I could have arranged for the services of soil scientists. Specialized knowledge of such kinds is now more of a routine part of archaeological operations, but it was certainly not unknown then to bring interdisciplinary aids to field work.

Lastly, the Virú settlement monograph now seems difficult for other archaeologists to use. If I were writing it over again, after my Introduction and the chapter on Environment and Inhabitants, I would devote a chapter on the Functional Classification of Sites. This was, after all, what I was primarily about. The sub-section on Classification would be shifted from the Introduction to such a chapter, where I would then present my case for all of the types and subtypes, with examples from each phase or period, using site maps and also constructing abstract or idealized drawings of each. The conclusions and the comparative section would follow. At the end would be the long, weary drill of site descriptions, one-by-one and period-by-period. This would be for the archaeologists interested in following up on particulars.

As to "second-guessing" from the perspective of the present, this has a special pertinence in that settlement pattern study has been resumed in Virú by a young colleague, Michael West (1971a, 1971b). In a very short time West has added more than another 250 sites to my original survey list of 315. But, more importantly, he has formulated an ecological model which, from preliminary tests which he has conducted, suggests important revisions in our ideas about subsistence for the earlier phases of the valley's prehistory and which is systemically linked to interpretations of socio-political organization. While the ecology of settlement was not exactly unknown to archaeologists in 1946, having been pioneered by British prehistorians long before that, its explicit systemic applications had not yet been developed so that an ecological approach is a significant innovation for Virú. In this connection it should be noted that ecological analyses of prehistoric settlement patterns have been carried out recently in other parts of Peru by a number of younger archaeologists, including T. C. Patterson and E. P. Lanning (1964), M. E. Moseley and C. J. Mackey (1972), and T. K. Earle (1972).

Another innovation that could well be applied in any Virú restudy, as well as elsewhere in Peruvian settlement studies, is what Moseley and Mackey (1972) have called the "Small Site Methodology." In fact, Moseley and Mackey developed the idea as a way of resolving some of the difficulties I had had with the functional classification of sites in Virú. The methodology involves the isolation of small, "uncontaminated" sites or features for which clear functions or uses may be determined by careful excavation. In this way the archaeologist may separate out the functional strands that go into the fabric of more complex settlements.

Still a third, and more widely known, innovation for settlement pattern study is Central-Place Theory. This theory was developed by cultural geographers and has been borrowed by archaeologists in a number of world areas (cf. Chang 1972, and various articles in Ucko, Tringham, and Dimbleby, eds. 1972). This theory might also play a part in any future Virú settlement pattern analyses. I see now that I was fumbling around with an amateurish approximation of this theory with my "Community Pattern" maps in the 1953 monograph. It might be interesting to see what could be done with the more formal "lattice" arrangements of Central-Place Theory. However, again, I would come up with my "dirt archaeological" caution that every effort be made to determine site functions in order to get the most of any such analysis.

The twenty-seven years that have passed since the Virú Valley settlement pattern study have seen revolutionary changes in archaeology, American and elsewhere, and settlement analyses have assumed an important place in these changes. The innovations I have mentioned as being possible new directions for future Virú or other Peruvian work are but a few of these changes. I shall not attempt to describe or list others, but the reader is referred to recent survey articles on settlement pattern archaeology in general (Chang 1972; J. R. Parsons 1972). I am not foolish enough to feel that all, or even very much of this has stemmed from my original Virú work. That archaeologists should have begun to take cognizance of the settlement record of the human past as it has been left upon or buried in the landscape was inevitable. The inspiration for such a perspective arose, I think, more or less independently and simultaneously in several places when we began to pass on from the temples, palaces, and rich tombs, or from the narrow pedantries of potsherd classification, to a broader vision of what the record of the past might tell us. I am pleased to have been one of those who participated in this transition.

References

BENNETT, W. C.

1939 Archaeology of the North Coast of Peru. American Museum of Natural History, Anthropological Papers 37; 1: 1–153.

1950 The Gallinazo Group, Virú Valley, Peru. Yale University Publications in Anthropology 43.

BENNETT, W. C. AND BIRD, J. B.

1964 Andean Culture History. 2nd ed. Garden City, N.Y., American Museum of Natural History and the Natural History Press.

BIRD, J. B.

1948 Preceramic Cultures in Chicama and Virú. *In* A Reappraisal of Peruvian Archaeology. W. C. Bennett, ed. Society for American Archaeology, Memoir 4: 21–28.

BUSHNELL, G. H. S.

1963 Peru. rev. ed. Ancient Peoples and Places Series, New York, Frederick A. Praeger.

CHANG, K. C.

1972 Settlement Patterns in Archaeology. Reading, Mass., Addison-Wesley Module in Anthropology, No. 24.

COLLIER, DONALD

1955 Cultural Chronology and Change as Reflected in the Ceramics of the Virú Valley, Peru. Anthropology 43.

EARLE, T. K.

1972 Lurin Valley, Peru: Early Intermediate Settlement Development. American Antiquity 37; 4: 467–477.

FORD, J. A.

1949 Cultural Dating of Prehistoric Sites in Virú Valley, Peru. Anthropological Papers 43: 1.

HOLMBERG, A. R.

1950 Virú: Remnant of an Exalted People. *In* Patterns for Modern Living. Chicago, The Delphian Society 367–416.

KROEBER, A. L.
1944 Peruvian Archaeology in 1942. Wenner-Gren Foundation, Viking Fund Publication in Anthropology.

LANNING, E. P.
1967 Peru Before the Incas. Englewood Cliffs, N.J., Prentice-Hall, Inc.

MOSELEY, M. E. AND MACKEY, C. J.
1972 Peruvian Settlement Pattern Studies and Small Site Methodology. American Antiquity 37; 1: 67–82.

PARSONS, J. R.
1972 Archaeological Settlement Patterns. Annual Review of Anthropology 1: 127–151.

PATTERSON, T. C. AND LANNING, E. P.
1964 Changing Settlement Patterns on the Central Peruvian Coast. Nawpa Pacha 2; 113–123.

ROWE, J. H.
1960 Cultural Unity and Diversification in Peruvian Archaeology. *In* Men and Cultures, Selected Papers, 5th International Congress of Ethnological and Anthropological Sciences. A.F.D. Wallace, ed. Philadelphia, University of Pennsylvania Press, 627–631.

STEWARD, J. H.
1937 Ecological Aspects of Southwestern Society. Anthropos 32: 87–104.

STRONG, W. D.
1936 Anthropological Theory and Archaeological Fact. *In* Essays in Anthropology. Honoring A. L. Kroeber. Berkeley, University of California Press, 359–368.

STRONG, W. D. AND EVANS, CLIFFORD JR.
1952 Cultural Stratigraphy in the Virú Valley, Northern Peru. Columbia University Studies in Archaeology and Ethnology 4. New York, Columbia University Press.

TAYLOR, W. W.
1948 A Study of Archaeology. American Anthropologist 50; 3: 2.

UCKO, PETER; TRINGHAM, RUTH AND DIMBLEBY, G. W. (eds.)
1972 Man, Settlement and Urbanism. London, Duckworth.

WEST, MICHAEL
1971a Prehistoric Human Ecology in the Virú Valley. California Anthropologist 1; 1: 47–56.

1971b Recent Archaeological Studies in the Virú Valley. Mimeograph.

WILLEY, GORDON R.
1948 Functional Analysis of 'Horizon Styles' in Peruvian Archaeology. *In* A Reappraisal of Peruvian Archaeology. W. C. Bennett, ed. Society for American Archaeology Memoir No. 4: 8–15.

1951 Peruvian Settlement and Socio-Economic Patterns. Selected Papers. 29th International Congress of Americanists 1: 195–200.

1953 Prehistoric Settlement Patterns in the Virú Valley, Peru. Bulletin 155. Smithsonian Institution, Bureau of American Ethnology.

1971 An Introduction to American Archaeology. Vol. II: South America. Englewood Cliffs, N.J., Prentice-Hall, Inc. Ch. 3.

CALIFORNIA

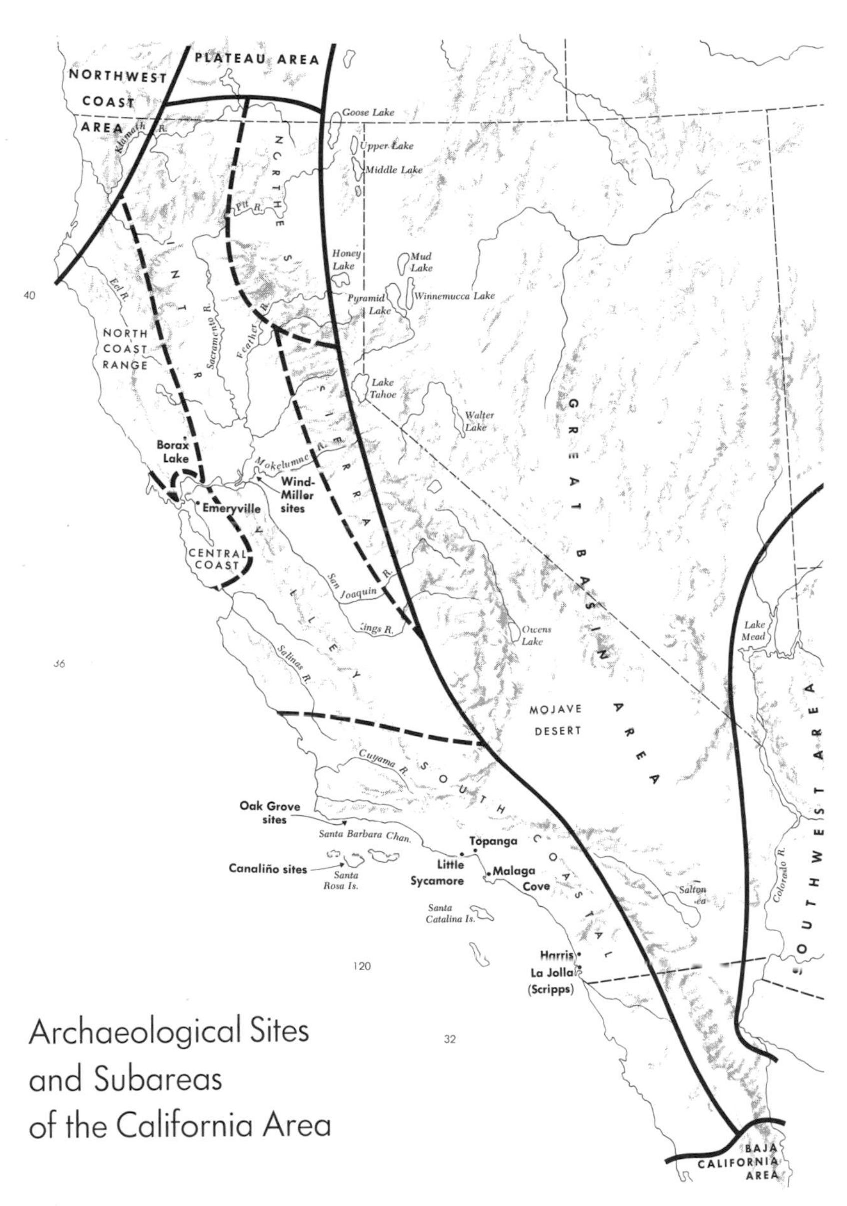

Archaeological Sites
and Subareas
of the California Area

(preceding page)

Map of California with archaeological subareas, regions and sites. The Windmiller sites which are discussed are located on the Mokelumne River in the Interior Valley subarea. From Gordon Willey, *An Introduction to American Archaeology*, Vol. I (Englewood Cliffs, N.J.: Prentice-Hall, 1966), p. 180.

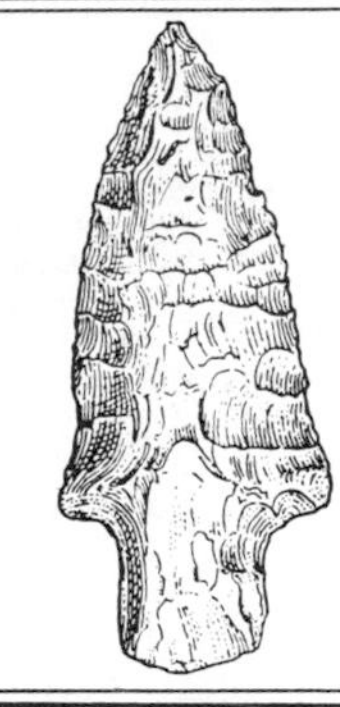

Studying the Windmiller Culture

ROBERT F. HEIZER

I have not found it easy to write a retrospective appraisal of a Californian archaeological research project which I had done in the past. Neither have I found it easy to recall all of the reasons why I did what I did over twenty years ago, partly because my memory is not that good, and partly because, in the interim, there have been any number of other research projects which have required maximum concentration and energy to get them started, then carried out, and finally written up. After thirty-five years of doing this, my recollections have become hazy, and I can only hope that they are sufficiently sharp to enable me to communicate here the interest I had at the time I did the research.

Introduction

When I began college in 1932 there were no archaeology lecture courses taught, and no instruction in how to excavate. Archaeology, as we understand it today, was a non-subject. At Sacramento Junior College where I had to spend two years making up courses which were not taught in the seventy-student Nevada high school I had attended, I learned something about scientific excavation from the president, J. B. Lillard, and a very good archaeologist, Richard van Valkenburgh, whose support was being managed with a part-time job in the college library. The Depression was on, and van Valkenburgh felt himself lucky to have this much employment and at the same time to be able to practice some archaeology. Having removed my (academic) deficiencies, I went off in 1934 to Berkeley as a junior and there learned more about excavation, through digging in local shellmounds, with Waldo Wedel and Philip Drucker, who were already graduate students. Alfred Kroeber, head of the Berkeley Department was not exactly against his students doing archaeology, but you could not at the same time say that he was wildly enthusias-

Headpiece: Windmiller projectile point.

tic that they should engage in this pursuit. There were still old Indians to talk to and there remained some big gaps in the record of tribal ethnographies for California, and Kroeber was clearly more interested in training his graduate students by having them spend a summer talking to the few surviving Tolowa or Shasta or Atsugewi than he was in having them indulge themselves by digging up skeletons and arrowpoints. Kroeber understood the value and significance of the prehistoric record of humans. But in 1936, when I got my A.B., he had already come to the conclusion that California archaeological materials were so similar for any period that it was not possible to detect any development of culture over time. I say that Kroeber had concluded this, but in fairness I must admit I am not certain that in fact he had—I merely recall that everything he said seemed to indicate this as his belief. While he recognized that archaeological materials from one area of the state were different from those of other areas, he believed that the prehistoric peoples of each region had earlier settled on what kinds of material culture forms they would make and use, and once having made this decision, the local culture became a relatively immutable one which persisted in essentially unchanged form through time.

Our datum year is 1936 in this retrospective sketch. Before 1936, a certain amount of excavation data was published, but the number of such reports which dealt with quite local areas scattered over the state were so variable in the way the data were presented and so geographically discontinuous that it was impossible to try to draw from them any kind of a general picture of prehistoric development. What Kroeber wrote in 1909 and 1925 were still about the best statewide surveys of prehistory. The pre-1936 archaeological literature ranged from discursive narrations of ill- or non-documented collections made by people that nowadays would have to be classed as "pothunters," to controlled stratigraphic samplings of sites such as Olson's work in the Santa Barbara mainland and Channel Island areas, to not-too-successful efforts to study the archaeology of an area such as the San Joaquin delta or the southern San Joaquin Valley through private collections. These were all honest efforts, but they represented particular forays into a complete void without a sense of problem, rather like exploratory operations by non-specialist surgeons with little knowledge of anatomy who operate merely to see "what is going on inside." Unfortunately, without a problem to direct their thinking and, therefore, the path of the scalpel, nothing much could be learned. The analogy is not a very good one, since the prehistoric "patient" was already dead.

The long neglect of California archaeology by the most active

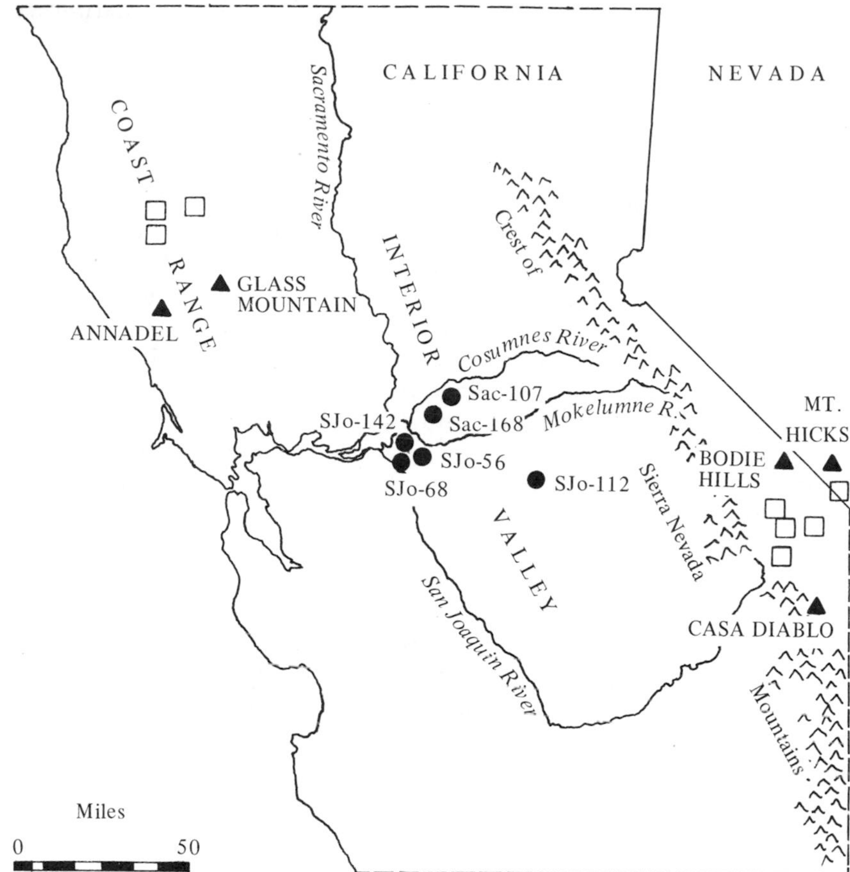

FIGURE 1
Map of Central California showing location of Windmiller culture sites. Five obsidian sources supplying implement material to Windmiller sites are shown as solid triangles. Known obsidian sources not known to have been used are shown in open squares.

anthropological research-oriented institution in the state (the Berkeley campus) was admitted, but at the same time justified, on the grounds that the archaeology could wait but the Indians and their languages and aboriginal practices were disappearing and must be recorded while there was still a chance to do so. As regards the last assumption, this was surely correct, but the first assumption proved to be false. Up to the mid-1930's California's growth (and acculturation of Indians) was a predictable one. What was not anticipated while what can properly be called "salvage ethnography" was being done, was that this period was also the last chance to learn about the archaeology of large areas which were soon to be plowed up for mega-farms and the urban-industrial sprawl which was to come with World War Two.

In 1936 J. B. Lillard, referred to above, and W. K. Purves (a music teacher at the Junior College with an interest in archaeology) announced in a pamphlet which they had written, that they could distinguish, in a series of sites in the nearby Cosumnes River Valley, three cultures which could be chronologically ordered. They did not name them, but distinguished them according to their order of depth occurrence as follows: Early, Intermediate and Late. Their type Early site was named Windmiller and is also referred to as site Sac-107. In 1939 Sacramento Junior College published a second pamphlet in which a considerably larger number of sites were discussed, and a modified culture sequence was proposed: Early (= early prehistoric), Transitional (= intermediate prehistoric) and Late (later prehistoric ending in protohistoric and historic), arranged chronologically. That sequence has remained the basic one for Central California for the past thirty years, although there have been numerous refinements as there has been more excavation and as archaeologists have finally succeeded in determining the precise temporal chronology through radiocarbon dating.

Some years before Lillard and Purves determined their three sequential cultures, a young farm boy, E. J. Dawson, who had considerable energy and intelligence and a true interest in archaeology assembled, through digging, a large collection of artifacts from sites in the vicinity of Thornton, about fifteen miles south of the area where Lillard and Purves made their studies. Dawson read what he could and thought about what he was doing, and through this self-training, learned to make systematic notes on his work. His observations and collection were published in 1929 with a co-author, W. E. Schenck who was a research associate of the University of California. Schenck was also self-trained, and as it turned out, less perceptive than Dawson who, in the course of his collecting activities, had analyzed his findings and had correctly identified the culture sequence which in 1939 was labelled Early, Transitional and Late. Schenck, it appears, was working with several preconceived ideas or assumptions. The first among these were that the time span of prehistoric occupation in the lower Cosumnes-Mokelumne River region was brief—he admitted that it might extend as far back as 1500 years. A second assumption was that the differences in the types and frequencies of artifacts such as projectile points, shell beads, and polished stone objects were assumed to be due either to regional differences (i.e., different customary procedures operating among populations living on sites sufficiently distant from each other so that there was no contact between them), or were the result of invention by individuals. Schenck admitted that the systematic differences between the similar aggregates of artifacts from groups of sites *might* be explained by assuming they were evidence of changes in culture through time—i.e., had chronological significance—but he seemed reluctant to accept this explanation. If Schenck had been more aware of the principle that changes in the form of artifacts and burial customs, when these are observed repeatedly in a series of archaeological sites, probably reflect changes in culture over time, his conclusions would have been nearer the mark. Dawson had correctly seen this, but Schenck refused to accept it. Schenck concluded that the ten sites excavated by Dawson could be sequenced into three "Groups": I, Late Historic (post 1848 A.D.); II, Late Prehistoric and Early Historic ("age between I and III"); and III, Prehistoric (maximum age about 500 A.D.).

After the war, I returned to Berkeley as a faculty member. There we were able to establish the Archaeological Survey in 1948, which insured that for the first time in any California university there was a staff archaeologist and the organization to carry out a systematic program of investigation. One of our main efforts was to carry out excavations in sites in the lower Sacramento Valley in order to get the local culture sequence, which had been so vaguely proposed by Lillard and Purves and Schenck and Dawson, more precisely defined. To do this meant more excavation in key sites, and especially meant making better records of what was found, as well as sitting down and doing detailed analysis of the information in hand.

We decided in 1947 to begin with the re-excavation of one of the Group III sites of Schenck and Dawson—the one known as SJo–68. We knew that it was very similar to the lowest level in a site (Sac–107) excavated by Lillard and Purves some fifteen miles to the north, and that it was also of the same age and culture as two others (sites SJo–56, SJo–142) situated nearby, these three lying inside the great bend of the lower Mokelumne River as it flows west to empty into the San Joaquin just before the combined streams empty into San Francisco Bay. With a group of six undergraduate students site SJo–68 was excavated in 1947 with as much care as we could practice. From that summer's work and some done earlier we recovered 154 burials; Dawson had earlier dug up 75 or 80 graves. From the Windmiller site (Sac–107) there were 46 "Early level" graves; from the Phelps site (SJo–56) there were 71; and from McGillivray (SJo–142) there were 51 graves. The total number of burials, for which we had controlled data, amounted to about 400. Because the Windmiller site was the first to be excavated, its name has been assigned to the culture.

In 1946 I completed a monograph which was published in 1949 in which the then-available data on the four Windmiller culture sites were presented and analyzed. Most sites of the culture (Figure 1) are cemeteries and, with the exception of SJo–68 which consists of dark carbon-rich occupation midden, are located on the crest of low clay knolls. The big bend which the Mokelumne River makes, and within whose inner arc lie sites SJo–56, 68 and 142, is caused by a great geological dome which contains natural gas. As the valley floor was covered with flood waters each year, silt was deposited over the floodplain, but the dome maintained its level and for that reason the Windmiller culture sites mentioned have not been covered with overflow silts. The geological phenomenon of isostasy has thus preserved, on or near the present surface archaeological sites, which are about 4000 years old. Outside of the Mokelumne bend dome a dozen or more feet of alluvial sediments have accumulated on the valley floor in the last four millennia. The villages where the people who buried their dead in sites SJo–142 and SJo–56 must lie nearby, but are now buried under silt deposits which are many feet thick.

The Windmiller Site

The Windmiller site (Sac–107) on the Cosumnes River is a higher natural clay mound, but the first people to use it lived off the mound and utilized the elevation as a cemetery. This practice of burying away from the village is not characteristic of most of California, and it may represent either a custom based upon the desire not to live on top of the graves of the dead, or it may have been based on the idea that it was undesirable for the cemetery to be covered each year with flood waters. The dead were buried, almost without exception, lying extended at full length on the stomach (i.e., ventrally) and oriented due west. This burial position was so rigorously followed that we can safely assume that it had an important religious significance. Skeletons are usually accompanied with artifacts.

Windmiller Artifacts

The most common grave offerings in Windmiller culture sites are shell beads and ornaments made of marine mollusks. In some cases it can be determined that these were sewed to a garment, probably of skin, as decorations. The abundant presence of shell beads and ornaments indicates either that these were secured by trade from people living over fifty miles to the west, on or near the Pacific shore, or that the local valley people occasionally visited the ocean coast to collect the shells from which they made beads and ornaments. Be-

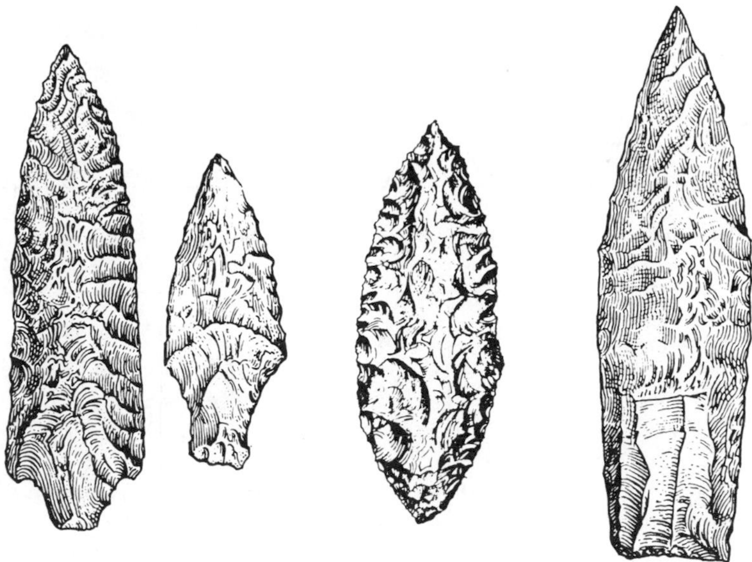

FIGURE 2
Windmiller culture artifacts: chipped projectile points.

cause there has been found no indication of the kind of industrial debris (useless bits of shell thrown away in the process of making beads) which we would expect to find if the Windmiller people had been making beads, we assume that these items were secured by trade, and that at the same time there were shell-gatherers and shell bead-makers living on the coast. Some round abalone shell ornaments have one or two drilled holes in the center, presumably for stringing or sewing onto a garment. But in Windmiller culture graves these central holes are often plugged with asphaltum, and the discs are commonly found over the left and right ear opening. The discs apparently served as decorative facings for wooden earplugs (now disappeared) being held in position with the asphaltum mastic. Since the surface of the disc is marred by the holes, it would seem that the discs were received with the holes already present, and this is another argument for their manufacture elsewhere—perhaps so far away that the Windmiller people had no opportunity to tell the distant makers, "please *don't* drill the holes in the discs." Thus, from these simple inferences, we should expect to find sites contemporaneous with the valley Windmiller sites on the coast. Since the coastal margin is subject to various kinds of physiographic alteration many, perhaps most, such old sites may have been covered or removed through erosion.

TABLE 1
Materials for charmstones

MATERIAL	SITE				
	SJo–68	SAC–107	SJo–68	SJo–142	
Andesite	–	2	–	–	2
Amphibolite schist	–	70	1	–	
Limestone	1	10	1	–	12
Alabaster	1	4	10	1	16
Diorite	1	4	1	1	7
Steatite	1	–	2	–	3
Gray schist	5	–	–	2	7
Granite	–	3	–	–	3
TOTALS	9	93	15	4	

Another common object in Windmiller graves is the "charmstone,"—a beautifully fashioned cylindrical or flattened spindle-shaped piece of stone selected for its color and beauty—often a banded blue amphibolite schist, or semi-translucent milky alabaster (Figure 3). They have almost invariably a drilled hole at one end and impressions in asphalt of fine cordage, indicating that they were suspended from a string. Curiously enough, charmstones from the three nearby sites in the Mokelumne River bend (SJo–56, SJo–68, SJo–142) are of rather different forms, and each site employed one preferred material.

From this, because the sites are only a short distance from each other, we must either conclude that the inhabitants of each village were not in communication with the others, or that local village custom demanded that the charmstones of each group be different. Possibly these were cult objects, and each village had developed its own and distinctive charmstone form. But, without knowing the answer, it seems more probable that the three villages were occupied at different times—otherwise we should expect to have more sharing of charmstone types than has been observed.

Of sixteen types, ten are unique to one or the other of the three sites, one type is shared with two sites and the one is shared with three sites. Some charmstones seem pretty definitely to be cult objects since they are made in the form of a phallus (Figure 4). No hints from the way they occur in graves tell us anything about such a cult or the significance of these particular stones in ritual or belief.

Another common item in Windmiller graves is clear quartz crystals.

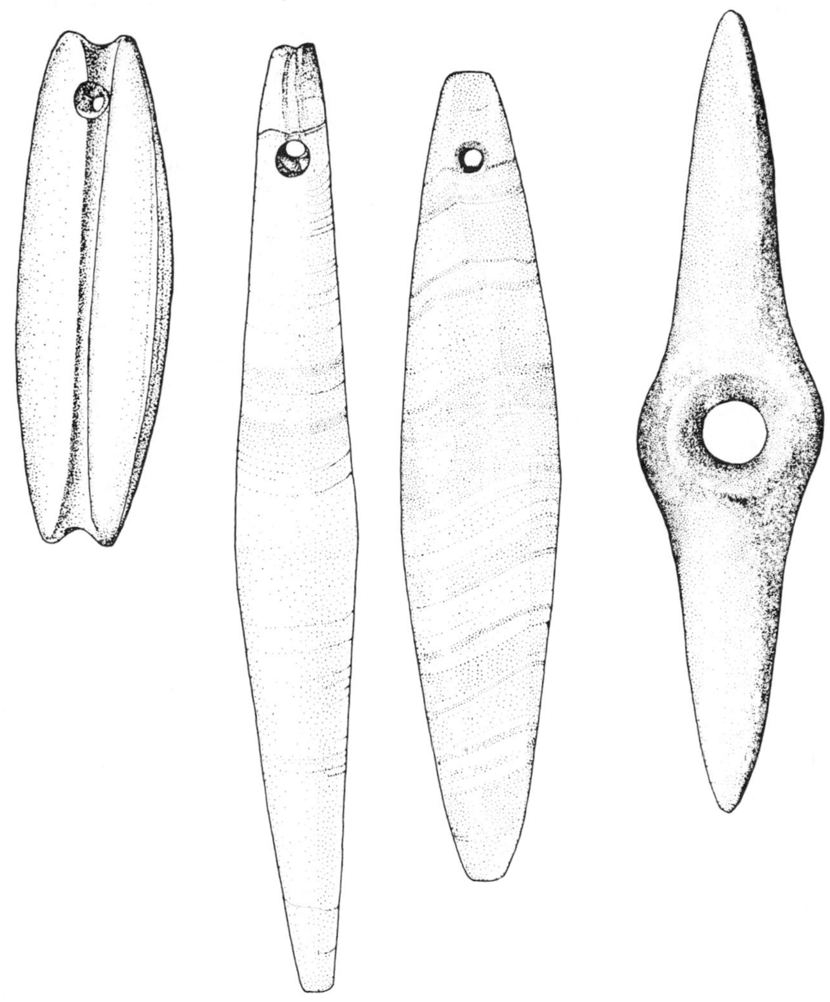

FIGURE 3
Some Windmiller charmstone forms.

Such crystals and charmstones persist into ethnographic times where they are reported as having magical properties such as, when manipulated by a trained shaman, being able to bring rain, to stop rain, or to attract fish, and being highly dangerous for the uninitiated to even touch. They, and charmstones, were believed by recent Indians of California to be capable of self-movement, so that a shaman who buried his precious stones might return to discover them gone, an absence he attributed to the stones not liking him any longer and having departed by burrowing through the ground. Whether such beliefs were in existence forty centuries ago in the same area we cannot, of course, tell. All we can say positively about this is that the charmstones in the Windmiller culture graves we excavated did not burrow their own way out to escape.

Chipped stone projectile points, usually fairly large and heavy and probably used to tip the shafts of atlaltl darts, and made of obsidian or flint also occur commonly in graves (Figure 2). All of these stones had to be imported, and here again we are faced with the problem of trying to decide whether the Windmiller people took the long walk west to collect obsidian and chert or to the nearer Sierra Nevada foothills to the east where chert and flint (but not obsidian) occur. Perhaps the obsidian came through inter-tribal trade, and at least some of the flint materials were gathered by the people themselves.

Seed grinding implements seemed, on the basis of the first Windmiller sites excavated, to be limited to the flat grinding slab (metate). And in 1946 on the basis of what was then known, I wrote that the stone mortar was not used, and further, that by reason of the abundance of chipped projectile points, hunting was the main economic base of the people. Excavation of site SJo-68 in 1947, however, showed that the stone bowl-mortar was present, and this finding threw into question the too-facile conclusion reached earlier that the Windmiller people were mainly meat-eaters. The stone mortar is practically a necessity to the recent California Indians for grinding acorns into meal, and its apparent absence in Windmiller culture sites suggested that the great California Indian staple diet item, the acorn, was then not much used. Assuming that the stone mortars from SJo-68 were used for grinding acorns, the earlier conclusion that the Windmiller people had not exploited the food value of the acorn (fully equivalent to maize or wheat), or did not know how to extract the unpalatable tannic acid contained in the meat, was incorrect.

Windmiller culture ornaments also include squared or trapezoidal

TABLE 2
Occurrence of charmstone types

CHARMSTONE TYPE	SITE			
	SJO–68	SAC–107	SJO–68	SJO–142
A	–	19	1	–
B	9	18	7	2
C	–	4	–	1
E	–	4	1	1
F	–	–	2	–

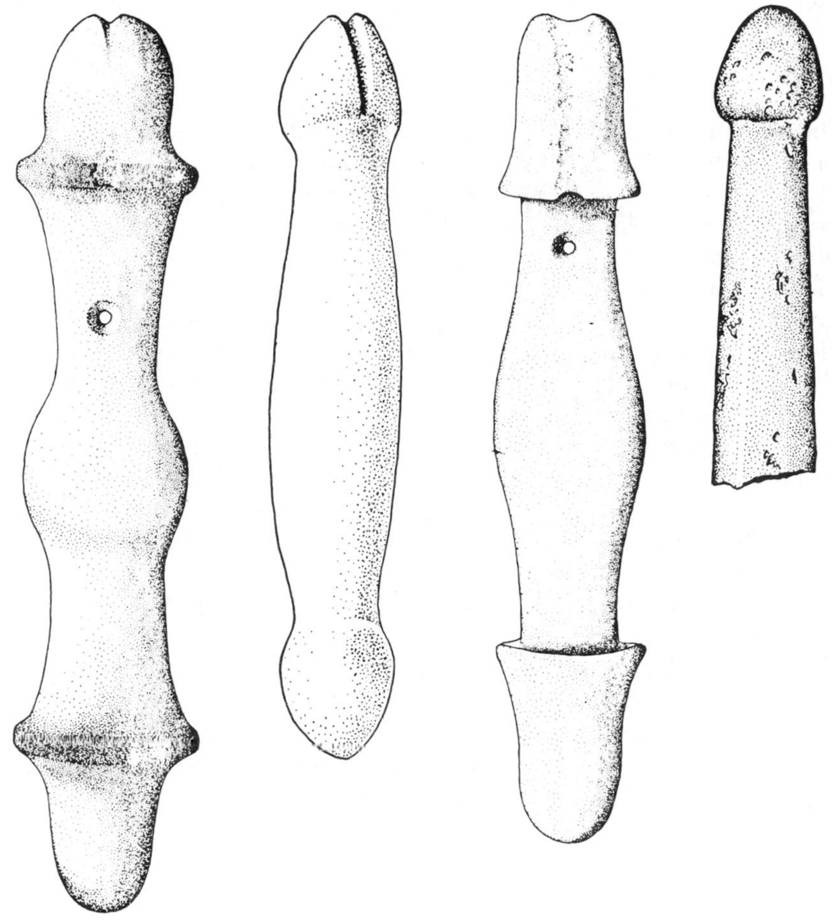

FIGURE 4
Phallic form Windmiller culture charmstones.

pieces of turtle plastron with shell beads affixed with asphaltum, pendants of mica and polished slate and birdbone beads. Two tubular stone pipes, presumably used for smoking, have been recovered. There is a variety of bone implements which include thin flat pieces whose ethnographic use was to scrape sweat from the skin. One C-shaped bone fishhook was recovered. A variety of fiber-tempered baked clay objects the form of which ranges from round tennis-ball size pieces to French roll-size specimens with flattened surfaces bearing negative imprints of twined basketry and pecan-size bipointed pieces, either bearing a longitudinal groove or ungrooved, occur in some quantity. The larger pieces, often found in fragments, probably served as surrogates for stone pot-boilers used in basket-boiling of a mush made of seeds. The smaller baked clay pieces may have been ornaments, fishline or net sinkers. Taken all in all the technological abilities of the Windmiller people to flake flint and obsidian, mold and fire clay objects, fashion shell ornaments, and shape from refractory rocks the beautifully symmetrical charmstones were of a high order. We do not know whether they were woodworkers, and we get only a tantalizing hint of their basketry from impressions in clay cooking stones. By and large, if we ignore the difference in shapes, we have something very close to the material culture of the Indians of Central California when they first came into contact with Europeans (Spanish explorers and missionaries) in the late eighteenth century.

In brief, the Windmiller culture is an early phase in what must be an unbroken cultural tradition—a conclusion which Kroeber had reached as early as 1909. No vestiges of housefloors have been found in any Windmiller culture site. We cannot assume that the people had no houses, but we can suppose that they may not have been very elaborate structures which were lived in for long enough periods of time to create a hardpacked floor which would survive as an archaeological feature. Flimsy houses made with a framework of willows and covered with rushes or matting of a general type used by some ethnographic groups in Central California may have been the house form of the Windmiller people. If so, no obvious traces of these would have survived after forty centuries.

Dating of the Windmiller Sites

In 1946, when I wrote my review of what we knew about the Windmiller culture, it seemed necessary to try to provide an estimate of the age of the sites. There was not much to go on as a precedent, and radiocarbon dating which has made age determination in many instances as simple as ordering a hamburger (though an expensive one) had not yet been developed. Schenck and Dawson's age estimate of their Group III ("prehistoric") materials which included some Windmiller culture sites, allowed only 1500 years B.P. Wedel had found in the bottom levels of a site at Buena Vista Lake in the Southern San Joaquin Valley extended burials which reminded us of those from the Windmiller sites. His estimate of a maximum antiquity of 1200 to 1500 years B.P. for these came close to that of Schenck and Dawson. To me such age did not seem to allow enough time for the Windmiller and the two following cultures to have developed. There were estimates that earliest occupation of some of the big shellmounds on San Francisco Bay might go back as far as 1000 to 2000 B.C., and since these earlier shellmound cultures were related to a post-Windmiller culture, then Windmiller should be older than 1000 to 2000 B.C. So I concluded (risking the choice of a long chronology over a short one) that the Windmiller culture was in operation about 2500 B.C., a suggestion which ran counter to what most people who might have been interested would have believed. But, there were several things we had observed about Windmiller culture sites which indicated that their antiquity was (respectable)—in terms of late 1940's thinking. One of these things was the fact that the occupation or burial sites seemed to have been established directly on a red clay soil which had since undergone a certain amount of erosion, and in some instances had become partially submerged under gray alluvial fill resulting from the annual overflow of the Cosumnes and Mokelumne Rivers. Further, the human bones lying in grave pits dug into and filled with this red clay were mineralized to a pronounced degree—that is, they were appreciably altered in the direction of becoming fossilized. Bones from graves of more recent periods in the area showed no, or only slight, evidence of mineralization. At several sites a thick layer of calcium carbonate (lime hardpan) had formed after the site was occupied. This was clearly proved by human burials imbedded in the hardpan which resembled a concrete sidewalk in color and consistency. Projectile points made of flint or chert were often patinated (oxidized on the surface in such a way as to alter the original color and chemical composition of the stone). So, all of these could be taken as supporting a fairly considerable antiquity of the Windmiller culture.

As of 1949 we had reached the point where we could identify the Windmiller culture as an entity; had established that it was the earliest known culture in the lower Cosumnes—lower Mokelumne region, and that it might date back to around 2500 B.C., but that this date was admittedly only a guess. There still were all sorts of unanswered questions about the Windmiller culture and people, however. Four occupation or cemetery sites had been excavated, and while obviously all belonged to the same culture, there were inter-site differences which might be interpreted either as evidence of village populations which lived by themselves and had little close contact with their contemporaries occupying sites in some cases only a few miles away, or which might be explained as the evidence of a sequential series of living and cemetery sites of a single small population which moved its location from time to time, and over the course of decades was changing certain details of its ways of making and doing things. Furthermore, so little archaeology had at that time been done in California that there was little information on other sites the possible age of the Windmiller culture.

Waldo Wedel, as mentioned, had reported extended burials in the deepest levels of a site at Buena Vista Lake, about 250 miles to the south, and in the Santa Barbara region we had reports of similar burials in the earliest identified culture which was called "Oak Grove." Elsewhere in northern California and Oregon, and across the Sierra Nevadas in the Great Basin there was nothing which looked at all similar to the Windmiller culture. These were slim leads to finding broader connections or relationships, and for all practical purposes the Windmiller people simply appeared in the Mokelumne-Cosumnes area as though they and their culture were created there. It was obvious that more work was needed in order to explain why the culture items in the graves of sites Sac-107, SJo-56, SJo-68 and SJo-142 differed not only in form and frequency, and also it was obvious that the guess date of 2500 B.C. should be tested by some other approach and either verified or corrected.

It was clear that human bones from graves of the earliest period were much more mineralized than those from the late prehistoric period of a few hundred years ago. I succeeded in interesting a colleague, Sherburne F. Cook who was Professor of Physiology at Berkeley, in a research program on the chemical analysis of large numbers of human bones from different periods in the hope that we could discover the time-rate of mineralization. If, for example, bone from a grave which could be placed at 1800 A.D. because it contained glass beads of an identifiable and dated type showed X degree of change from fresh human bone, we thus had two points on a curve, and could extrapolate backward to calculate that bones from Windmiller graves which showed 10X degrees of difference were 10X times as old as the 1800 A.D. burials. We did several years of laboratory experimentation on this problem, and while we learned that buried bones can be proved to progressively lose bound water and nitrogen and to increase in carbonate with age, we failed to determine a *fixed* rate of uptake or decrease of H_2O, N_2 and Ca. We could, in short, arrange bones from separate cemeteries in their proper order of time, but we could not invest the "time curve of mineralization" with precise or absolute (chronometric) age in terms of elapsed years. Happily for us, our lack of success was not serious because of Willard F. Libby's important development of the radiocarbon age determination method. In 1956 and 1957 J. B. Griffin of the Phoenix Memorial Laboratory at the University of Michigan, and W. F. Libby at the University of Chicago dated four organic samples from site SJo-68. One sample was too small and the date was considered inaccurate; the three others (samples C440/552, M-645, M-647) gave ages of 4052 ± 160 years B.P., 4100 ± 250 years B.P. and 4350 ± 250 years

B.P.—i.e., about 2000 to 2400 B.C. It would be nice to say at this point that my earlier guess date was nearly perfect, but that little bragadoccio is tempered by ten additional radiocarbon dates secured since 1957 from SJo-68 and several other Windmiller culture sites which give what seems too great a *floruit* for the culture—an age spread which runs up to 545 B.C.

Most simple and obvious conclusions often turn out to be incorrect, probably for the reason that they appear to be obvious and simple because they are based upon too limited data. To put it another way, you can prove anything if you have few enough facts. As of the time of the writing of this retrospection, we are uncertain as to the precise age of the Windmiller culture for the reason that we are unable to discriminate, with any assurance, those radiocarbon age dates which are correct and those which are in error. But in assessing the fourteen radiocarbon dates we now have, I still believe that the Windmiller culture was operating in 2000 B.C. How long it lasted is more difficult to say. Assuming that the radiocarbon dating method is correct in theory, it is nevertheless also the case that many age determinations do not accurately measure the absolute or true age of the sample. While technical errors in the radiocarbon laboratory can occur, it is equally or more probable that something may have happened to the organic sample during its long burial in the earth which is unknown to the archaeologist. Or it may also be the case that the archaeologist himself has failed to perform his job of recovering the sample to be dated with sufficient care. But here again we encounter that old problem of having to choose between better and worse judgments, and when you really have no good grounds in terms of expert knowledge on how to make a choice, you simply say: "It is still a problem." It seems that the exact age of the Windmiller culture sites remains today undetermined.

An attempt was made by D. Clark of Stanford University to apply the obsidian hydration dating method to the SJo–68 chipped points, but the results he secured were confusing, since obsidian artifacts from the same grave were calculated in some instances to differ in age by nearly a thousand years.

The problem of trying to seriate (time order) the four Windmiller culture sites was beyond my capability to solve in 1946. I guessed that since the obsidian used for implements came from some nonlocal source, and was probably secured by trade, that the older sites would contain less obsidian than the younger ones on the assumption that trade relations with distant groups would increase as time went on. Using this argument I selected site SJo–68 as the most recent and Sac–107 as the oldest of the Windmiller culture sites. In

TABLE 3
Suggested time sequence of four Windmiller culture sites, 1947–1972. References to publications can be found in Ragir (1972). SJo–68A, SJo–68B refer to upper and lower levels of this site.

↑ Time	SETZER 1947	HEIZER 1949	HEIZER AND COOK, 1949	BELOUS 1953	DEMPSEY AND BAUMHOFF 1963	RAGIR 1972
	SJo–68	SJo–68	SJo–56	SJo–68	SJo–56	SJo–142
	Sac–107	SJo–56	SJo–68	SJo–142	SJo–142	SJo–56
						SJo–68A
		Sac–107	Sac–107	Sac–107	Sac–107	Sac–107
	SJo–142	SJo–142	SJo–142	SJo–56	Sac–107	SJo–68B

1968 Sonia Ragir, in a detailed study of the considerable mass of information on site SJo–68, applied statistical analysis to two of the most common kinds of stone artifacts in graves, charmstones and projectile points. Since her data comprised nearly the entire contents of the site, she could differentiate five phases of occupation, each phase being identifiable with a series of graves distinguished by horizontal location, depth below surface, sex, age, and kinds and numbers of grave offerings. Using this sequence (of unknown duration in numbers of elapsed years) as a guideline, she compared the SJo–68 data with those from other Windmiller culture sites. The analysis involved 203 separate comparisons, and her sequence was: (oldest), lower levels of SJo–68; and (most recent) SJo–56. Table 3 shows the results of several attempts to decide the time sequence of the Windmiller culture sites. Belous, Baumhoff and Dempsey applied statistical methods to the data reported by me in 1949. Setzer's sequence was based upon soil chemistry (pedology). Heizer and Cook in 1949 developed a sequence derived from the "index of fossilization" of bones. Ragir in 1972 took a new crack at the problem and used computer analysis. Which of the various sequences shown in Table 3 if any, are correct, I am unable to say.

In 1949, as already mentioned, the search for related cultures was not very productive. And even today there is nothing similar enough to the Windmiller culture discovered in any area outside California to allow us to point to it as a parent culture. One can conclude from this that the Windmiller culture has historical roots in California, and that it is not an imported culture but rather one which had long development in the general region. There are hints of Paleoindian people of 8 to 10,000 years ago in Central California, their presence being indicated by fluted points of Clovis type. But whether the

Paleoindians remained to become the ancestors of the Windmiller group of later times we cannot tell. One indication—despite the failure of archaeologists to discover or recognize sites of pre-Windmiller culture age—that California was already well settled by 2000 B.C. is seen in recent studies of obsidian points from Windmiller sites which are aimed at determining the geologic source of the obsidian raw material. Table 4 shows the results of comparing a limited number of Windmiller obsidian artifacts with geological source samples. While not a very extensive series, one can draw certain conclusions about communication in Central California around 4000 years ago from these samples. (For location of obsidian sources and Windmiller culture sites see Figure 1.)

The valley Windmiller people were securing obsidian (either as raw material, preforms, blanks, or finished implements) from two main zones: (1) three trans-Sierran obsidian flows situated at a distance of 150 miles to the east, and; (2) two contiguous obsidian deposits in Napa County in the Coast Ranges lying 65 miles to the west (Figure 1). These distances are fairly considerable, and judging from ethnographic analogy of recent California Indians, it is more probable that the obsidian from the several sources reached the Windmiller people through inter group trade than by actual treks to the several obsidian localities to the west and east. If this fact is admitted, the Windmiller people seem suddenly less impersonal and less isolated. We can see them in a role as recipients of obsidian secured through tribe-to-tribe exchange between groups living in the space between the obsidian geologic sources and the sites where this material finally was received and utilized.

So, the proved contemporaries of the Windmiller people extended geographically, at the very least, as far as the western fringes of the Great Basin to the east and the Coast Ranges to the west. The abundance and variety of shell beads and ornaments in graves of the

Table 4
Geologic sources of obsidian implements

Geologic source	Archaeological site		
	SJo–68	SJo–56	SJo–142
Bodie Hills	7	2	1
Mt. Hicks	2		2
Casa Diablo	1		1
Annadel	1		
Glass Mt.	5	1	3

Windmiller people have not been tracked back to their precise places of manufacture along the Pacific shore, though we know enough to say that these must have lain somewhere in the zone, fifty miles to the north and fifty miles to the south of San Francisco Bay. So, gradually and as yet dimly, the Windmiller village populations which we saw in 1949 as isolated and unrelated to any others, began to come into focus as participant members of an ancient "Oikumene" (a Greek word signifying "the known world" and applied by Kroeber [1948] and Willey [1955] as a culture-historical term). We know, in short, that Central California must have been pretty well-settled with permanent populations in or around 2000 B.C., and that there was communication between groups which ranged from the Pacific shore eastward through the Coast Range, the Interior Valley, the Sierra Nevadas, and into the arid Great Basin. Since village sites of these several coastal, mountain, and desert populations have not come to light, it may be suggested that we have been looking in the wrong places and that on this time level the environmental regime was different and the choice of best-favored living spots occupied somewhat different positions than are suggested by present-day conditions. Or, possibly, permanently occupied villages at which deep deposits of occupation refuse built up do not exist, and the traces of peoples' presence at this time, in at least some areas, is scattered rather than concentrated. Still another possibility is that physiographic changes such as elevation or subsidence of the ocean shore, or wind or water erosion, or alluvial deposition which can cover sites, may have operated to either destroy or conceal what we believe to have been present and which we cannot find. Whatever the reason, be it human lack of perception or natural forces of obscuration, the evidence is somewhere, and in time it will come to light.

Other Prehistoric California Cultures

In 1949 we did not know much, but we were interested in learning how the prehistoric peoples of Central California lived, and what they did, and why we found sites and their contents in the extant condition. In the effort to try to gain some insight into living and activity pursuits of these peoples, we carried out an extensive program of digging 5 by 5 foot testpits in occupation sites, excavating by 6 or 12 inch levels, screening all of the earth in each pit through a one-quarter inch mesh screen, washing the material retained by the screen, separating this into constituents (rock, baked clay, shell, obsidian, bone, etc.) and tabulating the results. When dozens of sites were compared, we could see all sorts of differences, and these were explained (albeit crudely) in terms of site location (stoneless alluvial valley floor, mountains, coast), distance from available sources (e.g., obsidian, mollusk shells). What we were doing was a crude form of environmental or ecological archaeology. From this process we learned much, because we could bring into fairly sharp focus the human exploitation of some portions of the environment. Our efforts to develop a method for determining age of sites through quantitative changes over time in the water, nitrogen and carbonate content in human bones from graves has already been mentioned. We applied the "direct historical approach," pioneered by W. D. Strong in the Plains, with some success. We also carried out investigations into the chemical nature of, and differences between, archaeological site soils whose general time order, or sequence, we had determined from stratigraphy and cultural classification. These analyses provided us with interesting data on changes which occurred over time in the several sorts of archaeological sites, but they offered no reliable leads for development of a system of precision age-dating. In short, we did a lot and learned a lot. Much of what we learned, while interesting, did not fulfill our hopes for developing exact age-determination methods, but that failure does not automatically mean that our efforts were wasted. I have observed from experience that an idea may be sound, but that its successful application is prevented by our not possessing sufficiently finely developed techniques of demonstration or proof. For example, in 1947 we attempted to compare the chemical composition of obsidian artifacts from Windmiller sites with samples from geological deposits of obsidian. They all looked pretty much alike in certain elements, and it was not possible at that time to associate particular implements with source localities, the reason being that the common elements of this natural glass are everywhere similar—we learned, in brief, that obsidian is obsidian because it is obsidian. But with newer methods of neutron activation and X-ray fluorescence analysis, very precise quantitative determinations of dozens of rare elements, measured in ppm (parts per million) were possible, and these methods now can readily provide the answers we want. (See Table 3.) I believe that we should not shut the door to attempts at developing an independent dating method based on progressive changes in the chemical composition of buried bone. Somewhere, hidden in that ultra-complex process of post-mortem chemical change in bone, there may be one component which follows an orderly alteration through time. Dr. Cook and I thought the vital lead might be in the amino acid fraction, but with methods available to us at the time we could not pin it down, and we are hopeful that better minds and methods may make the progress we were unable to achieve.

TABLE 5
Age groupings of SJo–68 population. Sex in adolescents is difficult to determine. Table does not include fragmentary remains of 24 individuals (15.6% of total) who could not be assigned sex or age class. These 24 are included in the "unknown" total.

SEX	AGE GROUP				
	0–12	12–21	21–45	50+	Total
Male		6 (3.9%)	37 (24%)	7 (4.5%)	50 (32.5%)
Female		3 (1.9%)	22 (14.3%)	7 (4.5%)	32 (20.0%)
Unknown	25 (16.2%)	4 (3.2%)	15 (9.7%)	3 (1.9%)	72 (46.7%)
Total	25 (16.2%)	14 (9.1%)	74 (48.0%)	17 (11.0%)	154

Among other things we and others failed to do when the Windmiller sites were excavated was to fully exploit the available methods for reconstructing the botanical environment of the time(s) of site occupation through pollen analysis. Experts in this field were few and such analysis would have cost something, and that something was in even greater short supply than palynologists. This paleobotanical inquiry can and no doubt will be made in the course of time. Analysis of faunal remains from Windmiller sites was carried out, but no unexpected forms were present—all species were present-day residents in the area.

The human skeletal materials recovered were studied in part by R. Newman in 1955 who compared the Windmiller physical type with those of the later cultures in the same area. K. Kennedy in 1958 studied Windmiller and later period human dentitions with the aim of observing differences in tooth wear which might reflect changes in diet and/or culinary utensils, but found nothing very significant. The teeth of the skulls of Windmiller people did show somewhat more pronounced tooth wear than those of later people from the same area, but these differences could not be causally linked to diet or material culture. They surely mean something, but at this point we cannot suggest the explanation. Perhaps this will come in the course of more work.

The 154 skeletal remains from site SJo–68 were made the particular object of a study of pathology. Fifty-five percent of the individuals had some osteological or dental pathology. Arthritis and dental caries were the most common complaints of these people. One fractured skull was observed—the owner had survived. Only two broken bones (both lower arm bones) which had healed, and only one instance of a stone projectile point imbedded in a bone were noted. In general, if we ignore arthritic joints and bad teeth, the

SJo–68 population represented in these graves seemed to have had good health and did not die in numbers through warfare carried out with stone-tipped projectiles. Mortality figures for the SJo–68 groups are shown in Table 5.

Table 5 was drawn up to summarize a very careful assessment of age and sex by an advanced graduate student working under faculty supervision. The study of skeletal pathology was done by another graduate student, also working under faculty supervision. These two examinations produced somewhat variant sets of results. In one the sex determinations were: male, 38; female, 40; unknown, 76. In the other: male, 50; female, 32; unknown 72. Whether some bias crept in (one student was female, one was male); whether the expert supervision was unequal in quality; or whether (as I suspect) sex determination of prehistoric skeletal material is subject to wide error, we cannot tell, but holding the thought in mind, it is surely true that when we talk about the pathology of a prehistoric people we are studying, it is important (even essential) that we know whether it was a man or a woman who got shot with a stone-headed arrow or spear. It is also necessary to be certain, when we are trying to draw conclusions about ownership of different classes of property which occur in graves, whether the individual in each grave is a male or female. Archaeologists try to explain, although at times on a fairly superficial level, what they find. A grave containing two adults may be that of one male and one female, two females, or two males. If you like to explain (or speculate) think of the possibilities in this case. But at the same time note that two of the possibilities are impossible and the single correct one depends on the accuracy of the physical anthropologist who is making the sex determinations for you.

I believe that the several Windmiller culture grave populations will in future be re-studied in an effort to penetrate more deeply into the socio-economic-sex associated practices of the society. Were the individuals buried in site SJo–68 whose graves contained charmstones ancient shamans? If we accept one of the graduate student's sex-age studies mentioned above, it seems that there were charmstones in 8 male graves, 2 female graves, and 5 of unknown sex (2 infants, 1 child and 2 adolescents). If there is a pattern of consistency here, it is difficult to spot. The variations in the kind and quantity of objects (shell beads, chipped stone implements, shell ornaments, charmstones, etc.) occurring in Windmiller graves cannot be due to wholly unpatterned or random behavior. These items must have had some real value, and an individual whose grave contains a wealth of one or more of these different items must have occupied a different social or sexual status position or role than the person in a nearby grave

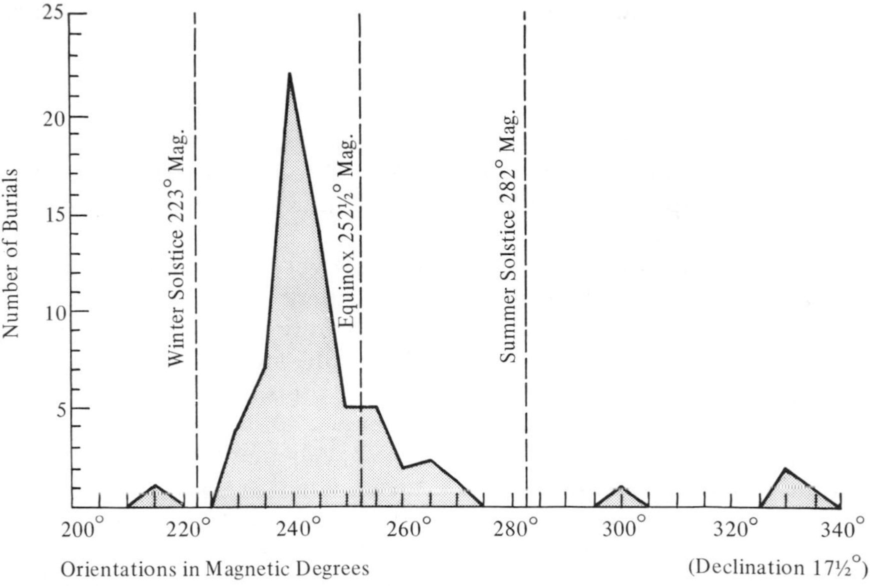

FIGURE 5
Magnetic orientation of 70 Windmiller culture burials from site SJo-68. From P. D. Schultz, Solar Burial Orientation and Paleodemography in the Central California Windmiller Tradition. (Center for Archaeological Research at David, Publ. 2.)

where all such objects are absent. An assessment of the sociological implications of Windmiller burials has not yet been done, but the data are on file and available for study.

If I were excavating Windmiller sites today I would try to use some of the recently devised methods for extracting hard-to-see elements. These would include flotation and ultra-fine screening. I would also attempt to apply a wholly new and untested kind of investigation which I have earlier called "chemical archaeology." It is known that most plants have special affinities for absorbing specific elements from the soil they grow in. Some plants concentrate in their stems and leaves gold, others molybdenum, others copper, or zinc, or aluminum, and other elements. These elements are present, of course, only in small quantities, measured in parts per million, but if a population living on a single spot for a long time was concentrating its diet on certain plant foods, there should occur in the soil of the living site a markedly higher concentration of those trace elements which occur in high quantity in plant foods being eaten in large amounts. In a village of hunters and gatherers it can be assumed that the inedible plant residues (stems, hulls of seeds, etc.) as well as the human wastes (feces and urine) produced by persons who ate the edible portions, will be a part of the midden soil itself. The high level of specific trace elements could be determined quantitatively with

FIGURE 6
Early Windmiller burial, from SJo-68.

several analytical instruments now available. In the case of Windmiller culture sites it would be interesting to try to learn whether these people were or were not eating acorns in large amounts. Trace element chemical archaeology has, I believe, very real possibilities in providing us with information through identification of chemical residues which we cannot secure by the grosser methods of collection and visual inspection of physical residues.

An examination of the orientation of Windmiller culture burials (the compass orientation of the main central axis of the skeleton) has been made by P.D. Schulz (1970). He determined that in four Windmiller sites there was a heavy preponderance of orientations lying between 223° and 282° magnetic which are, respectively, the positions of the sun at the winter and the summer solstices. Within this arc of 59°, a notable peak occurs at 240° which seems to indicate that the burials were concentrated in late autumn (October-November) or winter (mid-February). By dividing the distribution curve at the equinox (252° magnetic) it is seen that roughly 80 percent of burials (assuming corpses at the time of burial to have been oriented to the setting sun) were made in the winter half of the year. The SJo–68 burial orientation graph is shown here in Figure 5.

Whether this seasonal difference in numbers of deaths and burials reflects times of full or partial occupation of local sites due to the requirement to leave the valley floor sites at times of river flooding in the spring due to snow melt in the Sierra Nevadas, or to seasonal shifts to richer food-producing areas when game and plant foods were in scarce supply on the Mokelumne floodplain, or to seasonal peaks in endemic disease, we do not now know. H. McHenry's radiographic study of Windmiller culture femora showed that Harris lines were frequent in children, and from this he concludes that seasonal food shortages amounting to near-starvation occurred. (McHenry 1968). This suggestion provides a direct avenue of inquiry into the adequacy of Windmiller diet, and further exploration of the problem should be made.

In Conclusion

Of the four sites we have been talking about, Sac–107 has been nearly destroyed by the ranch-owner to secure fill and provide a level storage area for farm machinery which seems to have been bought only to abandon and turn to rust; SJo–142 was ripped out years ago to make a rice field when that crop was bringing good prices. SJo–56 has been mostly dug out, but something probably remains to be excavated, and the same is true for SJo–68, which is threatened with final destruction by a large canal which will help move surplus Mokelumne River water to thirsty Southern California. In the latter case, it is "One man's drink is the other man's archaeology." Two additional Windmiller culture sites (Sac–168, SJo–112) have been discovered and excavated since 1950, and they add a bit to our total knowledge. However, it seems probable that the most obvious and best of the Windmiller culture sites have been already found and excavated. Most of these are now so completely dug over (SJo–56), destroyed (SJo–142, Sac–107) or threatened with imminent destruction (SJo–68) that we probably have in hand nearly everything we will ever know about them. The prehistory of the valley floor of Central California has been essentially destroyed by cultivation and urban development. I believe that the most useful activity I engaged in in this area from 1932 to 1947 was to dig those sites. When I say this it is not with any sense of pride which comes from a job well done, since much of what we did is quite inadequate by modern standards, but because we saved at least that much from the bulldozer. What we found is safely stored in the Lowie Museum of Anthropology, and our notes and maps are deposited for the use of students still to come. And they will come, because for much of California the Archaeology for future study lies not in the ground but in museums and archives.

Surely there are at least a few more Windmiller culture sites, and when these are found they should be either protected from disturbance, or if that is not possible to guarantee, they should be excavated with the greatest care and attention due "an endangered species." Anyone in a position to carry out such a project will have read the spate of recent literature on "processual archaeology," "research design," "archaeological strategy," and the like. I believe that there is enough detail now known about the nature of Windmiller sites and their contents already excavated to allow anyone with proper training to do the right kind of job by today's standards when another Windmiller culture site comes to light. This future work, which I confidently expect will come, will be differently prosecuted than the work we did in the latter half of the 1930's and early 1940's. Our investigations were done with practically no financial support at all, and we were essentially untrained. We used our own cars (mine was a 1926 Dodge sedan; Alex Krieger had a later and better car—a 1930 Lincoln touring model) and we lived on very little cash plus large contributions of food supplied (at night) by neighboring farmers whose acquaintance we avoided in the daytime. While I say this in a kind of Proustian sense of recollection, I leave you with the hope that practicing archaeology will be as much fun and be accompanied by as much a feeling of accomplishment for today's reader as it was for me at a young age.

References*

Beardsley, R. K.

1948 Culture Sequences in Central California Archaeology. American Antiquity 14: 1–28.

Heizer, R. F.

1949 The Archaeology of Central California, I: The Early Horizon. University of California Anthropological Records 12; 1.

Heizer, R. F. and Cook, S. F.

1949 The Archaeology of Central California: a comparative analysis of human bone from nine sites. University of California Anthropological Records 12: 85–112.

McHenry, H.

1968 Tranverse Lines in Long Bones of Prehistoric California Indians. American Journal of Physical Anthropology 29: 1–18.

RAGIR, S.
1972 The Early Horizon in Central California Prehistory. University of California Archaeological Research Facility, Contribution No. 15.

SCHENCK, W. E. AND DAWSON, E. J.
1929 Archaeology of the Northern San Joaquin Valley. University of California Publications in American Archaeology and Ethnology 25; 4.

SCHULZ, P. D.
1970 Solar Burial Orientation and Paleodemography in the Central California Windmiller Tradition. Center for Archaeological Research at Davis, Publ. No. 2: 199–208.

WILLEY, GORDON R.
1966 An Introduction to American Archaeology. Vol. I. Englewood Cliffs, N.J., Prentice-Hall, 361–380. (General reference on Windmiller culture).

*Publications of persons referred to in the text can be found in Ragir 1972.

MESOAMERICA

(preceding page)

Map of Mexico and Central America, showing the locations of the Sierra Madre Oriental, Sierra de Tamaulipas, and the Tehuacan Valley, locations which bear evidence of the origins of Early Agriculture. From Gordon R. Willey, *An Introduction to American Archaeology,* Vol. 1 (Englewood Cliffs, N.J.: Prentice-Hall, 1971), p. 92.

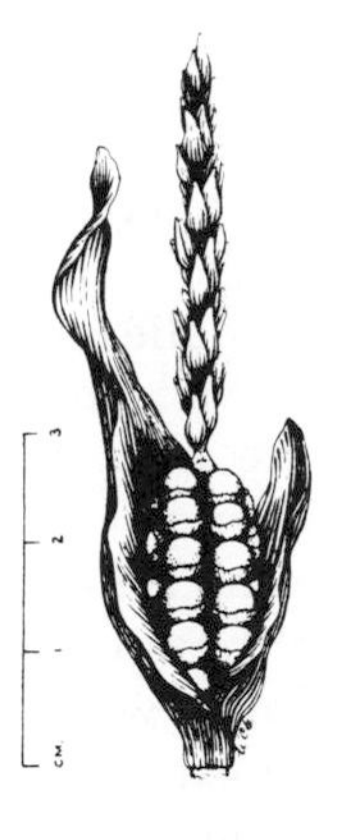

Reflections on My Search for the Beginnings of Agriculture in Mexico

RICHARD S. MACNEISH

My participation in the interdisciplinary Tehuacan Archaeological-Botanical Project on the search for the origins of agriculture in Mesoamerica began one hot afternoon in January 1949 on the dirt streets of Los Angeles in the Sierra de Tamaulipas. I had just returned from Nogales Cave in the Canyon Diablo after closing down that dig. I had left La Perra Cave two days before having instructed Alberto Aguilar to clean up the walls of our test, being careful because there might be plant remains, to draw the profile, load up the equipment and take it back to Los Angeles and to pack the jeep so we could move out of the Sierras.

When Alberto met me on the trail outside of Los Angeles and was clearly unpacked I was somewhat dismayed. However, when he produced a box labelled "northwest corner of square N15SW5, depth 14 inches," my interest intensified. As I opened the box, I reflected that other artifacts from a depth of 14 inches were certainly Preceramic—some three or four thousand years old. Then, there it was! A fragment of a woven mat and three tiny corn cobs tied with a string.

We returned to the Canyon Diablo and spent the next six weeks excavating La Perra Cave—literally peeling off from vertical faces layer after layer of preserved plant remains including more tiny corn cobs. At this time, these were certainly the earliest corn cobs in

Headpiece: Wild corn (actual size—or total height 6.5 centimeters) reconstructed on basis of a fragment bearing male spikelets and kernels. From an early level of a Tehuacan Valley cave site. The husks probably enclosed the young ears completely but opened at maturity, permitting dispersal of seeds. The kernels were round, brown or orange, and partly enclosed by glumes. From Mangelsdorf, MacNeish, and Galinat, "Prehistoric Wild and Cultivated Maize," *The Prehistory of the Tehuacan Valley*, Vol. 1. (Austin: University of Texas Press, 1967), pp. 178-200.

Mexico, and although few were to believe me for years to come, they were, in my opinion, of earlier origins than the ones from Bat Cave in the Southwest. If these cobs were in fact earlier, as I believed, they were concrete evidence that corn had spread from Mexico to the United States. I became, thereafter, involved in the hunt for the origins and spread of corn agriculture in the New World.

Our work during the rest of the '49 season yielded no other direct evidence dealing with the origins of agriculture, although we did establish the first Preceramic sequence for Mexico. Later, we discovered that agriculture began in the Preceramic, so my excavations at Basket Maker II sites of Arizona, Laurentian sites of New York, and the Faulkner site of Illinois were to pay handsome dividends later. Later in this season two sets of geologists visited our digs to give opinions about whether or not we had discovered artifacts of "Early Man." This first exposure to interdisciplinary studies was unfortunate because the opinions of the geologists were diametrically opposed to each other. However, the experience was educational for me; I learned much from my contact with them and felt that the interdisciplinary approach had a lot to recommend it—if it were undertaken in some sort of manner in which there was a real dialogue and interstimulating discussion and research with a common problem in mind, rather than being independent research with unretractable opinions the result.

In retrospect, the final months of the '49 season were a period of great insecurity as well as a race against time. In the first place, I was running out of money. Dr. Fay-Cooper Cole of the University of Chicago had backed my 1945-46 Tamaulipas thesis effort, and had promised to help with getting the department to match any funds I could get from the Viking Fund. But, when I received my grant from the generous Viking Fund, Dr. Cole had retired and the other members of the department had "no interest" in my project. I went ahead anyway, using my last summer's savings from the high-paying archaeological salvage job I had done for Major Webb in Kentucky, as well as some money from an article I had written for International Services, Inc. The latter would be enough to get me to my next job in Canada to survey the Northwest Territories. So, by scrimping and saving, and by "living worse than the ancient inhabitants in their caves," as Helmut de Terra—then doing prehistoric research for the Viking Fund—described our dig, we somehow managed to continue and to do some analysis during the last two months.

From my point of view, the analysis had to be done, and the material had to be written up, since I felt that we had found the remains of the first Early Man—the first complete Preceramic se-

Figure 1
Chronological chart of Preceramic phases and traditions in Mexico. The key Tamaulipas and Tehuacan columns are indicated, among others.

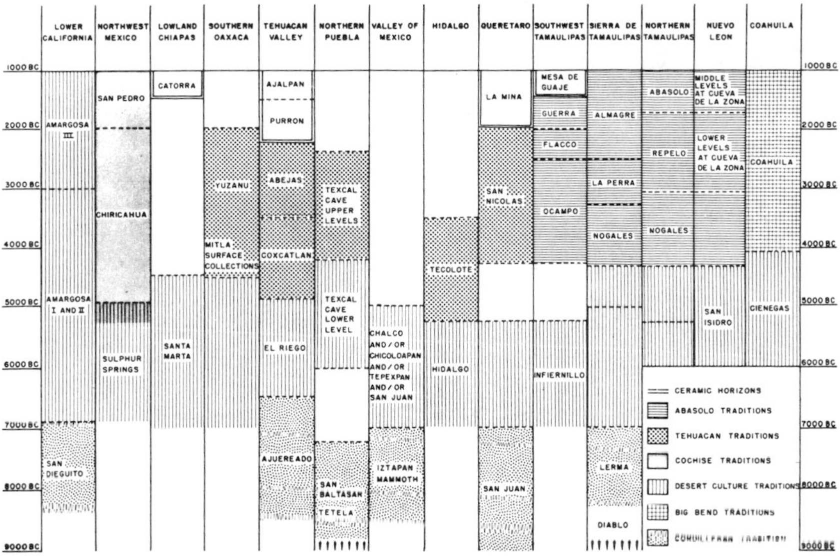

From MacNeish, Byers, Nelken-Turner and Johnson, The Prehistory of the Tehuacan Valley: Non-Ceramic Artifacts (Austin: University of Texas Press, 1967). Reprinted by permission.

quence, and the earliest corn of Mesoamerica. Although some of my colleagues were criticizing my Tamaulipas data because my digging techniques weren't any good, I felt otherwise. From 1936 to 1948 I had consciously set out to learn good field techniques. Ralph Beals in 1937 had suggested that the best method seemed to be to dig in as many different kinds of sites as possible, under a host of archaeologists with the best digging techniques. Even then I realized digging techniques couldn't be learned from books.

Field Work Experience

In 1936, I had started digging with Mort Howe on Iroquois sites and also at the Brewerton site in Upper New York State. Howe was a real artisan with a trowel and he taught me how to dig with one. Then, in 1937, I had worked on a Pueblo I pit house in northeastern Arizona under Ralph Beals, former head of the Department of Anthropology at UCLA. This was a true lesson in relating archaeological finds to ethnographic people. In addition I learned from Watson

Smith during two or three weeks' digging burials how to dig with a paint brush and spoon. In 1938 with the Rainbow Bridge-Monument Valley Expedition in the Tsegi not only did I work on another pit house with Beals and help Watson Smith of the Harvard Peabody Museum excavate Pueblo II architectural features on Black Mesa, I became also George Brainerd's—then of Carnegie Foundation—number one helper. I helped on a Basket Maker III pit house, dug in a stratified talus with preserved plant remains in Swallows Nest Cave, and even helped with the trenching of a Basket Maker II open village site. Although it is seldom noted, Brainerd was a magnificent field man and he tutored me in plane table mapping, using a transit, architectural drawing, taking photographs and using a light meter. He also showed me how to clean archaeological floors, and how to peel off strata in caves. But, more importantly, he talked archaeological techniques morning, noon, and night, and, like a hungry puppy, I devoured it all. The next year I was assigned to Roger Willis and Joe Chamberlain, then graduate students at the University of Chicago, to work at the Baumer Early Woodland Village site near Kincaid, and at a Middle Woodland stratified site near Sandoval in central Illinois. There, I learned the "Chicago method" and the vertical slicing technique that Thorne Deuel had developed in Fulton County, Illinois. Then, as was the custom for University of Chicago students, I went to Kincaid in the Black Bottom of the Ohio River. Four months in 1940, eight months in 1941, and even four months in 1942. During those months I dug in all kinds of sites—the village site Mx_o2, Mx_vIB, and Mx_vIA; the Lewis village Pp_o10 and the burial site Pp_o2, the palisade Mx_c36, the mounds Mx_o36, the mounds Mx_o4, and Mx_o10, and even my own beautifully stratified mound Mx_o7. But, more importantly, Dr. Fay-Cooper Cole had amassed a group of great graduate students for his summer "field school", and we taught each other. One to whom I'm particularly indebted, in terms of learning digging techniques, is Roger Willis. Others were Paul Maynard, Norman Emerson, "Chan" Rowe, Moreau Maxwell, Don Senter, and Ritz Ritzenthaler.

The days at Kincaid were days of great advances in American archaeological field techniques. This was a period of Works Progress Administration (WPA) and Tennessee Valley Authority (TVA) archaeology, and there were digs all over the southeastern United States being undertaken by fine archaeological technicians. You could learn field techniques either by word of mouth, or by a week's visit to see how it was being done at literally hundreds of government-sponsored digs by people whose names now read like a *Who's Who of New World Archaeology*.

After a brief period of service in the Armed Services, I returned to Chicago and, somewhat by default, became Dr. Cole's main field man for the Department of Anthropology. I ran the lab analyzing the Kincaid materials, and was in charge of any digging that was done.

In 1944, Joe Caldwell at the Illinois State Museum and I went back to southern Illinois to dig the Faulkner site—the first Preceramic site in Illinois. During the summer of 1945 I worked with John MacGregor, then acting director at the Illinois State Museum, on the Havana mounds and found the first Hopewell house. MacGregor and I uncovered there and also at the Weaver site, the first recognizable Hopewell stratigraphy. In the fall of 1945, working with Sally Tucker, I tested the Historic and Late Prehistoric Illinois village near Kaskaskia, Illinois.

From there I went to Mexico in November of 1945 to work in Tamaulipas until my money ran out in the fall of 1946. After that I was in Michigan, working for Jimmy Griffin, moving force and Director at the Museum of Anthropology at the University of Michigan, and with Bill Ritchie, then archaeologist of the Rochester Museum and leader in northeastern archaeology on Iroquois ceramics.

This project terminated with digs on stratified Delaware sites in eastern Pennsylvania together with my compatible field companions Al Spaulding, now a professor at the University of California, Santa Barbara, and Johnny Witthoft, now at the University of Pennsylvania. The year 1948 was less hectic since I was doing some testing of Iroquois sites in Upper New York State and then was working with Bill Haag, now of the University of Louisiana, and Doug Schwartz, now Director at the American School of Archaeological Research at Santa Fe, at Wolf Creek Dam in southern Kentucky, before starting my second season in Tamaulipas.

Analysis of Canyon Diablo Finds

I concluded that with all my good training there could be nothing wrong with my digging technique in the caves at the Canyon Diablo. Perhaps it was in my chronological analysis of these materials? The more I laid out my artifacts by strata on the tile floor of my hovel in Cuidad Victoria, and the more I compared these materials with those from the fine work of Alex Krieger, now at the University of Washington, and J. Charles Kelley, now of Southern Illinois University in Texas, as well as with those from the equally good work of Gordon Ekholm, at the American Museum of Natural History of N.Y., from nearby Panuco, Veracruz, the more convinced I became that my Tamaulipas materials were very old. I checked and I re-checked my artifact and ecofact stratigraphy and the answers about my chronology were always the same—the La Perra culture with its corn was under Late Archaic materials Ekholm dated at 500 B.C., and the points and scrapers were like Kelley's that he dated from 2500 to 4000 years old. I reasoned, as a consequence, that my finds had to be between 2500 to 4000 years old—and remember, these were the days before Carbon 14. The underlying Nogales culture with central Texas-like material had to fall in the period from 1000 or 2000 to 6000 B.C. The still earlier Lerma period had to be of "early recent times, 8000 to 12,000 years ago," and the underlying Diablo materials had to be still earlier.

I studied it all again, then wrote the artifact descriptions, photographed the artifacts, and suddenly the last bill for pictures left me with $30 to spare. With the season definitely over I went to Mexico City to turn over my artifacts and a copy of my notes to the Instituto de Antropología y Historia. The plant remains went to de Terra, who said he would have them guarded for me for future reference in the new Viking Fund Laboratory. Then, de Terra took my precious corn cobs and promised to turn them over to Dr. Paul Mangelsdorf, a Harvard professor who was working on corn for the Rockefeller Foundation. De Terra also asked me for bottles of "carbon" or plant remains from my various levels for a Chicago physicist who was working on a new dating technique. I gave them to him. The second day in Mexico City I submitted my report to Don Pablo Martíñez del Rio, who had shown some interest in my early finds and who said he would publish my report. From there I went to Ottawa, Canada.

For the next five days, between naps from sheer exhaustion, I had time to reflect on my work. By the time I got off the train in Edmonton, Alberta, I was beginning to recover, and by the next day when I flew to Yellowknife, I was raring to get back to doing strenuous field work and my thoughts on the season were beginning to come together.

My thoughts at this point were roughly as follows: I thought my digging techniques were sound after all; that our La Perra technique of stripping actual strata from a vertical face was correct for digging caves where one wanted to reconstruct the paleoethnography of an actual temporally discrete occupation; and that digging in arbitrary levels was unwarranted for any reasons. I also remember thinking that my archaeological survey techniques were horrible! Oh yes, I found lots of sites in Pope and Massac County, Illinois, as well as many others in Tamaulipas, but this was just a question of lots of hard work and a bit of luck. There had to be a better way. Looking out the cracked window of Ingraham's Hotel in Yellowknife seemed to be a perfect place to start: if I could develop survey techniques to find sites here then one could find them anywhere.

My other retrospective thoughts were about my analysis. The sort of typology for setting up a chronology which I had learned from "Poppa" Cole, Johnny Bennett, Jimmy Griffin, Jim Ford, and more recently Alex Krieger, was fine and good, but that Ivy Leaguer, Walt Taylor, was right—there should be more to archaeology than just chronology. What about all those bones, plant remains, shells, and bottles of dirt that I had left in Mexico? Wouldn't they have much to tell about ancient environments and subsistence systems? I reasoned that when I was later in Ottawa, I would somehow find some experts to work on them, and then I would take their data and mine and put it together into a full report. This seemed like an inefficient way to do things, and I can remember thinking at that time the whole system of archaeological work—dig now, analyze later—was just plain wrong, and that maybe someday I would try to think up a better way.

Dating of Canyon Diablo finds

The next couple of years in Ottawa were busy ones: I not only worked for the National Museum of Canada, but I found time to get my Panuco report written and to contact lots of experts about the Canyon Diablo materials. But, unfortunately, the materials still were in Mexico. One bottle of carbon that I had given Helmut de Terra had been sent to Dr. Willard Libby who, with his new Carbon 14 technique, had dated it 658 years ago ± 150. This seemed impossible for the oldest corn!! So I wrote Libby, asking about the provenience of the specimens, and, sure enough, de Terra had sent him the bottle from the top deposits with late Los Angeles ceramics and none of the earlier bottles. Further, Libby said he would be glad to date the others if I could get them to him.

On my winter vacation I went off to Mexico City at my own expense. Although Jose Luis Lorenzo helped me, the botanical specimens were not hard to find, for there they were sitting in the same spot in a corner of the Viking Fund Laboratory, in the same boxes just as I had left them. Lorenzo soon found the boxes of bottles elsewhere, and they were intact except for one compartment labelled "Late—not important," which was empty and, of course, the one sent to Libby.

Next, there was the task of getting a permit to export these materials, but this was no problem for "Nogie," Dr. Eduardo Noguera, who was head of Monumentos Prehispánicos of the Instituto, and was, like myself, a friend of "Jaime" Griffin—and in Mexico there is the time-worn adage that any friend of his is a friend of mine. Getting the specimens back for redistribution to the correct experts was not very difficult, although there was one comical moment when the U.S. Customs man in Miami, with good bureaucratic sampling techniques, gingerly picked out a large well-formed, 4000 year old, human fecal specimen—interdisciplinary studies hung in the balance!

By the time I left for the field in Canada in May of 1951, all the specimens had been redistributed to the correct experts. When I returned to Edmonton at the end of September I found a telegram from Chicago, which said, "Your corn has a radiocarbon date of 4445 years ago ± 280." Another letter from Mangelsdorf in Cambridge contained the statement, "Yours is the most primitive corn yet found in Mexico. When can you come to Cambridge?" My response was joyous. I grabbed all the letters and walked across the street to the Canadian National telegraph office and sent the words of Libby's telegram to Mangelsdorf, sent Mangelsdorf's message about corn to Libby, and sent the texts of both to Dr. Alcock, Director of the National Museum with a request for permission to go to Cambridge.

The next morning my ex-wife, June, and I were in Dr. Mangelsdorf's office at the Botanical Museum putting the corn specimens in chronological and stratigraphic order, for "these pine cones" had been badly jumbled by United States Customs. As I was sorting out the cobs by square and level, Paul Mangelsdorf asked, "Do you know anything about botany?" I answered honestly "not much," as archaeologists in U.S. institutions spend much of their time learning phonemics, personality and culture, esoteric kinship systems, and strange customs of primitive peoples. As a consequence, they do not have time for frills like botany, zoology, pollen analysis, soils, and geology—all fields they will have to use. Paul's next statement was, "Well, you have put the cobs into a precise evolutionary sequence."

The rest of the morning and afternoon Paul Mangelsdorf and I spent examining the specimens—he would ask me about them and explain to me what they meant. A number of times he even ventured to say that we ought to find more specimens like these.

At tea time late in the afternoon we finally took a break, feeling pretty pleased with ourselves. But Paul was still serious, particularly about my returning to Tamaulipas to get more corn specimens and about our starting a long-term archaeological-botanical program to solve the whole corn problem. Where was it domesticated? When was it domesticated? What was its wild ancestor really like? I realized finally that he was serious and I told him quite frankly that, while I was pretty sure there were more caves with corn in Tamaulipas, it might take two or three years to find them and that it might take a lot of money—say, twenty thousand dollars to guarantee it. Mangelsdorf insisted that money was no problem, and that I should start setting up some plans and figuring out ways to get free time from the National Museum of Canada.

That night I couldn't sleep. I sought out a typewriter and paper and began to outline a third Tamaulipas corn-hunting project. First of all, we would get some decent equipment, including a couple of good jeeps so we could really survey. We would survey southern Tamaulipas with the help of good, eager, graduate students with the survey techniques I had developed in northern Canada. When we found the good caves with corn—and I was certain we would —then we would excavate them with the La Perra Cave horizontal natural layer stripping from a vertical face technique. We also would run a laboratory, and from our laboratory tables we would make policy decisions about the digging program. Also, we would line up our specialists *beforehand.*

I paused with my typing, then pressed on, thinking about someone in Canada currently working on the La Perra feces who would be good; or of a zoologist, or ecologist, named Paul Martin who ought to be helpful. We should get someone from Paul Sears to work on the pollen; De Witt from Geological Survey of Canada could work on the soils...We would get money for a whole mess of carbon dates—like twelve! Paul could get a young student botanist like C. Earle Smith who was working on the La Perra remains, to handle the general botany, and Paul would handle the corn. Then, there would be a year to finish the analysis and write up the report.

I pecked away at the typewriter, tore up sheets, rewrote them, and finally I finished and sat back to reread them about 7:30 A.M.—just in time for breakfast. Bill Caudill and his wife Susan, with whom I was staying, discussed my proposal, and by 8:30 A.M. it was ready and, shortly thereafter, on Paul Mangelsdorf's desk.

Mangelsdorf and I talked further about corn and the project and then, about 10:00 Paul pulled out application blanks to research foundations and we began filling them out.

The Third Sierra de Tamaulipas Project

The year, 1952, was one in which I performed my normal Canadian archaeological duties, filled out project application blanks, waited for money to come through, and got ready for the third Tamaulipas project.

By the end of November, 1953, all was finally ready and we took off. I had two good jeeps and two better companions. Peter Grant was a 70-year-old amateur from Manitoba who had worked with me there on survey and, because of his long years in the bush, caught on quickly to survey techniques. Dave Kelley was a bright young Harvard graduate student, willing to give his all and full of wonderfully provocative ideas.

We worked hard throughout much of December and found many sites, although not the kind of dry cave we were looking for. Fortunately, there was a reference in my preparatory notes to a cave in Canyon Infiernillo in the Sierra Madre in southwest Tamaulipas. Here, in 1937, Javier Romero and Juan Valenzuela had found mummies and preserved materials in their tests. I cross-checked my notes and noted that the climate was right in this region for preservation of ancient food remains for it was so dry that even the bacteria of decay which would destroy such could not live and what is more, it geologically had a good possibility for many caves. We sought out Don Ignacio Guerra who lived in our territory and who had been Romero's and Valenzuela's guide, catching him finally at his ranch near Ocampo celebrating Christmas. We had a glass or two of his fiery mescal, explained our interest in the caves he had reported to Romero long ago, and before nightfall we were making plans to visit the caves the next day. Since we had only planned a visit to the caves we were ill-prepared for the memorable days ahead.

The Caves in Canyon Infiernillo

The first day of our journey to the caves we rode some thirty miles on horseback. This was particularly trying for us as we were not accustomed to the wooden saddles of the mountain rancheros. Worse still, it was cold and rainy that night, and we were without tents or waterproof sleeping bags. Next day we survived another fifteen miles and then we camped in an uncomfortable shelter on the mountain top, reputedly just above the cave. We searched in vain all the next day for the trail to the cave, but the thick, thorny brush had overgrown the trail since 1937. That night two local ranchers saw our fire, dropped in for a visit and immediately recognized Don Ignacio as that famous revolutionary (bandido?) leader. They knew about the caves and said that they would help us find them the next day. Although I had some doubts about this, as well as about the characters of these well-armed men, Don Ignacio assured me they were reliable. He then served up a mighty draught of mescal and put his faithful thirty-eight automatic under his pillow, and we went to sleep.

In the morning the ranchers returned and took us to two magnificent caves, which looter holes revealed as having beautiful stratigraphy with abundant preserved plant remains. We had found what we sought way ahead of schedule. Now we could start our excavations, set up our field laboratory, and maybe find a few more good caves in our spare time.

After a month or so of preparation, Dave Kelley, Peter Grant, and still another student, Peter Pratt, and I began excavation in Romero's Cave (Tc 247). It was unbelievable, for there were seventeen beautifully stratified layers, with not only lots of artifacts, but literally tons of preserved remains—baskets, mats, whittled sticks, string, feces, and plant remains. We used our La Perra technique and it worked like a charm, but we began to notice new significant information that was to modify our digging techniques and our recording of data.

As we stripped off our floors, it became apparent that there were concentrations of certain kinds of artifacts on different parts of the floor. For instance, on Floor II, the chips and cores were mainly over on the squares to the southeast, the wood artifacts and whittled sticks in three squares to the northeast, and the mats and string around the fireplace in the center. In other words, the people who had been busy doing different things on the cave floor were doing them in different areas of the floor. Our recording of artifacts by five foot squares was just not exact enough, and we would have to record them by sub-square or by their actual *in situ* location if we were ever going to work out the exact nature of the tool kits for the various activities. This meant that we should be making (besides those traditional cross-sectional drawings of the vertical profiles of the stratigraphy) rather exact floor plans of each floor, as we dug it. When we started doing this, it became apparent that the feet and inches system for recording was very cumbersome; next time we would use the metric system.

Gradually, our companions learned my digging techniques. Later, we dug Valenzuela's Cave (Tc 248), which had nine stratified layers, and then much later, we excavated Ojo de Agua Cave with its twelve stratified zones. Meanwhile, Peter Pratt and I went to the southern part of the Sierra de Tamaulipas to do survey, and with our improved survey techniques we found more good caves and we set to work digging them.

The digging was proceeding well and we were to find lots of artifacts in beautiful stratigraphy. I was, however, still doing too many things at once—survey today, Peter's digs in Sierra de Tamaulipas for the next three days, then a glance at the laboratory, then off to Dave Kelley's digs for a few days, and in between times doing accounts, buying supplies, and getting things shipped off to experts.

Gradually, it dawned on me that my problems were not technical, but basically organizational. Eventually, I put the accounting and supply problems onto Peter Grant. This worked fairly well, but what I obviously needed was a full-time administrator who spoke Spanish and knew the local region. June began to look after the lab, but time was still mainly spent doing cataloging and putting numbers on washed specimens. What I also needed was a full-time trained specialist in archaeological analysis with whom I could spend considerable time working on crucial problems that would help direct the digging operations in progress.

In spite of these administrative and laboratory problems we did, however, work out a sequence of nine archaeological phases from 7000 B.C. to 1750 A.D. (with a few gaps in it, of course) and these phases were associated with abundant plant remains. Somewhat to our surprise, our Sierra Madre corn was of a different primitive type—Bat Cave or Pre-Chapalate race—and not really as old as our Primitive Nal-tel race from the Sierra de Tamaulipas. Furthermore, we found gourds and pumpkins far older than corn—in the Infiernillo phase from roughly 7000 to 5500 B.C. With this same complex were wild runner beans and some chili peppers. Also, older than maize were common beans (*Phaseolus vulgaris*) found in the Ocampo phase, dating from 4000 to 2300 B.C. During the Flacco phase, 2300 to 1800 B.C. amaranth and corn were added to these domesticates while cotton and warty squashes (*Cucurbita moschata*) came after them in the Guerra phase, 1800 to 1400 B.C. Teocentli, that important relative of maize, appeared in Mesa de Guaje from 1200 to 800 B.C. Walnut squash (*Cucurbita mixta*), manihot, and lima beans first appeared in Palmillas times, 300 to 800 A.D. No new domesticates were added in the final phases, San Lorenzo, 900 to 1300 A.D. or San Antonio from 1300 to 1750 A.D. Obviously, these various data meant that there were multiple origins of Mesoamerican agriculture happening at different times in different places.

As far as the interdisciplinary projects were concerned, they really didn't yet function in the field, and most of the pertinent specimens did not get to the specialists until the following season when we were making the final analyses of the materials. Even then the cross-disciplinary collaboration wasn't working out very well. *Why not?* Well, first of all, the specialists for the most part understood very little about our archaeological phases and even less about our archaeological techniques or the archaeological contexts of the specimens they were studying. Second, most of the specialists had never seen the cave environments, let alone collected their kinds of specimens from that specific environment or micro-environment. And finally, except for the corn, this was not a cooperative endeavor between the archaeologists and the specialists. The specialists were simply doing a job for the archaeologists and taking time from their busy careers in their own fields and getting few rewards. Obviously, a whole new approach was needed. In 1954, I wasn't sure what it should be, but I was determined to find a new way.

By and large the only interdisciplinary study that was really working was the collaboration with Mangelsdorf on the corn studies. Some specimens for some specialists did get identified and analyzed. And Jimmy Griffin did obtain a dozen Carbon 14 dates from the Michigan laboratory for dating our sequence. With the corn studies, however, our new evidence from southwest Tamaulipas was of a negative sort. During the year of my Guggenheim fellowship at Harvard, Paul Mangelsdorf and I talked at length about this problem, and concluded that the earliest maize remains now available, dating from between 2000 and 3000 B.C., (from two areas of Tamaulipas, and from Swallows Cave in northwest Mexico and Bat Cave in the Southwest) were all probably *north* of the center of origin of corn. Therefore, corn must have been domesticated well before 3000 B.C.—and there was no Neolithic revolution, but a Neolithic evolution. But the question was, how far south? Could it be that it really came from Peru, as Mangelsdorf and Reeves had conjectured a long time ago? Well, I was the practical field man who could find dry caves, and my answer was "How about looking somewhere between Peru and Mexico?" What about Honduras, which had some dry areas and where people working at Copan had reported caves? Or, perhaps the Zacapa Valley of Guatemala which Kidder had reported as being very dry? This seemed like a good idea to Paul and myself. We, therefore, applied for a small grant to the American Philosophical Society, which in the past had always generously supported us.

In 1958 I went to Honduras to look at caves around Copan. I found good caves with no preservation, and no Preceramic; so I went on to Tegucigalpa where I found good caves, some Preceramic, and no preservation. At Comayagua I found poor caves, some plant preservation, and no Preceramic.

The Zacapa Valley

After this discouraging journey, I moved into the Zacapa Valley of Guatemala with about the same results. In the high part of the valley in the tropical rain forest, plant preservation was impossible, although there were lovely caves; whereas in the dry bottom of the valley where preservation was possible, and where we did find Preceramic remains, there were no caves!

I decided at this point to try a little further north in Chiapas on the border of Guatemala where caves had been reported, and where one cave near Cintalapa, Chiapas had yielded in 1947 a preserved textile. Thus, in 1959, after a brief exploration around Comitan and Cuidad de las Casas, where there were caves in a climate too wet for preservation, I decided to try one named Santa Marta which Fred Peterson had found near Ocozocoautla.

It was a huge cave, and Peterson's initial test, as I read it, indicated there were stratified Preceramic layers. He had a beautifully preserved bone and I thought perhaps there might be a few patches of preserved plant remains. Anyway, Gareth Lowe of the New World Archaeological Foundation was willing to fund us for a couple of weeks of site testing and he was willing to provide all the equipment as well as skilled archaeological laborers. An important by-product of these Chiapas endeavors was the discovery of Fred Peterson. He was not only an efficient administrator, but he had lived in Mexico for fifteen years and thought more like a Mexican than most Mexicans. In addition, he was trained in archaeology. Here was the person to solve the kind of logistics problems which had plagued us in Tamaulipas in 1953.

Santa Marta Cave

The stratigraphy of the cave was almost perfect and we found ten stratified layers, five of which contained many Preceramic tools and bones, which dated from between 7000 and 3500 B.C. But more important to the corn problem than discovering these first Preceramic remains in southern Mexico was the pollen profile which showed corn pollen in the upper five strata but none in the ones older than 3500 B.C. Corn, therefore, was no older in the south than it was in the excavations in northern Mexico. In fact, it seemed that Chiapas was too far south while our earlier studies suggested that northern Mexico was north of the original center of domestication. But at least we were narrowing down the north-south perimeters of where the origins of agriculture might have begun. We also now had Sears' studies of pollen from the Valley of Mexico which showed domesticated maize there as early as 4000 B.C. Therefore, we could push the northern border still further south. And there were other facts to help us, for Paul's studies of our archaeological corn indicated that the wild ancestor probably was a highland grass that might have flourished best in a dry environment. A brief study of the maps of the area between Mexico City and Chiapas only revealed three major high dry valleys. These were southern Oaxaca, Tehuacan in southern Puebla, and the Rio Balsas in eastern Guerrero. We decided to go there next.

Oaxaca Caves

I'd been in Oaxaca many times and had seen some caves. At the end of the 1959 Chiapas season we had actually stayed overnight in Tehuacan and had even crawled into a couple of caves on our way into town. On this brief first visit to Tehuacan I had been pleased to see an old friend of mine from my visit in Yucatan, Ricardo Gutierrez, now the assistant manager of the Hotel Peñafiel. Around Christmas of 1960 after a brief but unsuccessful look around Mitla in Oaxaca for caves I returned to Tehuacan to see Gutierrez. He then arranged for Luis Vasquez, the director of the Museo de la Revolución Puebla, to help me in my search. Vasquez and a willing amateur archaeologist, Juan Armenta, equipped me with tools, camping baggage, assorted information about Tehuacan and, of course, those necessary letters of introduction to all the local Tehuacan authorities. Also, they lent me their museum's proudest possession, "el monstruo," a 1949 U.S. Army commando truck. This turned out to be a good vehicle—once the gardening crew of the hotel and I started it every morning by pushing it from its hilltop perch in front of the Hotel Peñafiel. With a little bit of luck it would run all day, almost anywhere, and through and over almost any kind of trail.

The first foray, in the company of a bored lieutenant from the Tehuacan army barracks who had been commanded to guard me, was along the highway between Chazumba and Huajuapan de Leon, in Oaxaca. In this early January trip we visited sixteen caves, but all were in volcanic deposits too porous to allow for the preservation of vegetal material. Four other caves south of Huajuapan, near the Pan-American Highway, were equally unproductive. A second trip, this time with a very perplexed sergeant, netted four caves near Zapotitlan in Puebla and one just past Tequixtepec, Oaxaca. The latter, and another one near Zapotitlan, had indications of stratigraphy and possibly preserved organic remains, but both were very small. Other visits, in the company of a sleepy army private, located five caves near El Riego just north of Tehuacan; three others just northeast of Tehuacan along the highway to Veracruz, and three more one kilometer south of Tehuacan. All had possibilities, but they were not ideal for the finding of early corn for they were either too moist for plant preservation or did not have deposits that were old enough.

After looking at some thirty-six sites without apparent success, I was beginning to get a little discouraged, but I still had "an ace in the hole." Luis Vasquez had collected a series of forms which had been filled out by the local school teachers of Puebla and three of these mentioned caves in the general area of Tehuacan. One form indicated a cave near Altepexi and another east of Ajalpan, both of which I visited at last without any military assistance. They revealed little of interest.

Ajuereado Cave

The final cave called Ajuereado was said to be located south of a town called Coxcatlan, and it was recorded on one of Vasquez's forms that had been filled out by a local school teacher, señorita Martíñez. On the 21st of January she arranged for a guide, Pablo Bolanos, and her brother, Hector Martíñez, to take me to this cave some 10 kilometers south of Coxcatlan along the edge of the mountains. After a hot, sweltering walk through the mesquite, we arrived at the cave. Even from a distance it appeared to have exciting possibilities—in fact, I felt that this was it! The cave was very wide and was on a cliff facing north. The surface collection, including 5000 to 10,000 year old artifacts, the rock shelter's size, and the vegetal material which turned up from under the covering layer of goat dung all indicated that this was a site that had to be tested.

From January 21st to January 27th the three of us, Pablo, Hector and I, tested this cave. We dug, by trowel, a 2.0 meter by 2.0 meter square to a depth of about 2.0 meters. This hole was located in back of a large rock roughly in the center of the cave and all the material we uncovered by trowel was taken out by bucket and put through a half-inch mesh screen. Slowly but surely, we peeled off the occupation layers and different strata. Starting at the top we had some Post-classic Period pottery remains. Under this layer we found some Classic Period debris underlain, in turn, by a little Formative Period material. Then came a sterile layer and then a thick dark layer which was obviously Preceramic. Just after lunch, on the 27th, Pablo stood up from his digging in the lower layer, reached over and dropped a tiny corn cob, onto my sorting screen.

Pablo had found the cob in the deepest and darkest corner of our test. Only half believing him, I got down in the hole, took his trowel and paint brush and began cleaning off the area he had pointed to.

After a couple of minutes I brushed out another tiny corn cob from the floor. I was beginning to sweat now, and before I started to dig again I looked at the wall of the stratigraphic cut to see if it might somehow be intrusive. Not possible. Clutching the tiny cob in my left hand, I started cleaning again, struck a small flat rock, cleaned around it, and there, sticking out from underneath the rock, was another cob. I stood up and told the men we were finished digging. They looked perplexed, so I said I'd pay them for the full week. We packed up everything. I dropped the workers in Coxcatlan, drove to Tehuacan, sent Mangelsdorf a telegram and then went to the bar of the Hotel Peñafiel to tell Ricardo all about it. The big push was on. We had found what we were looking for and this time, after all the years of doing the wrong things, we were going to run a project that was as perfect as I could manage.

After January 27th there was no more digging, but we explored the valley where we were about to start our intensive investigations. We also informed the authorities in Mexico City about our finds; and Jose Luis Lorenzo, who realized their importance, came down to visit us, saw Ajuereado Cave, and helped me plan my biggest project. Lorenzo was a great help, and continued to be for the next four years.

I went back to Ottawa, as my vacation was almost over, and then made a quick visit to Cambridge to show Paul Mangelsdorf my precious cobs. Mangelsdorf agreed that these were what we had been looking for, and we set about making specific plans for our big project. First, we sent a maize-associated carbon sample off to Michigan to see if it was as early as we thought. It dated at 3600 B.C. The next task was to line up our basic personnel. We obtained the services of Fred Peterson as our administrator and those of C. Earle Smith as botanist and Mike Fowler as archaeologist. In addition, I wrote to other specialists to see if and when they might be available to assist us.

What kind of organization could most successfully sponsor a project of this sort? We pondered if it should be an institution with many facilities and a large staff with experts we might use, or a small flexible institution with experience in such matters and the ability to call upon a wide variety of specialists from other institutions. I decided the latter was perhaps the better choice and the ideal type of institution of this sort was found to be the Robert S. Peabody Foundation for Archaeology. It had a long history of sponsoring well-defined programs such as the Southwestern Expedition which had investigated the ancient Pueblos of Pecos, and the Andover Harvard-Yukon Expedition, to name a few. Furthermore, the institution was interested in and capable of handling interdisciplinary programs such as they had done at the Boylston Street Fishweir, Grassy Island and Martha's Vineyard where botanists, zoologists, icthyologists, pollen men, soil experts and geographers had worked with the archaeologists. The Foundation's record of publishing the results of such endeavors was very well-known. Its staff, headed by Douglas S. Byers, as Director, and Frederick Johnson, curator, had the ability to administer an enterprise of this magnitude. During discussions with them at the 1960 spring meeting of the Society for American Archaeology in New Haven, we agreed to set about making plans for financing the expedition for a three-year period. I was appointed a Research Associate of the Robert S. Peabody Foundation for Archaeology by Mr. John Kemper, then Headmaster of Phillips Academy, Andover, Massachusetts.

Our plan was submitted to the U.S. National Science Foundation in September of 1960 while I was doing my field work duties for the National Museum of Canada in the Yukon. I say "our" plan for, in actual fact, while I knew roughly what I wanted to do, it was Fred Johnson who taught me how to present a proposal in an organized and acceptable form. This was a final part of my archaeological education that eventually paid off in rather handsome dividends. In brief, the proposal described our main problem as the "Investigation of the Development of Agriculture and Concomitant Rise of Civilization in Mesoamerica." The area of research was the Tehuacan Valley and we proposed to use an interdisciplinary approach. In December, we were notified that we had received our grant. And on January 1, 1961, the Tehuacan Archaeological-Botanical Project officially began.

What we did after this date, and what we found has been described in detail in our five volumes published by the University of Texas Press, and there is also a series of articles which summarize our findings (see References). Thus, there is little point in reiterating this sort of information, Rather, I would like to reflect on some of our activities in a retrospective and somewhat critical manner.

Retrospection on the Tehuacan Project

I shall first consider the *reconnaissance*. Fred Peterson, later assisted by Jim Neely and Dick Woodbury, found 456 sites in a survey area of some 1500 square miles. We netted about 504 site components that can be identified as to type of settlement, as well as to chronological phase or subphase. In addition, many of these identified sites had sherds and artifacts of other periods indicating almost an equal number of indeterminate occupations. Thus, in all, we had materials from over 1000 occupations. Within our limited area, this seemed an adequate sample for settlement pattern studies, as well as for selecting stratified sites to dig. Obviously, more sites would have been welcome, particularly on the Preceramic and Early Man levels; and more extensive use of aerial photographs, as well as better notes on site locations and site dimensions, would have enhanced our survey data. Collection by areal units on sites might have been useful, but I'm afraid the use of "Binford's dog leash" technique in mesquite filled canyon country would have been a disaster.

However, in spite of these limitations we did find twelve stratified sites that, upon excavation, yielded the first 12,000-year long unbroken cultural sequence for the New World. Later we were to discover that relationships between occupations in each of our five micro-environments were of key importance in the understanding of the development of agriculture. In view of this, we should have dug enough sites in each micro-environment to have provided a complete sequence of occupation in each. Even so, as it turned out, our own serious excavation gaps were for the Preceramic in the center valley steppe micro-environment and for the Formative Period in the El Riego micro-environment.

Our survey, in terms of yielding information for settlement pattern data, was also less than perfect. Although most of Peterson's notes were useful in this realm, our best information came from Jim Neely's resurveying. This was done after we had worked out our artifact and ceramic sequences which allowed us to classify most sites as to phase or subphase. We then selected four or five sites representing a range of settlement types for each of the ceramic subphases and sent Jim back to map them. His Brunton compass maps of these fifty or so sites are surprisingly accurate, but some could have been greatly enhanced by locally made aerial photographs, either in black and white, or infra-red; more detailed descriptions and photographs could have been collected on architectural features; and surface collections could have been made for each structure or significant area of the sites. The coding of this information and feeding of it into a computer for factor analysis would have been an aid to us in our interpretation. However, all of this would have at least doubled our expenditures! Furthermore, at the time, this was not considered to be within our "early agriculture" problem. Most of such settlement data would have pertained to the ceramic periods. Perhaps some day someone interested in the problem of these later periods will do the job we really should have done.

A discussion of our survey leads directly to a consideration of our *excavations*. While Mike Fowler, Angel Garcia Cook and Fred Peter-

TABLE 1
Basic Stratigraphic Sequences of Tehuacan Caves

Venta Salada	1500+ A.D.– 700 A.D.
Palo Blanco	700 A.D.– 150 B.C.
Santa Maria	150 B.C.– 850 B.C.
Ajalpan	850 B.C.–1500 B.C.
Purron	1500 B.C.–2300 B.C.
Abejas	2300 B.C.–3400 B.C.
Coxcatlan	3400 B.C.–5000 B.C.
El Riego	5000 B.C.–6800 B.C.
Ajuereado	6800 B.C.–about 10,000 B.C.

son did a great job of implementing and augmenting the cave digging methods I had developed long ago in Tamaulipas, we still made some mistakes, such as mislabelling strata in the final excavation in the east end of Coxcatlan Cave. We also made mistakes in our system of paying for artifacts found *in situ*. But, fortunately, these errors were corrected. A study of the profiles caught the former error, and the firing of the workman who was caught "discovering" the wrong type of artifacts from stratigraphically inconsistent layers, corrected the latter. Basically the stratigraphic sequence derived from our excavations is listed in Table l. So, the very fact that we have such a long sequence speaks favorably of our cave excavations.

Unfortunately, our excavations of open sites did not come up to such high standards. First, because we didn't do enough of them, and second, because what we did do was too limited. The two El Riego open sites, as well as the Coxcatlan open site, were just tests, while in one open Abejas component and the Abejas pit house site only small areas were excavated. The notes and digging techniques for these sites were acceptable, but we could not approach any very complete picture of the way of life of the people who lived during these occupations. At the Formative sites of Ajalpan, Canoas and Coatepec East, our notes were almost as good and our excavation techniques revealed good stratigraphy, but somehow we didn't uncover clear evidence concerning living features. In Coatepec West and Quachilco, both of late Santa Maria times, we not only didn't uncover any kind of living features, but our field notes left much to be desired. This is equally true for the two Venta Salada tests Tr 62 and Tr 65. Although I dug few of these sites personally, and even allowed two of them to be dug when I was away in the Yukon, it is my responsibility that they weren't dug better. My interests were with the plant remains in the caves so *my* cave diggers received the most supervision, with the work in the open sites being somewhat slighted.

Fortunately, these open sites and many more in the survey, are still available for excavation. Again, I hope someone with other interests will dig them more completely, perhaps getting more data about habitations, architectural features, the function of the various structures, as well as their arrangements, and, of course, information about various aspects of the social life of the ancient inhabitants. Burial grounds and tombs which we noted in survey and which we avoided consciously because of the local looting it might have caused, also would have provided much valuable information. It follows that there is much still to be excavated in the Tehuacan Valley, but I feel our sins were mainly ones of omission rather than ones of commission.

Retrospection on Interdisciplinary Studies

What were the results of our interdisciplinary studies? These studies, which had been so poorly organized in our Tamaulipas work, were vastly different because our approach was different. This resulted from considerable soul searching on the part of Mangelsdorf and myself. Also, I had discussed the matter of interdisciplinary research coordination at some length with both Dr. A.V. Kidder, and, more recently, with Frederick Johnson of the R.S. Peabody Foundation. Dr. Kidder, who besides having been the man who gently turned me down when I was thirteen years old for a job as waterboy for his digs in Yucatan, had been head of the long-term archaeological research program at the Carnegie Institution in the Maya area. This had been a reasonably successful multi-disciplinary project, and the contributions of the various specialists had sometimes had considerable relevance to the archaeological aspects of the dig.

Kidder's problem, however, had been one of integration and coordination. And although the "multi-disciplinary" approach had much to be said for it, philosophically, it was very different from the "interdisciplinary approach" of Frederick Johnson. Johnson's attack was more problem oriented. He conceived of bringing a group of scientists together to attack a single problem, such as peoples' relationship to their environment in a particular time or place. In this frame of reference the data derived from each specialized field was coordinated in such a way as to lead to its solution. Indirectly, of course, the "spin-off" might become a major contribution to the specific, non-archaeological field. In the Tehuacan endeavors we attempted to use Johnson's "interdisciplinary" approach in combination with some of Kidder's "multi-disciplinary" features.

In Tehuacan, we scheduled our specialists so that they came to the field (usually at our expense), alone or in small groups, relatively late in the season or after our excavation programs were underway. At the outset, they were given a grand tour of our area. Sites and archaeological finds were reviewed, and our problems explained to them in considerable detail. This was a sort of brain-washing, albeit, not only making sure they understood the problems that concerned both of us, but helping to show them the kinds and contexts of archaeological data that were to be studied by each. Next, they could "do their thing" with us, being provided with living facilities at the fine old Hotel Peñafiel, charmingly hosted by Ricardo. We even provided transportation and, if necessary, guides—bilingual, trilingual, or otherwise. All data which fell directly into their own specialized fields was theirs to use, analyze and publish as they saw fit. Finally, after they had thoroughly surveyed and gathered the data pertinent to their own special fields, we gave them our relevant specimens for identification and study in a coordinated attack on our mutual problems—such as the origins of agriculture, the ancient relationships of people to their environment, or the various relationships between cultural and subsistence systems. Their results in these identifications and studies were eventually published in the final Tehuacan reports.

Interdisciplinary endeavors in the Tehuacan Valley on the problem of the origin of agriculture were generally successful, with Mangelsdorf and Galinat studying the corn, L. Kaplan the beans, Stephens the cotton, Whittaker and Cutler the cucurbits, Callen the feces, and C. Earle Smith working on the more general botany. Although more studies of pollen, soils, and other specific domesticates would have added wider dimensions to our studies, the flaws and weaknesses in what we did lay largely in the coordination of the various results. Again, I accept the blame and responsibility for these, since I was in Calgary, Alberta, Canada trying to set up a New World Department of Pre-historic Archaeology rather than personally coordinating the data. As a consequence coordination often fell into the hands of editors of our volumes. A better arrangement would have been a series of conferences among the specialists involved, directed by myself—the archaeologist in charge.

The problem of the evolution of the Tehuacan subsistence systems was closely allied to those of agricultural origins. Obviously, much of the botanical data was also relevant to this, but in addition we had the fine zoological information amassed by Kent Flannery, as well as the studies of irrigation by Woodbury and Neely. I attempted to coordinate these data in terms of three general categories: sustenance, food preparation, and subsistence activities. In the sustenance section we studied the wild and cultivated plant remains, as well as the bones from many of the floors, and this information was transposed into bulk units of edible foods—liters of wild and domesticated plants, and liters of wild animal meat and domesticated meat.

The general trends obtained by these means revealed significant subsistence trends. In El Riego times, at about 6000 B.C., about 5 percent of the food came from cultivated plants; 40 percent from wild plants; and 55 percent from meat. This contrasted to Abejas times, at about 3000 B.C., where food was obtained as follows: 21 percent from cultivated plants; 49 percent from wild plants; and 30 percent from meat. These trends continued, ending up with 75 percent coming from agricultural produce; 8 percent from wild plants; and 17 percent from meat for the end of the Venta Salada phase at the time of the Spanish Conquest. Although this pattern can be said to be generally correct, there is little doubt that this type of information could have been presented in a much more sophisticated manner by cooperation with specialists in the field of nutrition.

In attempting to estimate changes in methods of preparing food, we again used this bulk refuse data, but now in conjunction with information derived from coprolite studies, and with inferences from artifacts that ethnographically were used in food preparation. Again, these trends, from the roasting or steaming of meat, the milling of seeds, and the eating of raw plant materials to an emphasis on the baking of tortillas, the fine grinding of corn, and the boiling of food, were demonstrated. In all of this, however, I freely admit that a greater use of ethnographic information from the area would have improved our analysis.

On a higher level of abstraction, we attempted to reconstruct changes in subsistence activities using archaeological foodstuffs and the associated artifacts that seemed connected with food-obtaining activities. Again, I believe the shift from hunting, trapping, seed and leaf collecting, on a seasonally scheduled basis in the early part of our sequence, to full-time agriculture, on a year-round basis, is valid. However, our quantification of these trends was admittedly naive. Ideally, a study of this sort ought to be based on some sort of energy input-output basis—such as man hours involved in the various subsistence activities, either seasonally or annually. This would allow us to work with a systems theory framework that would be more amenable to making scientific generalizations. In the studies of subsistence in Tehuacan we were pioneering, and obviously later studies will greatly augment our efforts.

Our interdisciplinary efforts in attacking the problem of peoples' relationship to their environment, as well as our attempts at the reconstruction of ancient environments was hardly a new endeavor; and from many standpoints, I don't think our answers were as good as the ones derived from our pioneering effort just discussed. However, the description of the overall region was well done, not only by the botanists and zoologists, but also by Brunet, our geologist, and by Byers with his study of geography and climate. Unfortunately, studies of soils and a more in-depth study of geomorphology were not undertaken. Nevertheless, what we did do was an adequate job and was done cooperatively.

Our definition of the micro-environments, or the environmental zones within our more general region, was equally good, although done in a somewhat different manner. The initial delimiting of these environmental zones was made by Jim Schoenwetter of Arizona State museum after only about a week's study of the region. It was a beautifully intuitive job. Later, his botanied zones were modified and more fully described by Kent Flannery of the University of Michigan who added zoological data to their formulation. Although the five environmental zones these scientists came up with are extremely useful as they are, and perhaps might not significantly change with further study, I believe a broader methodological approach might be applied in further micro-zone definitions. This would incorporate climatological soil, and geomorphological data, as well as those from botany and zoology. Perhaps such studies could lead to more detailed conclusions on the paleo-ecological record or the shifting of the environmental zones through the periods of human occupation of the Tehuacan Valley. Based mainly on our present zoological and botanical data from the cave floors, only one major environmental change is discernible at present—that between the Pleistocene and Recent. Even here the boundaries of the micro-environments in the final phase of the Pleistocene have not been worked out. No changes, even minor ones, have been noted within the Recent period, and because of the highly selective refuse evidence it has been assumed that there were none. This hypothesis should be tested by pollen examinations, analyses of the land snails, and studies of the orthogenesis of some of the buried soils. Pollen and land snail studies were attempted by us during our Tehuacan endeavor but produced no results. The analyses of humic soils were unknown to us at that time.

One aspect of peoples' relationship to their environment was explored, but the results are still inconclusive. This concerned seasonality of our occupation and scheduling of human activities in certain environmental zones at certain seasons. Thanks to the efforts of

Carmen Cook, who collected data on present-day gathering and uses of wild plants, plus additional information from Smith, Flannery, Kaplan and Callen, we can tell the season of many cave occupations in many of the micro-environments throughout the whole sequence. From this we are gradually beginning to understand how the scheduling factor operated throughout our long sequence; this is of key importance in understanding how people domesticated plants and how, and perhaps why, their subsistence system changed. Unfortunately, some of these data have been misused in illustrating arguments on "systems theory" in archaeology; and, in retrospect, I feel there should have been more field research on these problems which would have precluded some of these misapplications of the data.

The final aspect of our studies concerned the reconstruction of the culture of the ancient inhabitants. These attempts were not interdisciplinary, but rather "intradisciplinary," for we attempted to bring ethnohistorical and social anthropological information to bear upon the interpretation of our archaeological finds, and these fields and archaeology are now clustered together under the uncomfortable rubric of anthropology. Perhaps the kindest thing I can say about these studies is that they were a disaster and have not yielded any very relevant information. Maybe one of these days, prehistoric archaeology in the New World will be outside the field of anthropology and then perhaps we will receive the sort of cooperation we never received when we were classified within that field!

But the final aspect of our Tehuacan project was the analysis of the materials in the field. Early in the first season, after survey was well underway, and Mike Fowler had started digging in Coxcatlan, specimens began piling up, and we appealed to Jose Luis Lorenzo to send somebody to run a laboratory. He sent us Antoinette Nelken, then a student in Mexico, originally from France. By the end of the week she had devised a catalog system, and soon specimens were being washed and numbered so that we could start preliminary analysis. No doubt, a cataloging using computer tape would have been better than our notebook, but it would have cost too much and probably taken so long that it would have held up out preliminary analysis. Also, within a short time, she transformed our storeroom in the front of our headquarters into a room of shelves with shoe boxes of specimens. It was clean, well-lit, had chairs and desks as well as large tables and our landlady even had the floor tiled. Better than that, by the time Angel Garcia had been digging in El Riego Cave there were projectile points from Coxcatlan Cave laid on the table by strata and a preliminary typology could begin. From then on I shuttled between the excavations, with their steadily improving digging techniques, and the laboratory, with its increasing number of typed lithic artifacts. By the end of the season we not only had a sequence of preliminary lithic types, but we were able to correlate the stratigraphy of the two excavations, as well as to define complexes of types. By the third season, Mary Hill Gilbert was typing a first draft of our monograph on the nonceramic artifacts. As important as knowing what we had was knowing what we didn't have and where the gaps were in our sequence. With this information we could plan where and what to dig next. In the second season, our chronological studies of the nonceramic artifacts worked even better, for now it was buttressed by Fred Johnson's program of Carbon 14 dating. This well-run and coordinated laboratory system was the primary reason we obtained a 12,000-year unbroken cultural sequence.

The other facet of our chronological analysis concerned our half-million ceramics, and it did not proceed in such an organized manner. In the preface of Volume III (MacNeish 1970) I have reviewed how and when we did these studies, which lasted from 1961 to 1968. I have also criticized our methods in particular and ceramic studies in general. What I wrote then still stands, we described a vast amount of pottery, which gave us a chronology, and it is a basis for further studies; but at best it must be considered an initial effort. Certainly another laboratory, devoted entirely to ceramics, would have greatly improved this study. I'm sure that advocates of the "new archaeology" might say that statistical formulae and the magic computer would have solved all our chronological-typological problems. Maybe some day they will; but, at present, our methods and techniques give the same result at much less expense.

Other analyses were concerned with the interpretation of the archaeological finds in terms of the lifestyles of the ancient inhabitants of Tehuacan. Relatively little of this kind of analysis had been completed, although two aspects of it—the reconstruction of the environment and of settlements and populations have been finished, and I have discussed these previously. Other research of this interpretive sort is still in process, and I might best discuss what we are attempting to do.

As a primary division, we have attempted a reconstruction of the way of life in the sites of each of our five micro-environments or localities. This means the stratigraphic excavations and tests in each locality are presented in the same chapter; and our discussion of each site is made in terms of short paleo-ethnographies of each occupational floor. Our population studies of each floor, which consider the size of the floor, numbers of fireplaces and activities as well as the seasonality of the occupation, are reasonably soundly inferred. Often we can estimate how many people occupied the floor and what season or seasons they lived there. Our reconstruction of the subsistence activities of the inhabitants with all their food remains and feces, as well as the tools they would use in subsistence activities is equally good although such reconstructions could have been improved if we had used some sort of Serinov microscopic photography technique, in conjunction with experimental archaeology, to interpret the nicks, scratches and polish on these tools.

Our reconstructions of weaving, bark-cloth making bone-tool making and woodworking, because of association of materials in activity areas are satisfactory; but our interpretation of flint knapping, hide working and the making of ground stone tools, leaves much to be desired. There is also good evidence for trade and commerce on some floors. Reconstruction of the various aspects of the social and religious life of the occupants of each floor is at best vague, speculative, and unsatisfactory. Here, I have the feeling that we need a whole new set of analytical techniques so that we can better tackle these problems. Perhaps well-planned computerized programs might help.

To conclude, it is our hope to synthesize the local chronologies of changing ways of life into a grand reconstruction of the changes that took place in the whole Tehuacan Valley, particularly with regard to those periods when agriculture began. This should allow us to form hypotheses about not only how, but why agriculture began. Future endeavors in other centers of agriculture should give us data to test these hypotheses, and even now we are working in Peru—the other center of plant domestications in the New World.

As of now, after all these years of work on the problem of how and why agriculture began, I see no final answers. I have the discouraging feeling that there is so much to do and so little time in which to do it. Perhaps I should be satisfied that, in a relatively limited time, we have amassed a vast amount of pertinent information, and that I have had a part in developing new and better techniques and methods for attacking this problem. After all, I should be able to say to myself that this is quite an accomplishment and then I should be willing to retire and be satisfied to let future researchers carry on the work and, perhaps, get the ultimate answers. Yet, I'm not willing to let them carry on without me—I'm just getting started!

References

MACNEISH, R. S.

1958 Preliminary Archaeological Investigations in the Sierra de Tamaulipas, Mexico. Transactions of the American Philosophical Society 48: 6.

1964 Ancient Mesoamerican Civilization. Science 193: 3606.

1971 Archaeological Synthesis of the Sierra. Middle American Handbook 11; 2, ch. 24.

1972 The Prehistory of the Tehuacan Valley: Chronology and Irrigation. Austin, University of Texas Press.

MACNEISH, R. S. AND BYERS, D. S.

1967 The Prehistory of the Tehuacan Valley: Environment and Subsistence. Austin, University of Texas Press.

MACNEISH, R. S.; BYERS, D. S.; NELKEN-TURNER, A. AND JOHNSON, I. W.

1967 The Prehistory of the Tehuacan Valley: Non-Ceramic Artifacts. Austin, University of Texas Press.

MACNEISH, R. S. AND KAPLAN, L.

1960 Prehistoric Bean Remains from Caves in the Ocampo Region, Mexico. Harvard University Botanical Museum Leaflets 19: 2.

MACNEISH, R. S.; MANGELSDORF, P. AND WILLEY, G.

1964 The Origin and Dispersal of Agriculture in Middle America. Middle American Handbook 1.

MACNEISH, R. S. AND PETERSON F.

1962 The Santa Marta Rock Shelter, Ocozocautla, Chiapas, Mexico. Papers of the New World Archaeological Foundation 14.

MACNEISH, R. S.; PETERSON, F. AND FLANNERY, K.

1970 The Prehistory of the Tehuacan Valley: Ceramics. Austin, University of Texas Press.

THE SUDAN

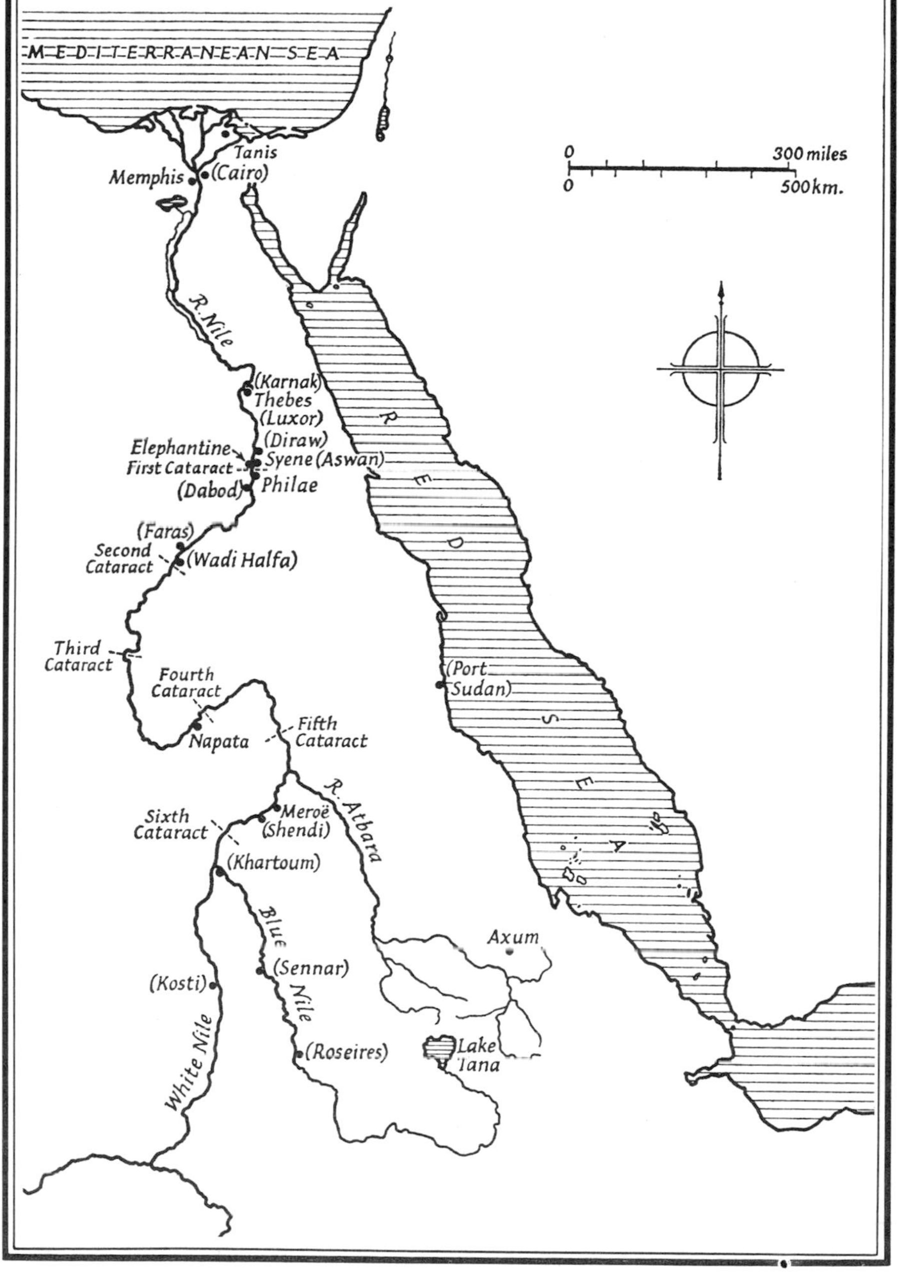

MEDITERRANEAN SEA
0 300 miles
0 500 km.
Tanis
Memphis
(Cairo)
R. Nile
(Karnak)
Thebes
(Luxor)
(Diraw)
Elephantine
Syene (Aswan)
First Cataract
Philae
(Dabod)
(Faras)
Second Cataract
(Wadi Halfa)
Third Cataract
Fourth Cataract
Napata
Fifth Cataract
R. Atbara
Sixth Cataract
Meroë
(Shendi)
(Khartoum)
Blue Nile
(Sennar)
(Kosti)
White Nile
(Roseires)
Lake Tana
Axum
(Port Sudan)
RED SEA

(preceding page)

Map of Nile Valley showing location of Meroe and other sites. From P. L. Shinnie, *Meroe.* (London: Thames and Hudson, Ltd. and New York: Frederick A. Praeger, Inc., 1967), p. 17.

Meroe in the Sudan

PETER L. SHINNIE

Background to Meroitic Culture

The town of ancient Meroe lies on the east bank of the Nile some 130 miles north of Khartoum, between the villages of Kijeik and Deragab, and two miles north of the market and railway station of Kabushiya. Meroe is to be distinguished from the modern town of Merowe, which lies far downstream.

Meroe contains all the components of an important ancient town—an area of royal residence, temples, mounds representing domestic occupation, traces of industrial activity, both iron working and pottery making, and both royal and commoners' cemeteries.

The site is in a region of semi-desert acacia scrub and short grassland with mean annual rainfall at present of about 100 millimeters, nearly all of which falls in the months of July and August. Temperatures range from a mean maximum of 87° F. in January to 109° F. in May and June. It is not infrequent for the rainfall to fail. In fact, during the years 1965 to 1970, in three years out of five the local inhabitants considered the rains to be inadequate to provide either sufficient grazing for their herds, or adequate moisture in the wadis, where in a year of normal or good rainfall considerable crops of sorghum are grown. The region is dependent on riverside irrigation for much of its crop growing, but less so than regions further north, where an almost complete lack of rain requires all agricultural land to be irrigated from the river—originally by simple lifting devices such as the counter-balanced pole (Arabic *shaduf*). This pole was complemented in about the third century B.C. by the wooden water wheel (Arabic *sagia*), driven by oxen, and in modern times by mechanical pumps.

The ancient town, which can be confidently identified with the town of Meroe—mentioned by a number of Greek and Latin writers—was the residence of a line of rulers, and the administrative center of a state of ancient Near Eastern type, stretching along the river Nile from a short way south of Aswan to at least as far as Sennar on the Blue Nile. The degree to which the state extended up the White Nile is not known, but can be assumed as far as Kosti. The chronological range of the culture represented at the town of Meroe is from about 750 B.C. to the fourth century A.D., with a received date of A.D. 350 for the end of the ruling dynasty. It is known that, at least further north, the main elements of the culture persisted for another hundred years or so, changing under the impact of new cultural influences from Egypt. One of these influences was Christianity, which began to penetrate the region during the fifth century A.D.

Terminology for the culture is somewhat confused, and it has been common to divide the period into two; Napatan and Meroitic, though sometimes the term Kushite, based on the Pharaonic Egyptian name for the region, Kush, has been used to encompass the whole period. The division between Napatan and Meroitic has been based on the assumption that the center of the country was originally at Napata, near where the earlier rulers were buried under mounds and pyramids. By about 300 B.C. royal burials were transferred to Meroe (the series of pyramids known in the literature as those of Begarawiya), though there is evidence from written documents that kings were living at the southern town for two hundred years or more before they were buried there. There has been considerable discussion as to the date at which the royal residence, or in modern terms the "capital," was transferred from Napata to Meroe. Argument about this date has provided one of the main talking points for the history of the time—the date currently most in favor is about 590 B.C.—during or just after the reign of King Aspelta. This view is largely based on evidence of an invasion as far as Napata by the Egyptian Pharaoh Psammetichus II in 591 B.C. and it has been suggested that military and economic reasons would have made a move to the south a sensible precaution. Aspelta's name is known from Meroe, but those of earlier rulers have also been found, and the presence of a name is not evidence of royal residence. The first mention of Meroe is in an inscription of a king, found in a temple at Kawa, a considerable distance to the north, and is dated in the second half of the fifth century B.C.

The argument concerning when the capital was transferred to Meroe has a certain air of unreality about it. No trace of a town at Napata has been found and, though the area was of an exceptionally sacred character, with the main temple of the state god, Amun, and royal cemeteries close by, there is no certainty that the royal house ever resided there. Since we know that Meroe was being occupied from at least as early as the eighth century B.C., it may be that it pre-dated Napata, and that the whole cultural and political development started from Meroe.

The main lines of Meroitic history have been known for some time. A skeleton chronology has been based on the excavation by Reisner, a distinguished American archaeologist, in the years 1916–1922 of all the known royal tombs in three main cemeteries (Kurru, Nuri, and Begarawiya). Reisner arranged these burial places in chronological order, based on a study of their location on the site, architectural features, and tomb contents. Generally his arrangement has stood up to several subsequent re-examinations, with only minor modifications. In many cases, inscriptions have provided the names of those buried, and on this basis Reisner compiled a list of rulers to which he attempted to give absolute dates. The close identification of the earlier rulers, such as Piankhy and Taharqa, with events in Egyptian history, with its firmly established chronology, made the dates of these kings reasonably accurate and formed a base line from which later dates could be calculated. Unfortunately there are only two approximate fixes in the whole period from about 700 B.C. to the middle of the fourth century A.D. And, since there is no certainty about the date of the last royal burial, the total period into which some sixty five to seventy rulers must be fitted still remains uncertain. Reisner assumed lengths of reign for individual rulers by using a fifteen year average, and then increasing the length of reign to twenty or more years for those who had large, well-built pyramids and rich grave furniture, and reducing it below the average for those whose tomb and tomb contents seemed poorer. Although no reliance can be placed on the absolute dates for individual rulers, the system gives an approximation, even if only to place a ruler in the right hundred year period. Further accuracy can on occasion be obtained from the presence of objects imported from further north. But, in view of doubt as to how long luxury objects might be kept in a royal household before burial, and difficulty in ascribing precise dates to the objects themselves, they do not take us much further, but act as a check on the chronology provided by Reisner's seriation. The dating of royal burials, however approximate, has provided some time-scale for objects found in the tombs—it has, however, not proved very useful in dating the pottery, or objects of domestic use, partly because of the special nature of royal burial furnishings, and partly because of the sometimes inadequate descriptions given in the publication.

Apart from the royal burials, the main evidence for Meroitic culture has until recently been confined to material from the most northerly part of the Meroitic state. Due to the intensive work carried out during the Aswan Dam salvage program, we now know that occupation and development of town and village communities was comparatively late—not pre-dating about 100 B.C. This occupation was based on intensive use of the *sagia* wheel for irrigation, and cannot be earlier than its introduction from Egypt, which is known to be about the fourth century B.C. In the southern area after about 300 B.C. a more distinctive culture, and the one usually described as Meroitic, developed. Here a few important excavations have been carried out. At Meroe itself, the capital and the largest town known in the area, Garstang excavated from 1909 to 1914, but this excavation organized in a wholesale way, and only summarily published, has produced more problems than it has answered. Careful excavations have been undertaken for many years at the site of Musawwarat es Sofra by the Humboldt University of Berlin, and this extremely important work is now in progress of publication. The large palace at Wad ben Naga has been excavated, but the results have only been published in preliminary form. Much further south, at the limit of Meroitic culture, a small cemetery and village were investigated in 1912 at Abu Geili. This is the present extent of knowledge, and the picture of Meroitic life is badly out of balance because of the emphasis on late material from the north. In the area known to ancient writers as the "Island of Meroe," the modern *Butana,* apart from cemeteries and those mainly royal, only monumental sites have been excavated. Although these have provided excellent information on architectural styles and some greater precision in chronology, many problems of Meroitic life have been left uninvestigated and unsolved.

As a result of the work of the last fifty years, though, considerable information has been recovered. There is a skeleton chronology for Meroitic history; the names of many rulers are known; and there is a mass of material objects which when finally analyzed, will provide the basis for a more detailed reconstruction of the nature of Meroitic culture. This culture is already seen as one that was highly susceptible to northern influences. In its early stage it was primarily an extension of that of Pharaonic Egyptian, and even after the move of the royal cemetery and perhaps administration, to the south, Egyptian influence remained strong. Changes in Egyptian artistic styles caused by Ptolemaic and Roman influence were reflected in Meroitic art, though more obvious indigenous elements become clearer after about 300 B.C. It is, presumably, not a coincidence that this is also the date of the move of the royal burials from Nuri to Meroe. In spite of all this work, many serious and important problems remain to be solved. For example, far greater precision is needed in the chronol-

FIGURE 1
Meroe, view of the main mound.

ogy, and until recently nothing was known about the nature of domestic life, except in the special case of the northern settlements. Also, no sequence of the main categories of artifacts had been established. In particular, the pottery was virtually unknown, and apart from that found in the royal burials, nothing was known about its styles earlier than the beginning of the first century B.C.

The Site of Meroe

To solve these problems Meroe was obviously the key site. It appeared that it would be decisive for the study of the cultural history of the central Nile Valley during the period of its occupation, and by its geographical position it was in touch not only with Egypt and the Near East, but presumably with other parts of Africa, and perhaps with areas further east. It seemed that this site, above all, would be the one that would answer many of the problems of chronology and history, and of the nature of the material culture. In view of the possibility of very considerable deposit, representing a long period of occupation, it was the one Meroitic site that was likely to provide a good sequence. Meroe was also likely to be of considerable importance not only for the history of the Nile Valley, but for Africa as a whole. It might also provide information as to early cultural contacts

FIGURE 2
Meroe, the Amun temple from the west.

with regions to south and west. As the only part of Africa this far south with any kind of chronology it could be of particular importance for the history of the continent, and in view of the widely held opinions by many scholars of African history that Meroe was a center from which ideas and techniques spread into Africa, and because of its assumed position as a center for the spread of iron working, investigation here seemed to be a matter of some importance.

As I have already suggested, earlier excavations were not very satisfactory—little attention was paid to stratification; the standard of supervision fell far short of what is now acceptable—even by the standards of the time it must be regarded as having been slap-dash. Also, the excavator, Garstang, published only a single volume covering his first season in a partial way, and later seasons were only described in preliminary reports. No further reports have ever been issued and many of the original records have now been lost. Fortunately, although the earlier excavations made very wide clearance in the Royal town and in the large temple and investigated other areas, most of the large mounds which were assumed to cover areas of domestic occupation, were virtually untouched, as was a great deal of the iron-working area. It seemed that there was a good possibility of finding a representative portion of the town that had not already been excavated. Since the earlier work had concentrated on temples and palaces it was felt that new work in the residential areas should give more solid results.

I had been interested in this site for many years, and it was one of the very first that I saw when I started work in the Sudan in 1946. I was taken there by A. J. Arkell, at that time Commissioner for Archaeology to the Sudan government, and was impressed by the size of the site and its archaeological potential. Arkell himself was deeply interested in it, and thanks to his efforts the damage that was being caused by illicit digging for soil, used as fertilizer on local agricultural schemes, was stopped, and the site well protected and preserved for subsequent workers. I had maintained my interest in the site for many years and had originally thought of working there in the middle 1950's. Unfortunately, political events in the Sudan made it impossible to pursue the matter at that stage. By 1965, when I was working in the University of Ghana, I had excavated once more in the Sudan, participating in the UNESCO-sponsored salvage scheme in Nubia, called for by the construction of the High Dam at Aswan. After digging a medieval town there for some seasons, from 1961 to 1964, I was able to think in terms of starting at Meroe.

Aims of the Expedition

Several years had been spent in considering the archaeological problems of the Meroitic period, while writing my general survey of the culture, which was published in 1967. So it seemed that the time had now come to try to get more precise answers to many of the problems that those of us interested in Meroitic culture had been discussing for some years. The work of the salvage operation in the north had also made the ancient Sudan a better-known and more widely understood archaeological phenomenon and had brought it to the forefront of interest in the archaeological community. Having given a lot of thought to the specific problems to be solved by restarting excavation at Meroe, I listed the following as being the aims of any such excavation:

1. To ascertain by modern stratigraphical methods the cultural sequence of the town, and to try to establish a firm chronology, not only for the beginning and end of the settlement, but also to attempt to date the main series of artifacts found and in particular to arrange the pottery chronologically so that it could be used as a tool in all future work on Meroitic sites.

2. To attempt to elucidate the architectural history of the Amun temple and other already excavated major buildings by further exca-

vation within and below them, and by examination of the many re-used blocks. This temple had already been completely cleared by Garstang, but he had treated it as a single period building, and had not gone into such questions as: Was there an earlier building underlying the present one? How many different periods of building were to be found? Ancient buildings almost always have been subjected to remodelling and re-building, and it seemed likely that this had happened in the Amun temple, which was the center of the state religion of Meroe after it had been transferred from Napata. It also seemed probable that an earlier building underlay the temple as it was discovered by Garstang.

3. To examine the iron-slag heaps to obtain information on techniques and dating of iron working. This was of importance in view of the widely-held opinion that the use and knowledge of iron working spread into Africa from Meroe. This is not a view with which I myself was in agreement, but it was one that had often been expressed, and since Meroe certainly produced iron on a large scale there were grounds for suggesting that it was from here that the technique spread further south.

4. The final aim of the excavation—and in this case not so much an aim as a hope—was that it might provide material that would help in the study and understanding of the Meroitic language. This language has the almost unique distinction, among ancient languages, of being untranslatable although the phonetic values of the signs with which it was written are quite well-known. This failure to understand the meaning of the words and, therefore, the texts, which have been found in considerable numbers has been a matter of frustration to scholars for many years. Anything that would help in the understanding of the texts would provide a great deal of extra information for the study of Meroitic history. The problem is that although words and sentences can easily be defined and their phonetic values understood, very little is known as to the actual meaning of words. No existing language seems to have any close relationship to Meroitic, and although the signs with which it was written are a simplified form of late Egyptian writing, the language was not connected with Egyptian. It may be that it was one of a group of languages which have now completely disappeared, or it may be that further research into African languages will provide clues. There is also always hope that a bilingual inscription may be found; it could be either in Meroitic and Egyptian, or perhaps, in Meroitic and Greek. So far none have been found, but if there were such, Meroe seemed as likely a place as any to produce such a document.

In the result, a number of these aims were not fulfilled during the course of the five seasons that have now been completed, and other questions and problems not originally thought of have arisen, and have diverted attention from some of the points that I originally set out to examine. The optimistic idea that material for understanding Meroitic language might be found has been disappointed, and an extremely small amount of written material has been discovered. This in itself is interesting, since it suggests that among the ordinary domestic areas which have been investigated, literacy was not common, and that the knowledge of writing was restricted to a small class of educated scribes. Apart from the failure to find inscriptional material, some of the other aims have also certainly not been fulfilled. For example, investigation of large buildings previously excavated has not been carried out, nor was it possible, as originally hoped, to link the new excavations with the earlier work in an attempt to understand the chronology of the part of the town already excavated. It was at one time intended to continue digging from the new areas, with their hopefully, clearly-defined stratification, to link up with the other areas to help in their dating. In actuality, Sudan authorities, for good reasons of their own, restricted the work of my expedition to those areas that had not previously been excavated, and I was not permitted to carry out any work in the areas investigated by Garstang. I was, therefore, restricted to the large mounds that he had not looked at. In many ways this restriction was a blessing; the finances of the excavation were never on a very strong basis, and each season was very much a hand-to-mouth activity. As a result, the amount of digging that could be done was limited, and it became necessary to concentrate the aims of the work. I do not think this has been harmful, and it enabled what, in many ways, are more interesting and important problems to be looked at. It caused greater emphasis to be placed on the establishment of the basic sequence, as well as on investigation of matters of domestic life. Since these were the two problems for which there was least information prior to the start of the work, it is probable that the enforced concentration on these areas was beneficial.

The First Season

The first season was early in 1965, when I went to the site with a group of Ghanaian students and started the work in the name of the University of Ghana. This first season was mainly devoted to making a detailed examination of the site, and producing a map by plane table survey, since no suitable one was available. The close study of the site, which such a survey entails, was of very great value in getting to know it in detail. The following winter I was involved in teaching duties in England and was unable to go out to the Sudan, but full work started in the season of 1966 to 1967 when I had accepted an invitation from the University of Khartoum to head the Department of Archaeology. The move to Khartoum had a number of advantages; it meant that transportation costs for getting to the site were very much reduced, since I and some of my colleagues were already in the country, and it also meant that I could be in touch with the site even during the non-excavation time of the year. This was helpful for a site where I had put up permanent buildings, both for living quarters and work rooms, and where a considerable quantity of furnishings and technical equipment was maintained. The permit to excavate was transferred to the University of Khartoum, and that university undertook the main financial responsibility for the future work, except for the season of 1970–1971 where most of the expense was covered by a grant from the Canada Council.

Techniques of the Expedition

The techniques employed in excavating this site were in many ways different from those normally in use in the Nile Valley. I had already tried to impose standards of the type that are normal in Europe and America in the excavation at Soba many years before, and it was possible to develop these further at Meroe. Archaeological methods in the Nile Valley, particularly in Egypt, have lagged far behind those used in other parts of the world and there still remains a lack of understanding of the nature of stratification. One distinguished British archaeologist had even stated, "There is no stratification in the Nile Valley." This is certainly not so; wherever man has lived in one spot for any length of time different layers of deposit will have accumulated, and the excavator should be able to differentiate them. Meroe, and Soba before it, had some positive advantages over other parts of the Nile Valley, in that the more compacted soil made it possible to dig in neat units with vertical faces, whereas over a great deal of the Nile Valley massive deposits of wind-blown sand make this very difficult. But in general the lack of attention to the finer points of excavation so noticeable in much Nile Valley archaeology arises from the emphasis on tomb and temple clearing at the expense of excavation of occupation sites. The work at Meroe was above all an investigation of such a site, and suitable methods were called for. One of the more obvious differences between the work at Meroe and that at other places, was in the use of tools. The customary tool in the Nile Valley has been the broad-bladed mattock or hoe (Arabic *toria*). I had already substituted the pick and shovel for this at Soba and continued to work with these tools at Meroe finding them more precise and more satisfactory in every way. The other change was to use wheelbarrows instead of basket men to remove the soil from the excavation. The introduction of these tools had been very successfully carried out at Soba and no difficulties were encountered at Meroe either. The other, more radical change, was to abandon the use of the trained and experienced Egyptian workmen, those known as Guftis, from their original home in Upper Egypt, Guft. These men originally trained by Petrie in 1893–1894, have for four generations been the backbone of every digging team throughout the Nile Valley. I had worked with them on many of my earlier excavations and have profound admiration for their skill and experience. However, they suffer from a number of defects which for the type of excavation I wished Meroe to be, made them unsuitable. The length of time they have been in archaeology and their great experience make them think that they know more about the work than the director, and in many cases this is true. But in view of the nature of excavation in Egypt they have no knowledge of stratification; it is almost impossible to slow up their rate of energetic and determined work, and as experience at Soba had shown they were not adaptable. Their instinct, born of years of work under different circumstances, is always to go down to a floor level. Since it was important for me to keep the material from different strata separate, it was certain that use of Guftis would not be helpful. It was difficult to do without men whom I had known for many years, some of whom were close friends, but I felt that under the circumstances it would be disastrous to have them teaching their methods to the raw local labor. It seemed far better to train this labor myself, in the way I wanted it to work, and since I hoped that the Meroe excavations would be carried on over a number of years to build up a local team who were trained in my methods. This imposed a lot of extra work in the early stages, and we suffered in the first season from the lack of the stiffening, discipline, and order which the use of Guftis bring to a labor force. This was overcome; we trained our team, found our local foreman, and I am convinced that we are now getting better results by using only local men who have no pre-conceived ideas as to how the work should be done, than we would have done by using Guftis. There is also, since finances were always limited, an important financial question here. The Guftis are much more expensive, in view of their experience and skill. They demand and receive higher wages than the local Sudanese labor, special arrangements have to be made for their housing, and they expect to be paid from the day they leave their home at Guft until the day they return.

After the making of the map, a grid was laid out over the whole site of 10.0 meter squares with the axes of the grid north-south and east-west. The lines from east to west were given letters of the alphabet, and those from south to north numbers. The squares formed by this grid became the main units of the excavation, although they were not dug to the full 10.0 meter size. In view of the soft nature of the soil and the tendency for it to cave in, it was found necessary to leave 2.0 meter baulks between each square so that the area excavated was 8.0 by 8.0 meters, but baulks between squares could be, and frequently were, removed. The laying out of the grid lines north-south and east-west, was subsequently found to be rather unsatisfactory, since it meant that with the low winter sun, the south face of the square was always in shadow. Had we paid attention to what Arkell had said in his report on his excavations at Shaheinab many years before, we would have avoided this difficulty, and would have turned the grid through forty-five degrees, so that every side of a square would have been in full light at some time of the day. The disadvantage of having one side of the square always in shadow was by no means disastrous; it meant that examination of the strata in the face was often easier since it was not in the bright sunshine which tends to make all levels look alike, but it did make it more difficult to get adequate photographs. On any subsequent work I would certainly arrange the grid lines north east–south west and north west–south east. But once having got the grid established on our site it was not possible to change it.

A consideration of the problems of the site and the overwhelming requirement of obtaining a good sequence and investigating the domestic areas suggested that it would be wise to put a trench across the northernmost of the two mounds, and to look at the southern edge of it in the first place. The northern mound was chosen because it was the larger and perhaps the more important, and the southern part of it was investigated first because I did not want to go into the heart of the mound until I had seen what the special problems were, and discovered the kinds of stratification likely to be found. There was also a feeling that the occupation had spread down to the southern end in later times and that some of the latest material, which I was anxious to identify, was to be found in that area. Also, since that part of the mound was in close proximity to much iron slag there might be evidence for iron working. A trench was laid out along the north side of grid line fifty, and a series of 8.0 meter squares was dug from the east end, moving west. This provided what was in effect a trench with a series of baulks across it, and during the two seasons of 1966-1967 and 1967-1968 work was carried on along this line.

FIGURE 3
Meroe, trench in squares.

Some Results of the Excavation

Starting with square B50 the work was continued up to square L50, thus providing a trench 120 meters long and giving a very good vertical section through this part of the mound. The excavation showed that we were among a number of rather poor domestic buildings, and that there was occupation in the area over a considerable period of time. At the deepest point there were 5.0 meters of deposit, and four or five main periods of building. The buildings were all of sun-dried brick, and were all small. A number of kitchens were found, which indicated that the buildings were dwelling houses, presumably those of a poor section of the population. At the east end of the trench, we cut through a large mound of iron slag, and traces of iron working were found in many other parts of the trench. This suggests that the houses found were those of people concerned with the iron working, and the discovery of a complete mound of slag beneath the surface was of importance in showing that there was more iron working and over a greater length of time than the mounds on the surface alone might indicate.

A very good pottery sequence was obtained, and it was observed that the pottery in the lower levels was different from anything previously known from Meroitic sites. As already suggested, Meroitic pottery has only been clearly identified for the last few hundred years of Meroitic civilization, and the kinds of pottery already well-known, particularly a very fine painted ware common in graves, were found in the upper levels. The pottery from the bottom levels —and we were fortunate in finding a cache of complete or virtually complete pots right at the very bottom of the cutting—was something quite new. The shapes of this pottery were reminiscent of Egyptian pottery of the sixth and seventh centuries B.C., and some of the types could be duplicated from examples in the royal cemetery at Nuri. So here was the first good evidence that the town of Meroe had been occupied some time before royal burials began. This conclusion did not come as a surprise since there was evidence of burials from as early as the seventh century B.C. from graves in what is known as the West Cemetery—many of which were not royal.

It was also possible to get some evidence for the lowest level at which traces of iron working were found. Carbon 14 dating suggests that this was about 500 B.C., pushing the date back earlier than had been previously assumed. So the work of these first two seasons was satisfactory in making clear the nature of the occupation, in at least this part of the mound, and in giving a reasonable sequence of pottery types, and to some extent of other objects. Apart from pottery, a variety of small objects was found, mostly of a domestic nature, such as grindstones, hammer stones, fragments of iron tools and so on. A large number of beads and faience amulets was also found, but the important material, and the only one which showed distinctive changes in style at different periods was the pottery.

One of the problems in an excavation of this kind is exercising sufficient control over the work so as to be certain of the exact find spots of objects, and also to prevent mixing of materials from different layers. All the soil at Meroe is basically sand, and although sufficiently compacted to allow vertical faces to be cut, it is extremely difficult in working downwards to know when one level stops and another begins. Although we work with a high proportion of trained supervisors to workmen, that is, normally one supervisor to each square, in which there will be two digging teams, that is two men with picks and two with shovels, it is not possible to exercise the precise control which would always enable the exact find spots of objects to be discovered or to insure that there is no mixing from one level to another. Also, to maintain a reasonable speed of work, without which it would be quite uneconomical to operate at this site, it is not possible to put all the soil through a sieve. So a certain number of small objects are lost, however much care and observation goes into the original digging, and it is particularly likely that such things as stone arrow heads, beads, and small faience objects will be lost in this way.

To obviate the danger of getting a false picture of the totality of the artifacts, we adopted the policy of digging trial trenches from which all of the contents could be put through a sieve. These pits, 2.0 meters square, were dug into the face of the existing cuttings, thus making it easy to observe the stratification, and to exercise very tight control. These trenches were normally supervised by one trained archaeologist with a digging team of two men and with the requisite number of boys and barrow men to remove the soil. In this way it was possible to get a good sample of every kind of artifact which existed in the area. The first of these trials was dug to get a pottery series, and it was excavated, not by the observable strata, but by ten centimeter spits, which were afterwards superimposed on the drawn section of the cutting. By putting this material through a sieve it was possible to retrieve everything, including small potsherds that would have been missed in the normal way. We also found that a significantly larger number of the rather beautiful quartz and carnelian arrow heads, for which Meroe has been famous, were recovered in this way. The same system was used to get a sample of bone, since it became clear that bone as recovered in the normal digging was not an adequate sample since there was a tendency for the men only to keep the larger pieces. So the second trial pit was dug specifically to obtain a bone sample, and the analysis of this bone was undertaken on the site, by P. L. Carter of Cambridge University, during the 1968-1969 season.

The bone, all from domestic refuse, was found to be exclusively of domestic animals and provided extremely interesting information as to the dietary habits of the Meroites. It was noticeable that in the lower levels there was a considerable quantity of sheep and goat bone, as well as that of cattle, while in the upper levels cattle predominated—in some of the upper levels being as much as 80 percent to 90 percent of the whole. There was virtually no wild animal bone, suggesting that hunting played a very minor part in the Meroitic food supply. The switch from mixed meat of cattle, sheep, and goat to one almost exclusively of cattle is interesting and the reasons for this have not yet been fully understood. There is no doubt that the Meroites were cattle-oriented people, as are many of the Sudan peoples today, and we know from sculptured reliefs that they had large herds. Presumably one of the reasons that made Meroe attractive as a site was the possibility of grazing lands in the plains to the east of the river, an area which is so used today. The discovery that cattle were common in Meroitic times made me consider still further the possibility that there had been greater rainfall in the past. I had frequently wondered why, in an area of such marginal rainfall as there is today, a town of the size of Meroe could have developed, and I had suggested that there might have been a greater rainfall so as to provide both better grazing land

and better possibilities of grain growing in the beds of the wadis. This practice goes on today. After the rains, the semi-nomadic part of the local population moves off away from the river to the east taking their cattle to the grazing grounds and also planting sorghum in the beds of the wadis. This procedure serves very well in years of good rain but, as I have already pointed out, there are many years in which this is not a practicable proposition. If the large town of Meroe was to have had a sufficiently assured food supply it seemed to me likely that the rainfall was higher. Subsequent information to which I will refer below confirms this.

1968–1970 Excavations at Meroe

Having during two seasons driven a trench most of the way across the mound, I had for the year 1968–1969 to consider whether to continue the trench, and then perhaps dig right across to link up with the Garstang excavations, or whether to open up a new area. In view of the restrictions on digging in the previously excavated area, I thought little was to be gained at that stage from the first alternative; and therefore decided to open up a wider area than the existing trench at the highest point of the mound, to see if the story was the same, or whether, in view of the greater depth of deposit, even earlier occupation would be found at the bottom. Consequently, the two seasons of 1968–1969 and 1969–1970, were devoted to clearing an area covered by squares L, M, and N79 and 80. Subsequently, in view of the impossibility of clearing the whole of the area in the time available, the digging was restricted to squares M79 and N79 and only these two were taken down to bottom. This area showed a slightly different story from the original trench; again there were many buildings of sun-dried brick, but in this case they were much bigger, perhaps public buildings of some sort, though the nature of our cuttings did not provide a plan for any one single building. The walls were more massive, the rooms were larger, and the whole nature of the construction suggested something of either greater wealth, or greater importance. A noticeable feature of the area was that there had not been continuous occupation in the same part of the mound through the whole period of the town. It seems that building activity shifted about on the mound, and we found that in some places after a building had fallen into disuse large rubbish pits had been dug in the area sometimes as much as 4.0 meters across. In several cases it could be seen that after the rubbish pits had been filled, the area had remained unoccupied for some time and a considerable deposit of wind-blown sand had accumulated before

FIGURE 4
Meroe, post-holes of hut at bottom of square M. 79.

further buildings were put up. This evidence, though derived only from rather a small area in the mound, strongly suggests that the whole mound was never occupied at any one time but that there was a slight shifting from period to period. This shifting process makes it difficult to get an idea of the full extent of the town at any one period, and therefore, to make any assessment of population. A wider horizontal clearance will have to be done to see the plan of the whole town at different periods of time.

The excavation in this area was taken down to bottom, which was reached at a depth of 10.0 meters; seven main building levels were seen, all of them of sun-dried brick and all of them of fairly large buildings. It was observed, as it had been in the earlier trench, that brick sizes were uniform except in the very bottom levels, where the bricks were of smaller size. This should prove to be a useful chronological indicator if some precision in the dating of the different building levels can be obtained. A number of samples for Carbon 14 dating have been taken, and when the results are available it may well be possible to give dates to the different periods. At present it is guessed that the bottom levels are at about 600 to 700 B.C. —somewhat earlier than the occupation at the bottom of the first trench. What is certain is that there is distinctively different material, particularly in the pottery, at this depth as well as different brick sizes. At the very bottom of the cutting there was a layer of clean sand, presumably part of one of the small sand hills similar to those on which most modern villages are built. In this sand was a series of post-holes, which when cleared, showed from their arrangement that a hut, very similar to those still in use, had stood on the site. The date of this first occupation, pre-dating the first brick buildings, still remains to be discovered, but I assume it to be somewhere of the order of 700–750 B.C. and, therefore, approximately contemporary with the beginnings of the Napatan kings whose burials are known at Kurru. These kings, who by their conquest of Egypt became rulers there, are known in Egyptian history as the twenty-fifth dynasty. Based on the considerable new historical information that this assumption provides, we can guess that the town of Meroe goes back to the beginnings of the independent state and confirms the suspicion suggested by evidence from burials that there was considerable population at Meroe at this early period.

In addition to the main deep trench already described it was decided in the 1969-1970 season to make some investigation into Meroitic iron working, and I was fortunate in having the help of Dr. R. Tylecote, a metallurgist and historian of metallurgy, from the University of Newcastle-upon-Tyne. Although the slag heaps had been known for many years, and had caused Sayce in 1910 to describe Meroe as the "Birmingham of Africa," very little information was available as to the actual nature of iron-working techniques. It had already been discovered that iron working went back to approximately 500 B.C. at Meroe and was more extensive than surface indications suggested, but the work of the first two seasons although finding new mounds of slag, and fragments of what may have been simple bowl furnaces, had told very little more about the nature of furnaces and of the process of iron working. One of the main aims was to find a complete iron-smelting furnace, and it seemed likely that the best place to look for this would be near to one of the mounds of slag, on the assumption that the workers would not have moved the slag very far from the areas of smelting. So, taking one of the large mounds that lay on the east side of the town, a curved trench was laid out along the circumference of the mound. Clearance very soon showed a mass of the characteristic red ash of smelting areas, and lumps of iron slag, and soon after, a furnace in a reasonable state of preservation was found. This furnace, of shaft type, was presumably fired with charcoal, and the necessary blast produced by bellows, of which the clay nozzles, tuyères, had been a common find throughout the excavation. It is likely also that the bellows were of the leather bag type, still to be

FIGURE 5
Meroe, iron-smelting furnace.

seen in use by blacksmiths in the local market. This furnace is probably to be dated within the first century or so A.D. and is a very satisfactory example of the kind of iron-smelting furnace in use at that time. Furnaces of other periods still remain to be found. In particular, the moment at which iron production moved from the use of the open bowl furnace, apparently in use in 500 B.C., to the use of shaft furnaces some few hundred years later needs to be identified.

The excavations of 1969 to 1970 virtually completed the first stage of the work at Meroe, but in 1971 to 1972, after my move to the University of Calgary, I went back with a team of students to do a small amount of excavation and to make a study of the enormous amount of material that had been retrieved. In previous years the tempo of work had been such that it had not been possible to make anything more than a superficial study of the material. Full records had been kept, and on getting the team onto the site it was a comparatively simple matter to start work. A small amount of excavation was carried out, partly as a University of Calgary field course, and partly because the exact point in the sequence at which the evidence for iron working stopped, had not been absolutely clear from the earlier seasons. Iron fragments were found right down to the very bottom, but there was some doubt as to whether these were only manufactured objects, which could have been imported, or whether there were fragments of slag to be found at the bottom of the trench. One further square was excavated, square M50, and evidence was gained as to the earliest appearance of iron slag. This coincided very closely with the level from which the 500 B.C. Carbon 14 date had been previously obtained, and it can now be said with some confidence that this is the earliest date of iron working. When further dates have been obtained it may be possible to get greater precision. During this same season another 2.0 meter square trial trench was dug in the south face of square M79, in which, having been left open for two seasons, the stratification was extremely clear. This trial was dug to obtain a further sample of animal bone, to act as a check on the results obtained from the first sample. A good selection of bone was obtained, though it has not yet been analyzed. During the course of the excavation, seeds of the plant *celtis integrifolia* were found. This find was valuable evidence for earlier climate, since the *celtis* does not grow in the region of Meroe today, but is only found much further south and requires an annual rainfall of 400 millimeters. This evidence was the first positive information to support the suggestion that rainfall in Meroitic times was greater. Pollen samples for further evidence to reconstruct the ancient vegetation and climate were also required. Earlier attempts to obtain pollen failed. A number of samples had been taken from the main part of the excavation, but they proved not to contain any pollen. This season a trial pit was dug into the bottom of an ancient reservoir, about two miles to the east of the site in the hope that the earlier water-logged conditions which were likely to have existed in the bottom of the reservoir would have preserved pollen. These reservoirs are a distinctive feature of the southern region of Meroitic culture and a large number of them are known in the "Island of Meroe." They consist of artificially made enclosures, with an earth bank of roughly horseshoe shape with the open end facing into an area of water runoff. During the rains these enclosures would have filled with water, and would have provided long-term storage for domestic purposes, and for the watering of cattle. Those known are all associated with Meroitic monuments and there can be little doubt that they date from that time. The enclosure that was investigated lies very close to a small temple, lying two miles east of the town, and it was surely built for use by the inhabitants of Meroe. The samples obtained have not yet been studied.

Pottery at Meroe

Most of the effort during this last season went into a study of the pottery. The pottery at Meroe is of immense quantity—something of the order of a million sherds being found every season. The number of complete, or restorable pots is small, as is to be expected from a domestic site. However, enough have been found—some 320—to give an idea of the main shapes. The potsherd collections were sorted into the various types. Once these types had been established, a statistical analysis was made and the familiar "battleship" curves were drawn to show the waxing and waning of the different pottery styles. As a result, there is now a good picture of the main classes of Meroitic pottery, and it is possible to point to certain types which are particularly distinctive and diagnostic, and which can be used in the future as chronological indicators. Relative dating for the pottery styles is now clearly established; what still remains to be done is to get absolute dating. This must wait on further Carbon 14 dates, although a guess can already be made.

Details of the pottery styles are not called for in this account; I have already referred to the quite different pottery styles in the lower levels, and this phenomenon has been repeated in every part of the site that has been cleared. There was a distinct break in pottery styles at some date which I assume at present to be around 500 B.C., although perhaps a little later. The famous fine-painted Meroitic ware is seen to be, as had already been suspected, a phenomenon of very late times, perhaps spanning the periods A.D. 100 to 300. Other painted wares go a little bit earlier, but for most of the period of the occupation of the town site the pottery was predominantly of a plain red type. One of the intriguing questions that arises with regard to this pottery is the presence of two absolutely different traditions. One, which comprises perhaps 85 to 90 percent of all the pottery, is wheel-made, mostly red or reddish in color, with many of the shapes based on those current in Egypt and the Eastern Mediterranean. The other type is quite different; it is non-wheel made, black, decorated with incisions and impressions, and in many cases is based on gourd shapes, as is much of present-day African pottery. The latter represents almost 10 percent of the whole and is found scattered throughout all levels except the very earliest ones. Does it represent, as has been normally suggested, the pottery made by women, whereas the wheel-made red wares were made by men, or does it represent the pottery of a distinct social, or ethnic, group? It is not possible to answer this question at the moment, but if wider clearance of the town showed it concentrated in certain areas, then the latter explanations might be thought to be possible. This rather unusual pottery which is found throughout the whole length and breadth of the Meroitic state is of special interest since it is the only material suggesting links with Africa further south. All other Meroitic material is either clearly a copy of northern objects, or is distinctively locally Meroitic.

In Retrospect

Looking back at the excavations of Meroe after the completion of five seasons and considering what was achieved and whether a different approach and better methods would have provided more adequate answers, on the whole it can be said that several of the main aims have been achieved. The basic aim of getting a sequence right through the whole period of occupation of the town has been achieved. The various building levels can be seen, the material has been sorted, and can be given relative dating, and in particular there is now a very good pottery sequence which has been checked and re-checked from several trial trenches. There can now be no doubt about the pottery styles at different periods at least in this town, although to what extent this can be extended to other parts of the Meroitic state still remains to be seen. It will now be possible to tie in the pottery with that from the royal burials and both will act as checks on the other. Carbon 14 dates may help to get more accurate dating, but within the limitations of Carbon 14, and given the reasonable knowledge that already exists for Meroitic chronology, there must be some doubt as to the usefulness of this method until a number of dates have been obtained and have been checked against the chronology obtained by Reisner's seriation. Insofar as the pottery found in the pyramids can be identified with the classes that have been defined at Meroe, the results should be of very great interest. One of the problems is that much of the pottery is of a rather non-diagnostic coarse red domestic ware, but there are probably enough diagnostic kinds to provide the kind of chronological framework that was hoped for. The same can be said to a rather lesser extent for other classes of objects; these were not, in the main, distinctive or diagnostic. Beads, insofar as they have been studied, do not seem to show marked changes at different periods. The same can be said of the large number of small faience objects, mostly amulets, which are familiar from Egypt, and from the Meroitic tombs; they also do not seem to have changed very much over time.

In total, a large number of objects other than pottery were found —the number being something of the order of 3500, and it is reasonable to suppose that if adequate study is given to them that something will be discovered about time changes and varying patterns in this material. An elaborate program of study is being set up which hopefully will make possible a comparative analysis of not only the material from Meroe but of all published Meroitic material of a similar sort, stretching from the most northern towns near the Egyptian frontier to Abu Geili.

In addition to obtaining this sequence, a great deal has now been learned about the domestic building for the period and area, and differences between structures at Meroe and those from towns and villages further north have been observed. The differences are not very great, because the limitations of building simple rectangular buildings in sun-dried brick do not allow of much variation. However, one of the striking features was the small size of the buildings found in the poorer part of Meroe town. It is not possible to say what the full ground plan of a domestic house of the period was, since no complete buildings have been obtained.

Other information about domestic life has been obtained, however. There are many examples of kitchens, and of the curious way in which the Meroites used large pots from which they broke off the bottoms, turning them upside down to serve as fireplaces—a phenomenon that has been observed in many Meroitic dwelling sites. We also know something of diet, particularly with regard to meat, as the analysis of animal bones showed. And, we have a little information about other items. We are short of information about crops; traces of sorghum were expected but so far none have been discovered, and the only grains found—and these were found at rather low level in what was probably a grain storage silo of dried mud—on analysis were shown to be barley. This find was rather unexpected, because barley is not grown in this area today, and this may be another piece of evidence indicating changes in climate. In addition to the light thrown on the domestic aspects of Meroitic society, some advance has also been made in understanding the iron working. So, on the whole, the results can be considered satisfactory, though not spectacular. During the course of the work at Meroe there has been certainly in my mind a change of emphasis from investigation of largely historical questions —concerned with the dates of the beginning and end of the town, of links with buildings such as the Amun temple, and various buildings in the royal palace area—to a greater emphasis on questions of domestic life, and ecological change. It is quite clear that the excavation of Meroe town is never going to produce a large quantity of spectacular objects. A number of interesting objects have certainly been found, some of them beautiful, and even a few small items of gold were discovered. In the main, however, the material discovered has been trivial and unexciting. But, from the standpoint of understanding Meroitic life and of finding the things that were the normal objects of day-to-day life, then this excavation can be considered extremely interesting and extremely important.

Evidence for the economic basis of Meroitic life still remains to be made absolutely clear. Almost certainly it was based on cattle and the growing of grain, and there is no doubt that the evidence is available in this site. Failure to find more grain, and in particular to find sorghum is a disappointment, and rather surprising, but it was only in the last season that samples were taken for flotation and they still remain to be examined. A great deal of vegetable matter was obtained in this way and detailed study will, it is hoped, produce not only evidence as to crops, but also as to local wild vegetation with its implications for climatic change. It is, of course, hoped also that samples taken for pollen analysis will provide similar evidence of climatic change.

The other matter that grew in significance as the work went on was the value of observing present day life in the area to throw light on ancient times. We had been aware for some time that there were two completely different groups living in the region and both were represented in our labor force. The settled riverain population lives in villages of rectangular flat-roofed mud houses, and bases its livelihood on cultivating the river bank. Two methods are in use: one on the lower flood plain which is covered by the river every summer when the Nile flood comes down. Here a *seluka* stick makes holes in the wet mud after the river has dropped, and grain can be planted; no further irrigation is required since the silt retains adequate moisture. Today a considerable range of crops are grown on this flood plain: maize, sorghum, pennisetum millet—though this is not a common crop in this area—together with tomatoes, okra, and a variety of beans. The other method of cultivation which is also carried out higher up on the river bank is largely irrigation by mechanical pump, but some of the old fashioned, wooden water wheels are still in use. In addition to their agricultural activities, a number of people in these villages make their living in other ways. There are small shopkeepers; there is a small professional class; some people are school teachers or medical orderlies, and so on. From almost every family some members now go away to work in the towns. So there is varied economic activity going on in the riverside villages, although, until recently, agriculture must have been responsible for at least 90 percent of the villagers' livelihood. These people also keep a certain number of animals—cattle, sheep, goats, and donkeys. It is probable that the type of life has not changed very greatly since Meroitic times, and the ancient town of Meroe cannot have looked very different from the modern villages. One difference in construction is that all Meroitic houses were built of sun-dried bricks formed in a wooden mold and left to dry in the sun, whereas the modern houses are almost entirely made of what is called locally *jalus,* which consists of large slabs of mud, not formed in a mold into bricks.

There is another quite separate group in addition to these riverain people, which is very conveniently separated from them in this part of the Sudan by the main railway line which runs from Khartoum to the north. This group lives to the east of the railway, which divides the cultivated land from the arid acacia scrub country. These people are nomadic, or at least semi-nomadic; they are camel people, but depend to some extent on cattle, and they also own some sheep and goats. They are not true nomads in the sense that they are continually on the move, but they practice a trans-humance pattern by which during the rains they move further east away from the river to the grazing lands of the Butana where they take their cattle. They also plant crops in the beds of the wadis, where again, as on the river foreshore, there is sufficient moisture retained, if the rains have been adequate, for crops to grow without any irrigation. These people have a marginal money economy, existing primarily on herd raising and crop growing activities. They will to some extent sell both grain and cattle, usually to obtain certain luxuries like tea and sugar, on which they depend very heavily, and items of simple clothing. They are otherwise economically self-sufficient. In times of drought they often find it necessary to buy grain from the markets, raising cash by selling animals or going to work. Thus, the presence of an archaeological excavation which has employed up to seventy-five men on occasion has been a very useful addition to their scanty cash resources.

There seems no reason to suppose that this contrast of the two groups did not also exist in Meroitic times; evidence for this is still to be found, but it seems a reasonable supposition that the main ways of life of the area, which has not been subjected to modern influences until the last fifty or sixty years has not fundamentally changed. If this is so, then a great many interesting things remain to be done; present archaeological evidence illustrates the life of the settled riverain population, and nothing is known of the semi-nomads who may have been those responsible for looking after the large herds of cattle which it seems likely were the property of the Meroitic king. The first evidence gained for this supposition was the hut found at the bottom of the excavation, which so closely resembles, in the arrangement of its posts, the huts of the nomads today. In fact, when the post-holes were cleared and the pattern was visible, the local men immediately said that it represented the place in which a hut had stood. When asked how they knew this, they explained that of course they knew, since this was exactly how they arranged the posts when making a hut for themselves. These huts are made of wooden posts, and covered with matting.

The next excavations at Meroe should carry out a wide horizontal clearance of the mound already investigated, over an area of at least 100.0 meters square, for the purpose of getting town and house plans so as to provide better information as to the nature of urban life in Meroitic times and to get an idea of how closely integrated the town was, and enable some estimates to be made of population. I would hope that it would be possible to clear, building level by building level, over this wide area so as to compare the way in which the town had developed, and to see if there were periods in which there was greater or less occupation. The identification of artifact types with the different building levels is now clear enough and the work done already in establishing the basic stratigraphy of the site will then be of tremendous help in clearing on a wider scale.

I would be inclined now, if time and finance is adequate, to proceed at a rather slower pace than in the earlier seasons. A great deal of consideration has been given as to the best digging methods, and I have already made the claim that the methods used were superior to those normally in use. Whether they were themselves adequate, or whether a slower and more careful approach more akin to that used on small sites in the western world would be more appropriate, needs to be considered. This is a difficult question; if the whole area so far excavated had been approached in this way, if it had all been worked with a trowel, if it had been all put through a sieve, we would not have the information that is now available, nor would bottom ever have been reached, or if it had, it would have been in such a small hole as to be virtually non-understandable. I take the view that the methods used were appropriate to the task being undertaken and that, although small objects and a certain amount of precision were lost here and there, the digging of the 2.0 meter square trial trenches provided a sufficient sample of the full range of objects to more than compensate for those that were lost in the wider areas. These trial trenches were also adequate for obtaining a range of samples of non-artifact material, such as charcoal for Carbon 14 dating, samples for flotation to obtain examples of vegetable matter, and for many other purposes. By use of the trial trenches, together with more rapid and wider clearance of areas where more generalized information is required, the maximum can be gained in the most economical way.

For the future, however, if time and funds permit, an attempt will be made to combine the advantage of both methods. This involves working over a large area in a slower way, with much trowelling and sieving. An attempt should be made to isolate areas of different kinds of ancient activity in the course of this clearance, not only in different quarters of the town, but also within individual houses.

Kitchens have already been so identified, but it has not been possible to study them in relation to other parts of the houses in which they were found. In clearing a large area of this kind it will probably be necessary to clear it as a whole and not to divide it up into the squares with 2.0 meter baulks so far used. In seeing an overall plan, baulks of this width cause difficulty in connecting building structures. What I am proposing is that the whole area be marked out into squares by means of string, and that the baulks should be removed in stages, after their sections have been drawn, so that for any one main building level the whole area can be seen and planned as a unit without interference of observation from the baulks. When digging starts again after the removal of upper buildings, the stringing will show where the sections were taken and again the baulks will be left in place until another level has been revealed. In this way it will be possible to obtain a complete view of each level over the full extent of the excavated area as well as to maintain adequate vertical control.

Apart from work in the town two other matters need attention: a considerable amount of information is now available concerning the physical attributes of the northern section of the Meroitic population and all evidence points to a marked stability from periods far anterior to Meroitic times to the present day. No comparable information is known from further south. There are many graves in the neighborhood of Meroe spanning the whole period of its occupation, and both Garstang and Reisner cleared a number of them to obtain the funerary objects. It appears that no attention was paid to skeletal remains and it is not even clear whether these were recovered, or were left *in situ*. This lack of information can be remedied, since many graves remain unplundered, and one of the aims of future work will be to obtain a suitable sample of skeletal material. To do this it will be necessary to add a physical anthropologist to the expedition and no graves should be opened without his presence.

The other investigation which it would be useful to make would be to look for traces of the rural Meroitic occupation. If the division into settled and semi-nomadic populations that I have suggested is correct, the semi-nomads will have left some traces of their existence. To find these will not be easy since there will be no elaborate buildings remaining from a people who lived in temporary huts, nor will there be mound formation in view of the shifting nature of their occupation. But a scatter of potsherds, grinding stones, and pounders should lead to the discovery of hut sites identifiable by the postholes. A small group of perhaps two archaeologists and a guide, travelling on foot and by camel moving east from the river might find these sites. Several Meroitic sites are known to lie up the wadis, and traces of this population, might be found between the wadis and the Nile.

To carry out all these operations on a site of the size, both horizontally and vertically, of Meroe will require either longer digging seasons, or a much larger work force. Here there are two main constraints: the first, familiar to all archaeologists is finance, since this determines the number who can be employed. Although wages are low in the Sudan by western standards, work forces are large, $1.20 (50 pence) per day per person for one hundred people over a normal three month season amounts to a considerable sum. In addition there is the cost of transporting and feeding the supervisory staff, as well as of all the other items of equipment and supplies. The other constraint is of time and climate. Given the high cost of transportation to the Sudan, it is not economical to work for less than a three-month season, nor would any measureable results be obtained in less. Sudan climate only makes it possible to work during the winter months between November and March, with the best time being December through February. In view of the arrangement of teaching terms and semesters in many North American universities there is often a difficulty for those involved in the direction of the work being away from their universities at the appropriate time of year for consecutive years. This applies far less to European universities which are more able to allow directors of excavations to have the necessary time, and to regard it as a normal part of their academic activity. The spasmodic nature of activity by North American scholars in the Sudan is in marked contrast to the continuity of archaeological projects sponsored from Europe. This is a serious difficulty—a site such as Meroe, requiring close and unremitting attention over many years cannot be satisfactorily studied except by continuous work. It is not only a matter of the way in which a large site only becomes understandable by living in close proximity to it for regular periods of time, but also of the less tangible psychological problems of contact with the labor force, and of maintaining morale and skill among those on whose efforts the success of the enterprise depends. This means both local labor and supervisory staff, and twenty-five years of experience have made it obvious to me that the greater the stability and permanence amongst the staff the greater the chances of achieving the aims of the project. Archaeological excavation is a serious business which should not be undertaken lightly, nor without adequate resources. It is not a hobby, though some of us are lucky enough to have our work as our hobby. It is a determined endeavor to study the past of mankind and as such deserves the support and sympathy of academic institutions.

References

ARKELL, A. J.
1962 History of the Sudan to 1821. London, Athlone Press.

GARSTANG, J.
1911 Meroe, the City of the Ethiopians. London, Oxford University Press.

HAYCOCK, B. G.
1965 The Kingship of Kush in the Sudan. Comparative Studies in Society and History 7: 461–480.

1968 Towards a better understanding of the Kingdom of Kush (Napata-Meroe). Sudan Notes and Records 49: 1–16.

SHINNIE, P. L.
1967 Meroe, a Civilization of the Sudan. London, Thames and Hudson, Ltd. and New York, Frederick A. Praeger.

TRIGGER, B. G.
1969 The Myth of Meroe and the African Iron Age. African Historical Studies II: 23 50.

BETWEEN THE INDUS AND EUPHRATES

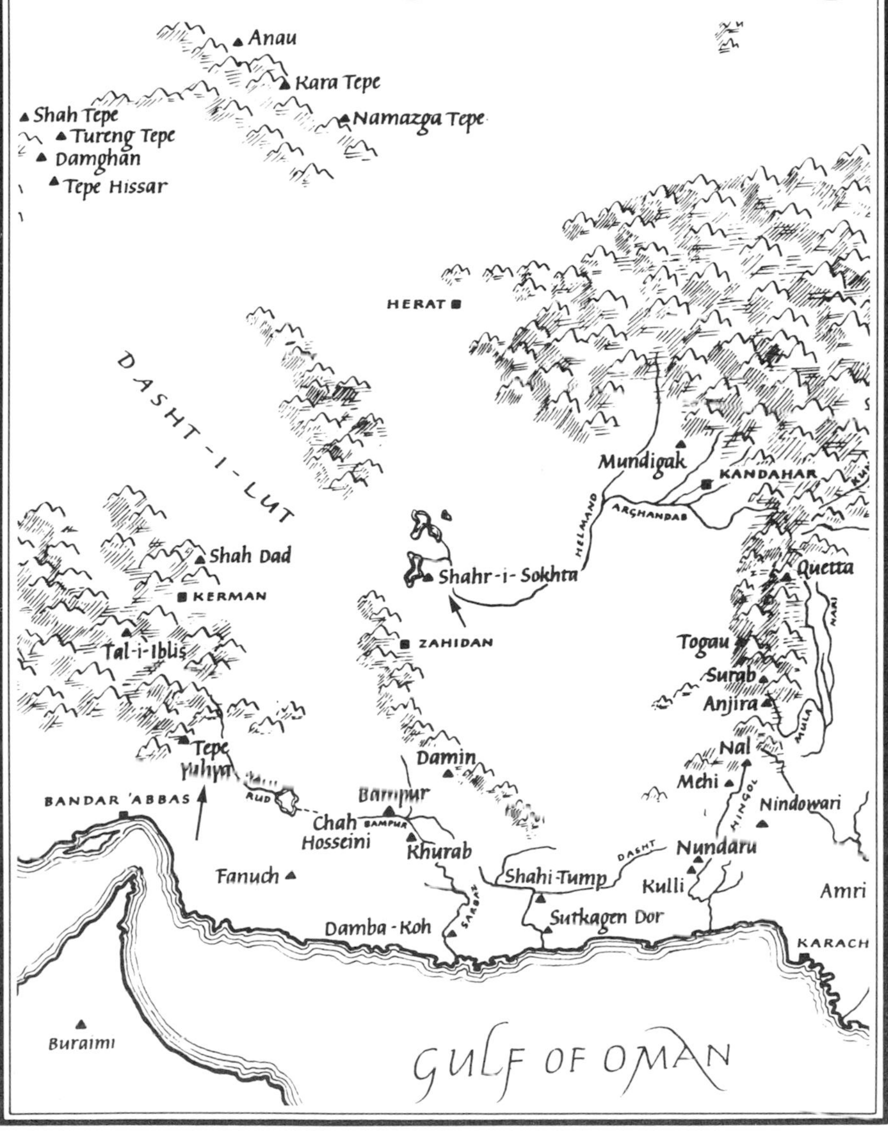

(preceding page)

Map of the principal sites of Sumerian Mesopotamia, showing the Indo-Iranian Highlands, and the Harappan Civilization of the Indus, about 2500 B.C.

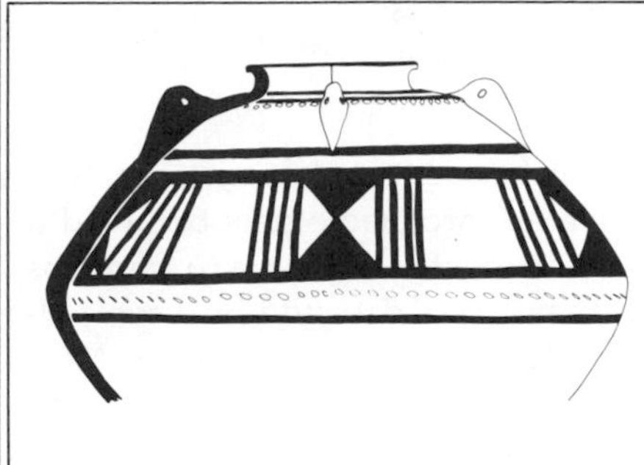

Excavations at Tepe Yahya

C. C. LAMBERG–KARLOVSKY

Tepe Yahya in southeastern Iran is one of the most isolated and remote archaeological excavations being undertaken today in the Middle East. Yet, the remains of this ancient city—today referred to by local villagers as Tepe Yahya—represent a major administrative city which was in contact with the major centers of the civilized world. The excavations at Tepe Yahya have been characterized by Sir Max Mallowan, a distinguished archaeologist, as transforming our notions of the extension of early dynastic and predynastic literate civilization in the Middle East.

The summer of 1973 will mark the seventh consecutive year of research and excavation at Yahya. Rarely does the excavator of a site have the opportunity to provide a biography of a research project which is still in progress. Unlike the other essays in this book, we are reflecting not on a completed task but on work "in progress." The manner in which the Yahya Project has "transformed our notions" is the subject of this essay. It is a biography of our research design, a review of our priorities, our memorable successes and our unforgettable frustrations.

The question is often asked of an archaeologist, "Why are you digging?" A more specific question is, "Why are you digging where you are and how did you come to dig at that particular place?" The answer to these questions is of special interest in considering the "accidental" discovery of Tepe Yahya in 1967.

The discovery of Tepe Yahya was indirectly brought about by the Six Day's War in the Near East. In June of 1967 I had hoped to lead a group of students to northeastern Syria to excavate a prehistoric site which I had located the summer before. The unfortunate outbreak of war abruptly terminated the possibility of an archaeological excavation in Syria. I had been studying the archaeological collections from southeastern Iran, gathered in the 1930's by Sir Aurel Stein for two

Headpiece: Jemdet Nasr type storage vessel.

years prior to our survey. I had begun to suspect that southeastern Iran was far from the "cultural backwater" archaeologists believed it to be, thus, my shift of archaeological interest from Syria to Iran was not a complete disorientation, but rather it was directed by a compelling interest in understanding the early urban process in the Near East and was stimulated by the archaeological collections gathered four decades ago by Sir Aurel Stein. I requested permission from the Director of the Peabody Museum where these collections were stored and from the National Science Foundation to use the funds allocated for our Syrian Expedition to lead a survey retracing Stein's footsteps, with the hope of locating a very particular type of site. Permission was granted, and we set out—by Land Rover—three students, an Iranian government representative and myself as chauffeur over 8,000 miles—to look for the suspected site. In order to best understand what we were looking for, and why, a background to the understanding of this area in modern and prehistoric times is necessary.

The Area

Our geographical focus of interest rests in the present province of Kerman, southeastern Iran. It is an area characterized by large tracts of uninhabitable desert and sparsely settled semi-arid areas in the plateaus of the Zagros Mountains. The key to human settlement throughout this area is in the availability of water. Rainfall in this corner of Iran ranges from one to six inches over the lowlands to a distinctly higher figure over the mountain crests and plateaus. To a very marked degree, cultivation resembles oasis development in a hostile environment. Agriculture is carried out where there are small but perennial streams, where motor pumps tap available underground waters, and through traditional irrigation canals and *qanats*. Dates, almonds, pistachios, cereals, and a wide variety of tropical and subtropical crops, including citrus and mangoes, are cultivated. Goats, sheep, cattle and camel are herded, either close to irrigated areas or on higher pastures. Pastoralism, based on sheep, goat, cattle, and even camel, characterizes a transhuman pattern of seasonal migration between the lowland and highland pastures. With the exception of a half-dozen cities, the population of this area today is very sparse and greatly scattered.

The first serious archaeological work in this area was undertaken by Sir Aurel Stein. The results of his pioneering excavations in the early 1930's were partially published in 1937. In that publication he stated that his motivating interest was to be "fully aware that the

TABLE 1
Chronological chart indicating the relations of Tepe Yahya with the nearby site of Iblis, related sites of the Iranian Plateau and Persian Gulf, as well as the influences of Mesopotamia on the above sites.

YAHYA	IBLIS	RELATED SITES	INFLUENCES	DATE
			Hassunan	5000 B.C.
		Sialk I		
VI-C-E				
				4500
VI-A-B	1			
V-C	1–2	Sialk II Bakun B1		4200
			Ubaid	
V-A-B	2–3	Sialk III Chah Husseini		3800
			Uruk	
IV-C Proto-Elamite	6	Susa C Shah-Dad (Early) Shahr-i-Sokhta III Bampur I-	Jemdet Nasr	3200
Stealite			Early Dynastic II–III	
IV-B Proto-Elamite		Umm-an-Nar Barbar I (Bahrein) Bampur VI Shahr-i-Sokhta IV		2800
?Gap?				
IV-A		Shah-Dad (Late)		2300
		GAP		
III			Iron I/II	1000
II			Achaemenian (?)	400
I			Partho-Sasanian	300 A.D.

——— Strong Ceramic Parallels
- - - - Tenuous Ceramic Parallels

results thus secured cannot lead to final conclusions as regards those relations of civilization and intercourse which in prehistoric periods linked the Indus Valley with Iran and the region at the head of the Persian Gulf (Mesopotamia). But I hope that a full record of my investigations may help to stimulate and guide more detailed researches in the future," (Stein 1937). His work was the first to investigate the manner of cultural relations which characterized the third millenium Sumerian civilization and the contemporary Indus civilization in the geographical area which separated the two. Unfortunately, Stein's work contributed little to our understanding of the interrelationships between these earliest contemporary civilizations of Asia. Following Stein's work, interest in the degree of socioeconomic exchange between Sumer and the Indus continued, but only through research conducted in the centers of those civilizations. It was decades before archaeologists returned to the geographically intermediate areas. Two sites in this intermediate zone, initially discovered and excavated by Stein, have been recently re-excavated. These are Bampur—under the direction of the British archaeologist Miss B. de Cardi in 1967; and Tal-i Iblis—under the direction of Professor Joseph R. Caldwell then of the University of Illinois, in 1966. The Peabody Museum, forty years ago one of the sponsors of Sir Aurel's research, returned to this area to conduct a survey in 1967 under my direction. Thus, after forty years, three separate projects, each unaware of the other, were launched. Excavations at Bampur and Tal-i Iblis were discontinued after an initial two months of productive results. At Tal-i Iblis Professor Caldwell recovered the earliest known metallurgical production site, dated to about 4000 B.C., while at Bampur excavations suggested long-range contacts with excavated sites from Oman on the other side of the Persian Gulf. In the setting of this skeletal outline of the prehistory of the area we discovered Tepe Yahya.

After seven weeks of survey we had depressingly come to accept Aurel Stein's conclusion—archaeological sites in this area are small in size, of limited occupation through time, few in number and distantly scattered. We had hoped to discover a single archaeological site which would allow us to establish the cultural history of this area. This would mean a site with a long period of human occupation—the longer the better. Only through the stratigraphic exposure of a successive series of superimposed settlements on a single site can the chronology and material remains be convincingly ordered. In short, we believed chronological control to be an imperative initial condition for this site. We reasoned that only after its establishment could the similar and/or different processes in the social, economic, and political developments within and between different culture areas be contrasted.

The Discovery of the Site

For years archaeologists had dismissed this entire area as contributing toward the development of the Mesopotamian and/or

FIGURE 1
View of Tepe Yahya and the principal excavations in the southern step-trench. Remains of the earliest architecture (4500 B.C.) are visible at the bottom of the mound.

Indus civilizations. Yet, a major enigma in the larger Middle Eastern archaeological record was the virtual absence of evidence for cultural relations between the civilized states of Sumer and those of the Indus. It remained to investigate the area between the two to shed light on this problem.

On the afternoon of August 17th, 1967 we first sighted the mound of Tepe Yahya. Actually, we were lost, since roads and maps are virtually non-existent, and we were becoming low on another scarce commodity in this area—gasoline. We had actually been fifteen miles from Yahya a month earlier, but, then I had decided to lead the survey in a different direction. Our return to this area was motivated by the incessant "nagging" of one of the students, Mrs. Denise Schmandt, whose hunch that this area would prove productive was correct. The small mounds fifteen miles from Yahya, found a month earlier, have since become of paramount importance in understanding the supporting population. Excavations over the past six years have not only provided an initial understanding of this large area but have altered earlier conceptions about the extent, distribution and very formation of Mesopotamian and Indus civilizations. Prior to our work at Yahya most archaeologists believed that the process of urbanization took place in southern Mesopotamia and later diffused to Iran and even further east, culminating in the Indus civilization. Excavations at Yahya and more recently at Shahdad and Shahr-i

Sokhta—all in eastern Iran—have dramatically challenged the pristine nature of Mesopotamian civilization. We anticipate here, however, the later results of our research.

The discovery of Tepe Yahya surely represents one of the most exciting moments of the ten years I have worked in the field. Driving over cropped fields and irrigation ditches we reached the mound only an hour after we initially sighted it. It was the largest mound we had seen all summer and remains today the largest known site in this corner of Iran. The possibility remained that it was a large Islamic site and would not provide the cultural longevity we had hoped for. Five of us spent that afternoon walking over the mound collecting from the surface the broken fragments of ceramics. We were to remain there a week undertaking a small exploratory excavation. Our initial suspicions were confirmed: ceramics littered the surface, ceramics identifiable from 300–500 A.D. to the fifth millennium, B.C. Here, indeed, was a site which would provide us with the information we were in search of—a site from which we could extrapolate on the cultural process both within this area and between it and other areas.

Description of the Site

Tepe Yahya is a typical Near Eastern archaeological site; measuring 19.8 meters above the present-day valley floor and 187.0 meters in diameter. It represents the built-up debris of millennia of human occupation. From the base of the mound, sherds are scattered over a distance of almost a mile in every direction. The site is located in the Soghun Valley, 1521.0 meters above sea level and 225 kilometers south of the provincial capital of Kerman. Today this small valley is dotted by small villages averaging between 50–300 people. Rainfall in the valley would not be sufficient for dry farming and mechanical water pumps are used today to water the fields of wheat and barley. It is in this setting and with this background that we returned to Yahya in the summer of 1968 for our first full season of three month excavations. The survey and limited test trenches dug in 1967, at and around Yahya, suggested to us that this site would best suit our purposes.

Results of the First Season

That first season was most difficult. With a group of ten students and a government representative from the Archaeological Service of Iran, and a cook from Teheran, we lived for almost three months in

FIGURE 2
A view from the mound of the excavations at Yahya and the expedition headquarters in the village of Baghin. The Kish-e Shur River flows seasonally past the mound and the village.

tents, cooking over open fires (mostly if not exclusively rice and goat), and trying to find secluded spots in the natural environment to serve as a privy. There was no running water, no electricity and not sufficient food available in the valley. At different times we were all ill, at times rather seriously. Most importantly we established excellent relations with the villagers, who even came to accept some of our bizarre behavior, such as boiling water and falling ill almost every other day. With our large supplies of medicine we took to not only doctoring ourselves, but our work force and their families.

Over the course of the first two seasons, we constructed and rented mud-brick houses and brought in gas stoves and lamps. It is still far from a resort, but a hard core group of stalwarts have been calling it their summer home for six years. Of the original year, there are four students presently completing their Ph.D.'s on different aspects of Yahya. If the first season included but a staff of ten, the 1973 season grew to a number of twenty-four, including students and professional colleagues who worked with us at the site. There has been a very fortunate continuity in personnel over the years, and invaluable aid in sustained field work.

In excavating a site the size of Tepe Yahya one is faced with the initial problem of where to dig. The surface exploration of the site indicated a generalized part of the mound which had the greatest variety of ceramics—most particularly a painted prehistoric ware. We chose to dig there. We set up a grid of five 10.0 meter square trenches, running from the top of the mound to its base. For two summers we excavated exclusively in these trenches, after which we opened a similar step trench from the top to the bottom of the mound on the opposite side of the mound. For the last four summers we have been digging in these step trenches. A final excavation goal remains to be accomplished; the cutting of the mound into two parts, removing a central slice from the heart of the mound. The strategy of such an excavation provides secure stratigraphic associations of directly superimposed materials. Eventually a slice of the mound is entirely cut away providing one with a controlled sample of its entirety. It is an approach which has proved most successful. The area in which we chose to place the trenches has not disappointed us —an enticing slice of less than 5 percent of the mound.

We turn now to a brief summary of our excavations and their far-reaching implications—results which would have greatly interested Sir Aurel Stein who sought some of the answers we have been able to provide while unaware of the new problems which our excavations have produced. We begin with a summary of the initial period of the settlement of the site and conclude with its final occupation, as well as prospects for future work.

History

The earliest remains of village settlement on the southeast Iranian Plateau are from Yahya, Period VI, about 4500-4000 B.C. We are not entirely sure where these settlers came from—perhaps they were not migrants from another area but were pastoral nomads who, for unexplained reasons settled down permanently to farm. The material remains at the site suggest only generalized parallels to contemporary sites of southwestern Iran. The reasons for establishing a settlement at Tepe Yahya remain elusive. Only further excavation and survey can determine whether an economic transformation of nomadic pastoralists or a migration from the west brought about the first settlement at Yahya.

The architecture of Period VI is entirely enigmatic. We have excavated eighteen rooms of a single architectural complex constructed of hand-formed mud, tempered with straw. Not a single room exceeds seven square feet; none have doorways, specialized features or distinguishable activity areas. Fragments of reed matting and timber found on the floors indicate the manner of roofing. The function of these rooms eludes us: they appear far too small to have served for human habitation. The sparse material remains found in rooms do not suggest specific functions. A coarse, chaff-tempered pottery and tools of chipped stone and worked bone, including hafted bone tools with sickle blades for harvesting cereals provide the limited inventory of material finds. On the floor of one of these rooms, however, we found a most remarkable stone female figurine; twelve inches in height and carefully rested over a cache of flint tools and carved bone implements. It clearly appears to be an intentional deposit. By whom and for what reason? Small rooms of this type are often interpreted as communal storage areas for grain. This architectural complex may have such a function. If so, can we interpret this female idol as intentionally deposited to protect the stored produce? If this conjecture is true, then we have yet to excavate the domestic quarters in which the people lived.

Our preliminary analysis of the economic subsistence at this time indicates that cattle were of principle importance, followed by sheep and goats. Rodents, equid and gazelle are also present and may have supplemented the diet. Analysis of the plant remains is underway and indicates the presence of domesticated wheat and barley. It is of interest to note that dry farming in the Soghun Valley would be impossible today. Crop raising necessitates the presence of irrigation. We have no evidence for prehistoric irrigation canals around Yahya. However, precipitation may have been greater in the past than today. An irrigation technology for this period would not be extraordinary, however, having been documented for Neolithic communities 1500 years before the initial settlement of Yahya.

The transition to Period V (4000–3500 B.C.) at Yahya occurs without a break in cultural continuity. From the material remains recovered it is evident that the occupants during Period V are the descendants of those that settled the site. The differences between what we refer to as Period VI and V are determined through quantitative changes in the material remains: a decrease in the coarse chaff-tempered wares so characteristic of Period VI and the appearance of a finer ceramic with painted designs. These quantitative changes in ceramics, the first appearance of painted wares, and the increasing complexity in the three architectural levels form our arbitrary reasons for separating Period VI from V. During this period, dated to the first half of the fourth millennium, we have our first direct ceramic parallels with sites 400 miles to the west, Susa and Bakun. These parallels clearly indicate a stronger cultural link to this area than was evident in earlier times. Throughout Period V there is a continuous increase in the utilization of imported resources, also unknown in earlier times. Such evidence further indicates the increasing expansiveness in the "foreign" relations at Yahya. Imported materials which appear for the first time from distant areas include alabaster, obsidian, mother-of-pearl, varieties of different flint, onyx, and turquoise. Alloyed copper-arsenic bronzes, smelted, hot and cold forged, appear in the form of chisels and pins. The presence of these remains support the contention of an increasing pattern of interaction within and between different areas of southern Iran.

The architecture of Period V indicates a specialized development beyond that of the earlier period. Individual living rooms measure 16 x 9 feet with hearth and chimney and numerous smaller adjoining rooms forming house complexes upward of eight rooms. Over 25 percent of the bricks are of standardized size indicating the first use of brick molds. Bricks are thumb-impressed, allowing a mud-straw mortar to infuse the impressions, thus providing greater structural strength to the building. Preliminary analysis of the faunal remains indicates a shift away from the earlier primacy of cattle toward the greater dependence on sheep and goat. It is difficult to interpret the reason or cause for this economic shift. A greater dependence on transhumant patterns, an increasing interaction with nomads, a decreasing suitability of the environment for cattle are among individual possibilities.

The majority of archaeological sites in the vicinity of Yahya date to this time period. They are all of rather uniform size—two to four acres—and are located around perennial streams. The size of these settlements is rather close to the size of the villages in the area today in which 50-300 people live. There is a clear shift in the settlement following this period: sites are far fewer but larger. This shift in settlement organization may be correlated with the development of a stronger centralization of administrative authority in the succeeding Period IV-C. During Period V a number of processes are set in motion that are of fundamental importance: (1) a clear increase in the number and size of settlements indicating a growth of population or influx of new peoples; (2) an increasing specialization of crafts and technological control in the production of ceramics, metals, and architecture; and (3) an increasing regional consolidation and interregional interaction between settlements throughout southern Iran. It is within the above framework that one must picture the totally expected settlement discovered at Tepe Yahya in 1970, that settlement directly overlying Period V, referred to as Period IV-C—the Proto-Elamite settlement dated 3400–3000 B.C.

The Proto-Elamite Settlement

This period consists of a single building complex dated by radiocarbon to about 3200 B.C. It consists of a most remarkable association of materials which have transformed our notions of the extension of early dynastic and predynastic civilization in the Near East. There is one fundamental aspect which must be appreciated prior to considering the nature of Yahya's Proto-Elamite Settlement. The area in which Yahya is situated was regarded as a cultural backwater which did not share in the principal developments of the urban world of Mesopotamia. The earliest literate civilization was believed to be entirely restricted to southern Mesopotamia or Sumer, from whence the "urban idea" drifted eastward to Iran and the Indus. The "cradle of civilization" was an honor bestowed entirely upon Sumer. Excavations at Yahya have expanded the geographical expanse of this "cradle" and challenged this simplistic notion of relying on Sumer for the origins of the process of civilization. Today an infinitely more complex picture emerges through the recognition of a Proto-Elamite civilization of southern Iran, as well as the Helmand Civilization in Iranian Seistan. For example, this latter civilization was excavated by Dr. Maurizio Tosi over the past four years. It is one of the largest of Bronze Age sites in Iran. Tosi recovered from this 176 acre site materials unparalleled elsewhere. Iranian archaeologists, under the direction of Mr. Hakemi, excavated the cemetery site of Shahdad near Kerman, where they are recovering from tombs an unparalleled wealth of materials which are stylistically entirely different from, but in wealth comparable to, the Royal Tombs of Ur where Sumerian queens and princes were buried. All of these distinctive civilizations can be dated to the early part of the third millennium. All can be seen to be contemporary with and, to a greater or lesser degree, interacting with the Sumerian world. Thus, we can conclude that the process was not one which developed in a single nuclear area but was the result and may have been defined by, the complex interaction of many cultures over wide areas.

The nature and extent of the interaction between the above areas remains to be clarified, and the process of urbanization in each area

TABLE 2
The Urban Process at Tepe Yahya

1.		2.		3.	
Increasing food production through domestication of plants and animals	---→	Procurement Specialization: irrigation, herding = surplus	--→	Population Increase	---→
4.		5.		6.	
Increasing goods demand craft specialization	---→	Increasing inter-regional interaction and competition	----→	Agglomeration into towns	---→
7.				8.	
Local distributive systems	=	defense necessities administrative problems city-nomad relations warfare increases	----→	Administrative Complex Centralization of State Functions.	

At Yahya the process of 1. and 2. are evident in Period VI, while 3.–6. appear throughout the development of Period V, 7. and 8. are only characteristic of Period IVC, the Proto-Elamite settlement.

may prove to be both different and distinctive. We have only the barest outline for each of the areas and still less understanding of the reasons and causes which brought about the great internationalism characteristic of the very end of the fourth and the beginning of the third millennium B.C. Archaeologists have detected during this period—from Egypt through Mesopotamia and the Persian Gulf to eastern Iran and Soviet Turkmenistan—distinctive urban complexes with material remains that align each of the civilizations to the other. The evidence indicates that Tepe Yahya Period IV-C was the site of one such urban complex. It was probably an urban center of the Proto-Elamite civilization which was contemporary, but distinctive from, the early dynastic traditions of Sumer and Egypt.

In the 400 square meters which have been excavated of the Period IV-C building, the following materials have been found. Stacked in a pile in a corner of one room we recovered eighty-four tablet blanks and six complete Proto-Elamite tablets; from another room three tablets and fragments of others. Proto-Elamite tablets have been found on three other sites in Iran: Susa, Sialk, and Tal-i Ghazir. These tablets differ in their signary from the earliest contemporary tablets found in Sumer. The early tablets of the Sumerians and Elamites have not been fully deciphered though they are different from each other as well as of contemporary date. Both the earliest of Sumerian and Elamite tablets appear to be economic account tablets, recording amounts of various unknown materials either produced, received, or shipped. The tablets of early Sumer, those of the Proto-Elamites, and

Egyptian hieroglyphs represent the earliest written languages of these three earliest and contemporary civilizations. Presently our evidence would suggest that the former two are eerlier than the formulation of the Egyptian hieroglyph, but perhaps not by more than a century or two. The discovery of Proto-Elamite tablets some 550 miles from Susa, the next closest site to Yahya with such tablets and the later capital of the Elamite Kingdom, provided unexpected evidence for the widespread distribution of this civilization. The eighty-four blanks found in direct association are of fundamental importance, for they suggest the presence of a scribe at Yahya and clearly indicate that writing was actually undertaken there. The signs on the tablets at Susa and at Yahya are so nearly identical that there is little doubt that the scribe at one site could have read the tablet written by the scribe of another.

We have also recovered over fifty cylinder sealings within the rooms of this building. These clay impressions, made by rolling an incised cylinder over moist clay, were used to seal entire rooms or vessel containers. In this way the contents of the room or vessel could be sealed. The presence of cylinder seals and broken sealings from vessels indicates both storage and trans-shipment of unknown materials. The account tablets, cylinder sealings and seals are all suggestive of an administrative complex engaged in the storing, recording and shipment of merchandise. In fact, the presence of these materials even though they are of different styles in the Sumerian world, suggests an economic redistribution system comparable to that in Mesopotamia. The presence of such an association within a single building suggests that in this far distant region there was a similar socio-economic system of redistributing material, such as the system which characterized the early Sumerian civilization. The cylinder seals, sealings, ceramics, and tablets indicate the close cultural relations between the site of Yahya and contemporary Mesopotamian sites to the west. The redistributive nature and administrative function of our IV-C building is further indicated by the materials recovered from the floors of the rooms: (1) large Mesopotamian type (Jemdet Nasr) grain jars in small storage rooms; (2) record keeping, both blank and written tablets; and (3) Jemdet Nasr cylinder seals and sealings, indicating the receiving and shipping of goods.

The ceramics of this period also attest to wide-scale contacts. Mesopotamian bevelled-rim bowls and polychrome Jemdet Nasr type vessels are associated with painted ceramics which are paralleled hundreds of miles to the east in Pakistan Baluchistan (Shahi Tump), and in Iranian Seistan at Shahr-i Sokhta which Dr. Tosi ascribes to the Helmand civilization. These ceramic types appear in small percentages compared to the total inventory which characterizes the distinctive local tradition of ceramic production. The urban settlement at Yahya at this time is in close contact with other far distant centers. Such evidence supports a previously unsuspected internationalism beginning around 3200 B.C. in which geographically separate urban centers were in contact with each other. The following Period IV-B at Yahya continues to maintain major trade relations with far distant areas. There are, however, striking differences in the nature of this community and that of the earlier IV-C settlement.

Period IV-B dates to the early and middle part of the third millennium (2900-2500 B.C.), contemporary with the height of the literate civilization of the Sumerian. In contrast to the earlier period at Yahya we have found no written tablets of this date. In fact, the minimal architecture recovered considering the rather large horizontal exposure, does not suggest the continuity of the early administrative function of the site. We have, however, recovered from poorly preserved domestic dwellings and from open surfaces materials which connect Yahya to the world of the Sumerians, the Dilmun culture of the Persian Gulf, and the settled communities to the east in Pakistan. The Sumerian tablets of the late third millennium make consistent reference to three important commercial centers: Dilmun, Magan, and Meluhha. It is from these three commercial centers that the Sumerians obtained the natural resources that they lacked in their homeland: ore, timber, precious minerals, alabaster, and diorite. The geographical location of these three commercial centers beyond the Sumerian world has long been sought by archaeologists. A Danish expedition under the direction of P. Glob and G. Bibby has undertaken numerous expeditions to the Persian Gulf, chiefly Bahrein, and have reasoned that the Gulf, most likely the island of Bahrein, is to be identified with Dilmun, referred to in Sumerian texts as the Paradise Land. It might be added that the Danish expeditions have brilliantly elucidated that distinctive nature of this Dilmun culture. The evidence for the two other Sumerian commercial centers are more contentious. Many scholars have identified the third millennium civilization of the Indus as Meluhha, and the lands between Sumer and the Indus, along the Gulf, as Magan. These identifications would place Yahya as a principal city of Magan. Our excavations have not confirmed any of the above identifications. Perhaps Yahya is part of Magan, perhaps Magan will be discovered on the other side of the Gulf in the largely unexplored territory of Oman and Muscat, where James Humphries presently is undertaking a survey.

At any event, strong links exist between the Dilmun culture of Bahrein, the Sumerian civilization and distant Yahya during Period IV-B in ceramics, cylinder and stamp seals, but most importantly through carved "steatite" vessels. The soft greenstone vessels so commonly referred to as "steatite" (actually analysis shows most to be chlorite) have an extraordinarily wide distribution. From the Sumerian site of Mari on the Upper Euphrates to the small island of Tarut off the coast of Saudi Arabia in the Persian Gulf, to the site of Mohenjodaro, principal site of the Indus civilization, archaeologists have recovered numerous "steatite" vessels of identical shape and sharing a complex syntax of design motifs. These incised designs include architectural façades, intricately incised geometric patterns, and more rarely combined scenes of animals (lions, hares, eagles, snakes), insects (scorpion), and humans. All are identically portrayed over this wide area. There can be little doubt that these vessels represent a shared belief system; that is, the meaning of the depicted art is shared over the wide area of distribution. It can be fairly asked if the shared ideology represented a diffusion of a religious belief system, and, if so, from where?

Following Professor H. Frankfort, archaeologists have for several decades attributed these "steatite" vessels to Sumerian craftsmanship. Results of the excavations at Yahya have contested this view. We have recovered over a thousand fragments of these "steatite" vessels, recording almost every known design motif as well as new design elements. It is surely one of the largest-known collections from a single site. More importantly, dozens of pieces show the process of their manufacture, many being incompletely carved, unfinished vessels. We have also found large chunks, up to 3 x 2 feet, cut from a mining source as well as smaller "ingots."

For three years we had tangible evidence for their local manufacture but were unaware of the source for the stone area. In 1970 Mr. Philip Kohl and I were guided by a keeper of a local shrine to a place far up in the mountains where he said this type of stone was to be found. That year we found small traces of outcrops which would not have justified our belief in a local source but confirmed our suspicion that the resource was locally available. The next summer Phil Kohl stubbornly explored the mountains for several days. He returned jubilantly to tell us what he had already reported on his Walkie-Talkie—the discovery of four localities, each of considerable size, with hundreds of meters of exposed "steatite" evidencing chisel marks for its extraction. Since that time Phil has undertaken a series of physico-chemical analyses to confirm these mining areas as the ones used in the production of Yahya's "steatite."

The situation seems clear. Yahya was one of perhaps several (but the first discovered), centers of "steatite" manufacture. These objects most assuredly were not produced here by Sumerians. From Tepe Yahya these vessels were exchanged with far distant rulers in an elaborate gift exchange. In Sumer such "steatite" vessels are almost always found in temples, palaces and in the rich graves (The Royal Cemetery of Ur). The exchange of these luxury items between rulers of different communities could well have aided the further socio-political relations between far distant communities. At Yahya there is surely no evidence for Sumerian enclaves of merchants or craftsmen, living in the community. These "steatite" vessels and their rare ceramic type are the only tangible links with the Sumerian world. However, it appears unequivocal that the artisans manufacturing these vessels at Yahya shared an ideology with distant Sumer, for they clearly understood the complex design motifs which they carried, as did the Sumerians who placed them in their temples. Without such evidence, the presence of such a far-reaching and widespread ideology would completely escape detection by the archaeologist. We are still at odds to establish the inspiration behind the motifs as that of Elamite or Sumerian.

It is obvious that at Yahya, from 3200-2500 B.C., there is considerable evidence for close cultural relations with far distant Sumer and the Dilmun cultures of the Persian Gulf. A trade in luxury items brought Mesopotamia, with its almost total lack of stone and other resources, into close commercial contact with the Persian Gulf, southeastern Iran, Iranian Seistan, and even Soviet Turkmenistan. These areas all controlled the natural resources which the Sumerians desired: pearls, carnelian, "steatite," lapis lazuli, mineral ores and wood, to name but a few. In return for these resources Sumerian tablets refer to the export of *tons* of textiles and grain, neither of which has survived in the archaeological record.

Thus, from the earliest time of the Sumerian civilization we see a picture not of the spread of the urban idea *per se* to backward areas, but of an interdependent relationship which involved a continuous cultural and economic interchange of goods and ideas among far distant areas. This process, which began at least by the end of the fourth millennium, resulted in the development of not only the highly literate urban centers of the Sumerian world but those of the Dilmun culture, as well as such sites as Tepe Yahya and even further to the east, the Early Harrapan Indus sites. In each of the above areas we can perceive an early and independent population nucleation process (at Yahya beginning in the middle of the fifth millennium) which, toward the end of the fourth millennium, saw a number of urban centers in different culture areas interacting. Rather than labelling one area—the Sumerian—as providing the energy for "civilizing" this large area, we see a number of interdependent interaction spheres: Persian Gulf, southern Iran, Seistan (Helmand civilization), Indus, Turkmenia, and the Sumerian.

Shahr-i Sokhta site

The recent excavations at Shahr-i Sokhta in Iranian Seistan have underscored this analysis. Here, Dr. Tosi has been excavating a site of equal size and complexity to any known in the Middle East of that period. Materials at Shahr-i Sokhta suggest elaborate technological achievements in metallurgy, architecture, elaborate stone and bead manufacturing, pottery manufacture (seen in an entire site of dozens of pottery kilns), as well as a cemetery with an estimated 20,000 burials. There is also evidence for large-scale lapis lazuli (that most precious of stones to Sumerians) manufacture and export. These material remains suggest direct cultural contact not with the Sumerian world but seem more to imply contact with Yahya and, perhaps most, to connect Shahr-i Sokhta with the sites of Soviet Turkmenistan. Dr. Tosi has referred to this site and the numerous settlements of Seistan as representing a "Helmand civilization." It might be added that Sir Aurel Stein was the first to discover Shahr-i Sokhta but did not recognize its importance. It appears evident today that Shahr-i Sokhta offered to other cultural areas that which it also received —participation in the interaction of the urban process.

At Tepe Yahya, as at Shahr-i Sokhta and so many other sites in Iran, the remains indicate that something happened around 2000 B.C.—an internal collapse. At Tepe Yahya a localized Period IV-A follows the internationalism of Periods IV-C and IV-B. There appears to be a "gap" in the occupation following IV-B times. That is to say, the site may have been unoccupied for a period of time before it was re-settled in IV-A times. The people who re-settled Yahya provided a puzzling picture. The site is virtually without any evidence for external relations. The ceramics and small finds are without parallel, save for Shahdad, on the entirety of the eastern Iranian Plateau. Very little has been excavated of this period which ties it to the outside world. A single Harappan-type sealing of the Indus civilization and rare occurrences of "steatite," most probably heirlooms, are singular exceptions. What caused this implosion from the earlier extensive relations which Yahya had with the outside world? The answer may rest in Mesopotamia which in earlier days acted as a demand center, drawing upon many different areas for obtaining its resources. Late in the third millennium this economic dialectic was broken down. The Akkadian conquest of the Sumerian civilization brought about generations of internal turmoil which are discussed in both the Sumerian and Akkadian tablets. A series of internal upheavals within the Mesopotamian world—internecine warfare—upset the ecological balance which in turn seems to have resulted in the internalization and localization of the cultures on the Iranian Plateau. Many of the earlier urban centers dependent on their interaction with Mesopotamia "collapsed." Period IV-A at Tepe Yahya reflects this internal consolidation and breakdown of foreign relations. Sometime in the early part of the second millennium Yahya was completely abandoned—its earlier wealth and importance a memory of a millennium past. This collapse of so many urban sites of the Iranian Plateau in the second millennium implies a sharp change in the pattern of social organization and systems of production.

The remains also indicate that Tepe Yahya was abandoned for almost a millennium only to be re-settled in the early part of the first millennium B.C. Excavations have yet to establish a coherent picture of this first millennium occupation which continues to about 500 A.D. After 500 A.D. the site was never again inhabited. The excavations at Yahya suggest an Iron Age settlement, followed by an Achaemenid settlement with ceramic parallels to Pasargadae, capital of the Persian Empire founded by Cyrus the Great. Materials from the settlement of the third and second centuries B.C. indicate Hellenistic influence, followed by Parthian and Sasanian. It would appear that these later settlements at Tepe Yahya were greatly influenced by the passing of dynastic traditions: Achaemenian, Hellenistic, Parthian and Sasanian. All are present, but only future excavations will elucidate the role they played in these empires. Our tentative evidence suggests that the site was a provincial outpost of these great empires: perhaps a local citadel in which resident feudal lords were intermittently established to strengthen and control the frontiers of the particular empire. Much work remains to be done in providing an understandable framework for these later settlements. The next three years of excavation hopefully will provide such a framework while work will continue on the earlier periods.

The Participants

Over the past six years, thirty-four students have participated in the Yahya Project together with numerous interdisciplinary colleagues working on environmental problems and analytical studies of metals, ceramics, and other materials. Their contribution, together with that of our artist, Miss Ann Hechle, whose excellent drawings were often produced under the most adverse conditions of blinding sandstorms, are to be credited with our successes. Perhaps one of the most pleasant tasks has been working with some of the students. Richard Meadow is one of these. As a junior undergraduate, with considerable archaeological experience in the American Southwest, he accompanied me on the initial survey which discovered Yahya, and after five seasons there he is completing his thesis on the faunal remains. Others have already been mentioned, and there are many more. They have transformed our understanding of an area almost entirely ignored, and in so doing have transformed many of our earlier conjectures on the process of urbanization within the area which stretches from the Indus to Mesopotamia. The future prospects at Yahya promise different rewards. A greater horizontal exposure of each of the periods is not only desirable but necessary for a fuller understanding of each period. In future seasons, Miss Martha Prickett will be undertaking intensive surface settlement analysis in search of the supporting population among Yahya. We are still largely ignorant of the number and size of settlements dated to each period in the vicinity of Yahya.

In Conclusion

Excavations at Tepe Yahya have underscored the strong correlation between cultural interaction and innovation. The striking regional differences extant in the secular world of domestic materials can be contrasted with the equally striking similarities in luxury items and iconographic themes which tie the different cultural regions together. Within independent regional processes, joined together by a social elite pattern of non-secular interactions one can detect the Great Traditions of religious, political and economic ideology which characterize a "civilization."

If one may perceive historical changes at Yahya it is evident that they are not the result of external cataclysmic cyclicality, as has been so often argued for individual archaeological sites as well as nations, but are rather determined by the capacity of the people to adapt to a broad spectrum of economic and social changes. A continuous dialectic is established between pastoralists, agriculturalists, nomads, villagers and city dwellers. The social organization of the Iranian Plateau and in Mesopotamia can be understood only in the interaction between all of these complimentary subsystems.

Excavations at Tepe Yahya have indicated unexpectedly complex patterns of prehistoric interaction between widely separated and dis-

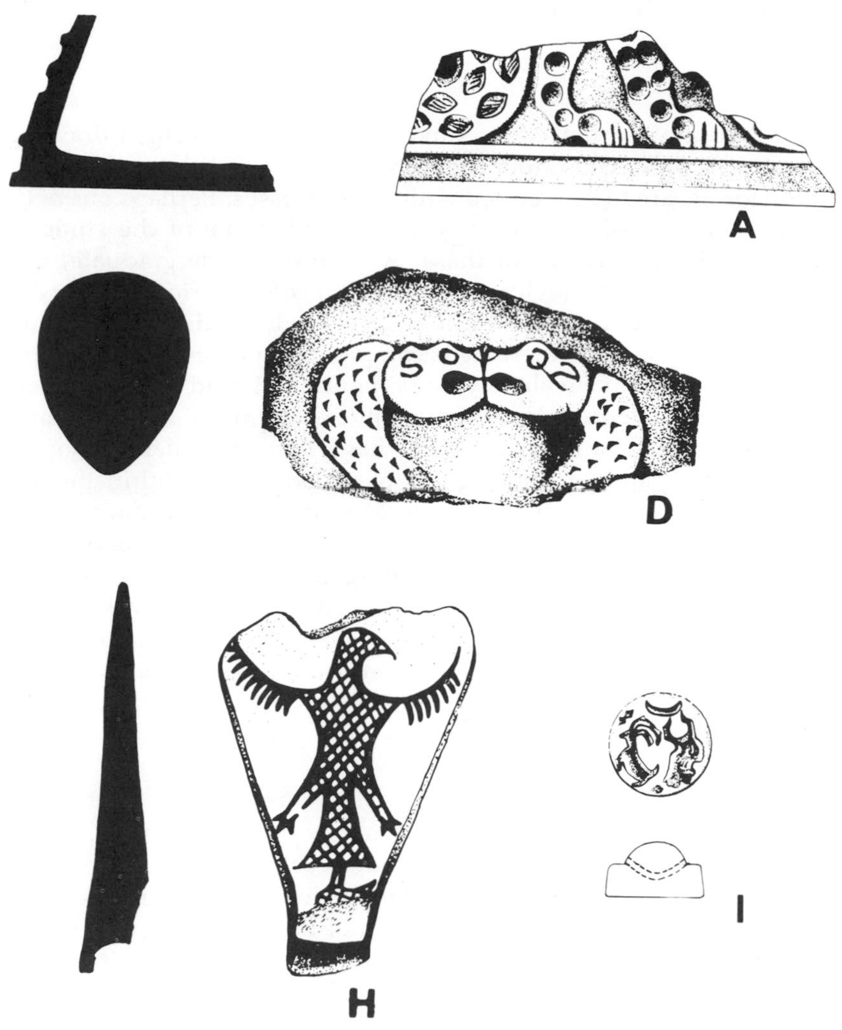

FIGURE 3
Fragments of carved "steatite" vessels from Period IV-B (about 2700 B.C.) at Tepe Yahya. Fragments identical to these have been found on most major sites of the third millenium B.C. in Mesopotamia.

tinctive cultural areas. In so doing they have pointed toward a more expansive understanding of peoples' most venturesome experiment—the invention of the city, an invention predicated by peoples' first international experience. The future prospects of research at Yahya promise to be as exciting as the rewards of the past years, although much more remains to be done. Many of our hypotheses must be tested and challenged, for great tracts of the Asian land mass are wholly unexplored by archaeologists and the research pursued in any one part may upset the conceptions developed in another.

As archaeology searches for new intellectual forms for an understanding of the past it is as important to refuse solicitations thrown up by the rapid march of "progress," where novelty alone is often deemed worth chasing, as it is to become entrenched in useless rearguard actions futilely defending outmoded methods for resurrecting the past.

A Prospective Appraisal

The editor of this collection has requested that I set down some thoughts of the "prospect" of archaeology in lieu of retrospect since I am the youngest of the present contributors. How will archaeological opinion regard my work twenty years from today?

Twenty years from now, there still may be, as there are already today, grave difficulties in interpreting the data from Yahya. Discussion would no doubt center on the manner and priorities in our techniques of data retrieval, and given these techniques, the methods used in establishing our interpretations, and their credibility. An evaluation of the Yahya Project twenty years from now may deem the project on the one hand, to be "site optimizing," and on the other, "problem optimizing." Archaeologists are increasingly tending toward problem optimization—collecting and emphasizing particular types of data with as yet imperfectly understood methods, to answer specific problems, i.e., environmental adaptations, demographic shifts, social organizational framework and so on. Twenty years from now, even if the methods for the resolution of the above problem are not at hand, the archaeologist will better grasp the constraints, boundary conditions, presuppositions, and implications of the methods he uses in the solution of specific problems.

Today we are directed to be painfully explicit in the formation of hypotheses prior to undertaking our field programs. In starting our work at Yahya I believe we had a sense of problem but surely not a rank-order list of hypotheses. The interplay between data and ideas carried us forward at different times in different directions and our priorities shift even today. Thus, our work has generated collaboration with geologists, geomorphologists, hydrologists, paleofloral and faunal specialists and has undertaken the analysis of a full complement of material remains recovered, including a pioneering effort of physiochemical techniques applied to steatite. These cannot, however, be seen as self-conscious efforts toward being "explicitly scientific." All too often in excavations dealing with an explicit hypothesis the archaeologist pays attention to the data base which bears on the hypothesis to the near exclusion of other problems, data and hypotheses. In the Near East, for example, we have seen sites excavated which maximize, for instance, an eco-systemic model of culture change. Bones, seeds and all environmental data are concentrated upon in the research design. A final report is published providing the different percentages of the above data through time, interpreted as the cause of social change, while the ceramic and architectural aspects of the site are all but ignored. (Alternatively, and more traditionally, some archaeologists have concentrated on the latter and thrown out the former.) Such problem optimization tells one a great deal about a limited aspect of the site.

Other archaeologists have been site optimizing, excavating and publishing an assumed representative corpus from the site but without a sense of problem. Here, digging proceeds with the inherent interest of what one is finding as an end unto itself. At Yahya we have rejected the rigidity of both approaches. This has been both its strength and its weakness. In future years we may well be criticized for not optimizing certain problems in favor of others, for not collecting particular types of data in a systematic manner in favor of other types of data, or for having at times excavated for the inherent pleasure of the materials recovered from certain periods.

There is no point in dwelling on the strengths of our program. Twenty years from now a younger generation of archaeologists will reflect on Tepe Yahya as a "classic type site" for the area—a site which provided the basic frame of reference for a very large area, previously little understood, and a new view toward the understanding of the interaction between even larger areas. Tepe Yahya will suffer the fate of all type sites—all of its errors in method, technique, and interpretation will be pointed out by the influx of younger archaeologists invading this once virgin area. Of its weaknesses we select but four which will loom large 20 years from today:

1. Our excavations have been oriented toward vertical exposure not horizontal. Given the minimal exposure for each time period our interpretations rest on minimal data. Perhaps it would have been better to maximize a single period horizontally, which would have told us a great deal about a single time period rather than little of a long time period.

2. Within the excavations our data retrieval has been often selective and not uniform. We have not sieved all areas, quantified all data, or even preserved all materials excavated. Nor have we utilized the full range of statistical and analytical tools at our disposal. Given particular goals, which may not be those of the future, we have quantified only certain types of data, sieved only certain areas. The decisions to do this were often predicated by our financial resources, time, per-

sonnel, and our own particularistic goals. Thus, our data will not allow archaeologists in future years to deal with the full complement of materials we actually retrieved. This is, in a sense, a problem inherent to all sites; the nature of the sample is predetermined by the sense of problem, while after the data are retrieved archaeologists often recognize new problems when the data are no longer available.

3. We have not and will not undertake an intensive survey about the entire area where Yahya is located. We have focused instead on an intensive survey of but one valley around Yahya. Thus, the land behind Yahya will be imperfectly understood and with that much of the understanding of the significance of the site.

4. Lastly, and perhaps most significantly for the future, is our lack of ethno-archaeological research. Within varying degrees of rigor we have collected an archaeological data base which can long be utilized toward the understanding of a multiplicity of problems. Whatever techniques and methods face us in the future, a well-dug site remains of enduring importance. Our absence of ethno-archaeological research around Yahya will be our most enduring failure. The Near East today is undergoing an astonishingly rapid rate of industrialization. This is particularly true in Iran. Twenty years from now we will not have the opportunity to study the interaction of nomadic tribes, with sedentary agriculturalists. In the six years we have been working at Yahya the area has been transformed before our very eyes through the introduction of mechanical irrigation. We have missed the opportunity of studying this transformation on the nature of nomad-village interaction and its political, economic, social and demographic structure. This ethno-archaeological research has been ignored, but it is an aspect which, once removed, will become all the more obvious to the archaeological understanding of an area. As few social anthropologists undertake this type of research today it becomes imperative that we do so. The mounds in the Near East have existed for centuries, and will remain for centuries. The cultural conditions most analogous to those once inhabited mounds, however, are very rapidly disappearing. The fact that we have not incorporated such research in our program will, I believe, in the future be seen as a serious shortcoming.

References

BIBBY, GEOFFREY
1970 Looking for Dilmun. New York, Alfred Knopf.

KRAMER, SAMUEL NOAH
1963 The Sumerians: Their History, Culture and Character. Chicago, University of Chicago Press.

LAMBERG-KARLOVSKY, C. C.
1967–1972 Articles and Preliminary Reports of the excavations at Tepe Yahya have been published each year in Iran, The British Institute of Persian Studies, Vol. VI through Vol. X.

1970 Excavations at Tepe Yahya, Iran, 1967–1969. Report 1. American School of Prehistoric Research. Cambridge, Mass., Peabody Museum, Harvard University.

1972 Trade Mechanisms in Indus-Mesopotamian Interrelations. Journal of the American Oriental Society 92; 2: 222–230.

LAMBERG-KARLOVSKY, C. C. AND TOSI, MAURIZIO
1972 Shahr-i Sokhta and Tepe Yahya: Tracks on the Earliest History of the Iranian Plateau. East and West 22.

MASSON, V. M. AND SARIANIDI, V. I.
1972 Central Asia, Turkmenia Before the Archaemenids. London, Thames and Hudson.

MEADOW, RICHARD H.
1971 The Emergence of Civilization. *In* Man, Culture, and Society. Harry L. Shapiro, ed. New York, Oxford University Press.

STEIN, SIR AUREL
1937 Archaeological Reconnaissances in North-Western India and South-Eastern Iran. London, Macmillan and Co.

WHEELER, SIR MORTIMER
1968 The Indus Civilization. 3rd ed. Cambridge, Cambridge University Press.

Glossary

amulet, object worn as a charm against witchcraft, disease, etc.
asphaltum, mineral pitch.
atlatl, throwing-stick used to propel a dart or short spear, a Nahua word (Mexican Indian language).
attribute analysis, analysis of artifacts in which detailed features or "modes" of the object are described, listed, tabulated.

backed blade, an unpointed blade with one, or in some cases two edges, steeply retouched by continuous, fairly abrupt removals.
baulks, in archaeology this term refers to unexcavated sections left between pits or trenches, usually for stratigraphic control and reference.
break burin, a burin formed by the intersection of a burin spall, or a group of such removals, parallel to the axis of the piece, and a broken surface, normally of a blade.
burin, a burin, or graver, is a special form of cutting tool the edge of which is formed by the intersection of a small removal with either: (a) another spall scar; (b) a retouched truncation; or (c) a broken surface of either a flake or a blade.
busked burin, an asymmetrical dihedral angle burin, the transversal side of which is convex and generally exhibits multiple removals that are often terminated by a notch.

calcareous, containing lime or limestone.
carinate, keel-shaped, with a central ridge.
carinate scraper, an end-scraper made on a thick flake with a cross-section in the shape of a reversed keel. The working end is delimited by the removal of a series of bladelets which are either short and broad or narrow and elongated.
celt, an edged instrument of stone or bronze, axe-like but without a hafting-groove.
Châtelperron point, piece with a sharp asymmetrical point made on a blade that may either be short and squat or elongated and slender. One edge is steeply retouched by abrupt removals that generally emanate from the bulbar surface.
chert, a flint-like quartz, also a term pertaining to various impure siliceous rocks.
Clovis type, Clovis point, an early (late Pleistocene, about 10,000–9000 B.C.) chipped stone projectile point type, occurring widely in North America. The point is characterized by a long, lanceolate form and fluted sides.
coprolites, preserved feces of humans or animals.

dihedral burin, a burin, the cutting edge of which is formed by the intersection at a dihedral angle of two flakes or groups of flakes called burin spalls.
doubly notched (or "strangled") blade, this is a variety of Aurignacian blade which normally exhibits two large and broad, medianly located notches that are more or less opposed to each other.
Dufour bladelet, a bladelet with a frequently incurved profile which exhibits fine, continuous, semi-abrupt marginal retouch, either exclusively along one of the edges

or along both edges. In the latter case it is disposed in an alternating (obverse-inverse) fashion.

faience, glazed earthenware or porcelain.

fléchette, a sub-losangic (losange-shaped), leaf-shaped piece with short, abrupt retouching—sometimes alternating—generally along the edges.

Font-Robert point, a point with a long axial tang clearly disengaged by abrupt or semi-abrupt retouching. The head is either of sub-losangic or elongated triangular shape with retouching often extending over the entire surface. In a few cases the latter is bifacial and involves particularly the distal extremity.

Gravette point, a point that is generally very sharp on a straight and slender blade with a steeply rectilinear or very slightly incurved back that has been steeply retouched by abrupt removals often originating from both surfaces. In some cases there is supplementary, either direct or inverse, retouch on the opposite edge either at the base, the point, or both.

horizon, a period of widespread significance in an archaeological chronology.

horizon marker, a trait, feature, or style whose presence serves to indicate contemporaneity of occurrence in two or more archaeological locations (sites, regions).

hydration dating, establishing relative dating of materials by the degree of their chemical change (hydration), as in obsidian hydration dating.

inverse retouch, small removals along the edge, or edges of a blade or flake from the dorsal (upper) surface downwards.

isostasy, referring to the equilibrium of the earth's crust, to movements of land surfaces in relation to oceans and seas.

kiva, a subterranean or semi-subterranean ceremonial chamber in Southwestern United States aboriginal societies.

knapping technique, this is the process of preparing the nucleus for the removal of blanks (blades or flakes) that are subsequently manufactured into tools.

lense, as used archaeologically it refers to a distinguishable feature of a deposition, usually a small stratum of earth, ash, or debris.

losangic-shaped bone point, or **sagaie,** an elongated and somewhat flat bone point, or sagaie, in which the base has not been split, or cleft.

metate, stone basin for grinding maize in which a *mano,* or handstone, was used with a sliding motion.

microliths, very small flint or other hard stone tools, including bladelets, scrapers, knives, etc.

midden, refuse resulting from human occupation or habitation.

Noailles burins, burins on the angle of a retouched truncation on a thin blade of small or very small dimensions. The burin spall removals are often stopped by a small notch. In many cases Noailles burins are multiple.

nose-ended scraper, these are very like carinate scrapers except that the working end exhibits a projection of a roughly nose-shaped form that has been disengaged by a series of bladelet removals.

obsidian, volcanic glass, usually black or grey in color.

obverse retouch, small removals along the edge, or edges, of a blade or flake from the bulbar (lower) surface upward.

obverse/inverse retouch, this is normally found on Dufour bladelets, one edge of which exhibits obverse retouch, while down the opposite edge inverse retouch has been applied.

onager, the wild ass *(Equus onager).*

paleomagnetic analysis, also archaeomagnetic analysis or dating, a branch of geophysics which deals with the earth's magnetic field and its changes through time, and which, as applied to archaeology is concerned with measurements of remnant magnetization of baked clay materials as a means of arriving at relative (and, eventually, absolute) dates for archaeological materials.

plastron (turtle), the ventral part of the animal's shell.

pollen analysis, in archaeology usually refers to the study of fossil plant pollens as a means of reconstructing the vegetational (and climatic) conditions of prehistoric environments.

polyhedral burins, a burin is considered "polyhedral" if more than one spall has been removed to form the cutting edge.

postmold, the residue left in the soil from a decayed post.

process (processual), in archaeology (and anthropology) this term refers to the conditions and circumstances of social and cultural change, particularly to the causes of such change.

provenience, the find location or context of an archaeological discovery, with reference to strata, to house floors, burial associations, or other artifacts and features, etc.

quern, apparatus consisting of two circular stones used in grinding cereals.

Raysse burins, a very complex type of flat-face burin, the spall removals on which are often nearly perpendicular to the long axis of the piece. Either the end or one lateral edge has been prepared as a retouched truncation.

retouch, abrupt retouch, blade or flake exhibiting continuous retouch along either one or both edges, which is neither abrupt (which distinguishes it from backed blades) or semi-abrupt of the scaled type (which distinguishes it from the so-called "Aurignacian blades").

seriation, the arrangement of data into series, especially time-ordered or chronological series, usually by the principle of similarity among the units, or by placing like next to like in the series.

sherd, a fragment of a broken pottery vessel.

sipapu, a small hole in a *kiva* floor, regarded as the mythical opening into the underworld through which human ancestors are supposed to have reached this world.

split-base bone point, or **sagaie,** a flattened more-or-less leaf-shaped or elongated triangular bone point, the base of which has been split, or cleft, presumably to facilitate hafting.

steep scraper, an end-scraper on a thick blade or flake, the working end of which has been formed by the removal of a series of bladelets.

stratigraphy, a study and description of strata in which the principle of superposition gives a relative chronological ordering (underlying strata are older than those on top of them), a method developed in geology but widely applied in archaeology.

talus, a geological term referring to a sloping mass of debris lying at the base of a cliff or the like, and which in archaeology refers to debris similarly disposed with reference to man-made structures.

temporally discrete occupation, archaeological site occupation which can be distinguished as pertaining to a particular period in a sequence and which is discrete from other strata or occupational levels at that site.

time-space systematics, that part of archaeology concerned with the chronological and geographical ordering of its data.

trans-humance (trans-humant pattern), a mode of life whereby a social group shifts its residence regularly, and usually seasonally, in response to the food quest.

truncation burin, a burin formed by the intersection of a burin spall, or a group of such removals, and a truncated extremity of a blade obtained by abrupt retouches generally from the lower (bulbar) surface, more rarely from the upper (dorsal) surface of the piece.

typology (typological procedures), the classifications of archaeological remains according to types.

unifacial point, a chipped stone projectile point which shows retouch, or trimming and shaping by flaking, on only one surface.

unimodal curve, a statistical term pertaining to one mode or the line or graph describing such a mode, as in the plotting of the frequency of occurrence of a feature on one axis, *e.g.*, time, in the case of stratigraphic study of pottery types.

wadi, Arabic term for a ravine or valley which in the rainy season becomes a watercourse.

well-struck blade, as the name implies, this is simply a long parallel-sided blade that has been removed from the parent nucleus by a well-directed blow. If the width of the piece exceeds twice its length the object is referred to as a flake.